Air Fryer Toast Oven Recipe Cookbook 2021

The One-stop Cookbook for COSORI, Breville Smart, Cuisinart, Instant Omni, Mueller Austria, Black+Decker, Oster, Kalorik & Iconites Air Fryer Toast Oven

By Jenson Homolka

Table of Contents

Description

This is a book that contains useful information on the air fryer toast oven. The content includes popular brands that offer this exceptional appliance, various functions, the benefits of cooking with an air fryer toast oven, and informative tips. And best of all, you'll get superb recipes to try with your new multicooker.

If you are looking to upgrade your kitchen appliances by getting an air fryer, or perhaps you just want to see and experience what all the excitement is about, then the air fryer toast oven might just be the one for you.

An air fryer toast oven gives you the power and flexibility of two already beloved appliances. With so many possibilities at your fingertips, getting a comprehensive guide in the form of a fine recipe book is as vital as picking your first unit.

Luckily, this Air Fryer Toast Oven Recipe Book provides practical information as follows:

- Popular air fryer toast oven brands
- Simple but useful functions
- Benefits of using an air fryer toast oven for cooking
- Various air fryer toast oven brands you can have
- Tips and cautions of air fryer toast oven usage
- A collection of carefully curated recipes for your air fryer toast oven

From filling breakfast meals to scrumptious dinners and exquisite desserts, the air fryer toast oven has a great potential to be your new kitchen workhorse.

Introduction

Many people are consciously making healthier options in terms of their diet, and with it comes changes in lifestyle as well. They may be keener on making and preparing their own meals at home. Thus, finding a kitchen appliance that can perform multiple functions is one of their priorities.

These days, it is difficult to keep up with all the new kitchen appliances in the market. Every year there is a newer and improved version of an already existed appliance, and we can't help but feel excited for it. They will, after all, bring convenience to the kitchen. But apart from that, it is an opportunity to try out recipes that we love and learn new ones to add to our favorites.

An air fryer is a multicooker that lets you enjoy fried food without the unhealthy grease and oil. It is one of the kitchen appliances that became extremely popular in the last few years as it has brought a revolutionary technology into people's kitchen.

While oven toasters have been around for as long as we can remember, they are one of the few kitchen staples that we grew up with and love due to its ease of operation.

Now, we have a combination of these two great appliances—the air fryer toast oven. You'll be able to save money and precious counter space with a single appliance that has all the cooking options you could possibly need.

Chapter 1: Essentials You Must Know

Popular Air Fryer Toast Oven Brands

Air fryer toast ovens are relatively young but there's already a handful of manufacturers in the market offering a great deal of brands at competitive prices.

One advantage of buying from trusted brands is that it will save your money down the line. Plus, reputable companies offer warranties and customer support in case your unit needs servicing.

With so many options available, it is easy to get overwhelmed with all the information out there.

To give you a head start in finding the best one for you, here are some reliable brands that offer air fryer toast ovens.

- Instant
- Ninja / SharkNinja
- Breville
- Cuisinart

- Nuwave
- Cosori
- Aaobosi
- Moosoo

- Black+Decker
- Emeril Lagasse

Simple but Useful Functions

Although different brands may offer varying functions for their models, you can expect most of these settings on an air fryer toast oven.

- Air fry
- Toast
- Dehydrate
- Bake

- Roast / Air roast
- Broil / Air broil
- Slow cook
- Rotisserie

- Grill
- Keep warm
- Re-heat
- Thaw / Frozen food

Other models will have dedicated options for specific foods like fries, pizza, bagel, cookies, and ferment, to name a few.

Benefits of Using Air Fryer Toast Oven for Cooking

Aside from its ability to cook all your meals from breakfasts to desserts, air fryer toast ovens have other benefits that will make you want to use it more often.

- Heart-healthy meals — The air fry function allows you to prepare tasty meals for your family with much less oil.   It is also great for people with strict dietary needs and those transitioning into a healthier lifestyle.

- Super easy to operate — Most models are equipped with several presets to go with most of your cooking needs.

- Amazing flavors — The air fryer toast oven's ability to give the food a delectable browning will make your meals taste as good as they look. The improved flavors, aroma, and textures are guaranteed to make everyone feel thrilled for whatever comes out of the air fryer toast oven.

- Compact and energy-efficient — They may be small compared to conventional appliances, but they are truly powerful kitchen tools. With a smaller size, they can heat up and cook faster than full-sized kitchen appliances. They are also better options for cooking or reheating food in smaller portions. This will not only take less time but will consume much less energy.

- Smaller footprint — For an appliance that can perform so many functions, it only occupies a fraction of your precious kitchen space. Just imagine all the space that your gas range, oven, grill, toaster oven, dehydrator, and microwave oven may take up.

- Easy to clean — Most air fryer toast ovens are made with stainless steel or metal. Not only do they look stylish and elegant, but they are durable and food-safe. The cooking chamber and removable components are usually coated with a non-stick material or made with stainless steel. The oven racks, air fry baskets, and other accessories are also dishwasher-safe.

Various Air Fryer Toast Oven Brands You Can Have

- Instant Omni Plus — From the maker of the renowned instant pot comes another bestseller in the multicooker category. The Instant Omni Plus offers a total of 11 functions and even comes with a rotisserie option as well as cooking accessories for your convenience. People love the Instant Omni Plus for its large capacity and smart functions.

- Breville — One of the top-rated air fryer toast ovens coming from the Australian brand, Breville. The BOV900BSS model features a powerful 1800-watt motor for faster cooking, a spacious one-cubic meter interior ideal for cooking for family and guests, 13 preset cooking functions, and a two-year warranty. The only downside to this model is the price and size, as it is a bit on the pricier and bulkier side.

- Cosori 12-in-1 Air fryer toaster oven — Aside from the sleek and appealing design, this model also features a 1800-watt motor, a large capacity with non-stick interior, a rotisserie function on top of 11 other cooking presets, numerous cooking accessories, and a recipe book. This air fryer oven has a 30-liter capacity and is suitable for a family of five to seven.

- Nuwave Brio 14Q—Nuwave's newest offering outshines its competitors with its whopping 100 preset menu selection. It also includes a temperature probe, the ability to adjust the wattage to suit your cooking needs, an all-metal interior, access to the Nuwave cooking club app, and a recipe book. The Brio can also automatically shut off once cooking is done. The accessories that come with the unit includes a popcorn maker/roasting drum, baking pan, and cupcake liners.

- Cuisinart TOA-60—This model is a toaster oven that has an air fryer function. It also houses a powerful 1800-watt motor but has a smaller capacity and only seven cooking functions as compared to the previous models from other brands. Nevertheless, it offers an affordable option for small families.

- Black+Decker Extra Wide Crisp n' Bake Air Fryer Toaster Oven — Similar to the Cuisinart previously mentioned, this unit is a toaster oven equipped with an air fryer setting. The interior can fit a 12-inch pizza and has five cooking functions to bake, broil, air fry, toast, and keep warm.

- Ninja SP101 — Ninja Foodi's take on the air fryer oven also features its digital crisp control technology. Unlike other similar air fryer ovens, the Ninja Foodi is wider at its sides and has a shorter height. Although it occupies a larger space when in use, the Ninja Foodi can be flipped upwards, making up for the size to some extent. The Ninja SP101 has the following cooking settings: air fry, air roast, air broil, toast, dehydrate, bagel, bake, and keep warm.

- Aaobosi B089W4NSQ3 — Aaobosi's sophisticated-looking air fryer oven has an impressive 10 cooking presets. It also features a 23-liter capacity, up to 450°F maximum temperature, adjustable temperature and time. This appliance comes with various cooking accessories such as an air fryer basket, removable crumb tray, rotisserie spit assembly, wire rack, and drip pan. It will also come with a free cookbook and a two-year warranty.

- Moosoo Air fryer Oven — This air fryer also doubles as a convection oven and showcases an elegant appearance, with a stainless-steel body and wide double-glazed glass door to see the food while it is cooking. It has a 23-liter capacity and has a maximum temperature of 450°F. The cooking presets include thawing, fries, air roast, air broil, toast, pizza, rotisserie, and dehydration. It also comes with accessories and a free cookbook containing 100 delicious recipes.

- Emeril Legasse Power Air fryer — This model's exterior is made from brushed stainless steel. It has a 1500-watt motor, a total of 12 cooking presets, a memory function, and a slow cook option. It is ideal for a small family as it has a 930-cubic inch capacity.

Tips and Cautions of Air Fryer Toast Oven Usage

As with any new appliances, one of the first things to do is to read the manual carefully and follow the manufacturer's guidelines to ensure safety.

Here are a few things to remember when using your air fryer toast oven.

- Wash the removable accessories thoroughly before the first use. Make sure that everything is properly dried before putting them back either for use or for storage.

- Do not leave the appliance unattended when in use, especially if there are small children around.

- Do not put anything else inside, such as wax paper or aluminium foil, as these may pose as a fire hazard.

- Never put anything on top of your appliance, especially while in operation.

- Exercise caution when cooking. Use oven mitts to avoid any burns.

- Your unit will naturally heat up, so leave ample space around your appliance and keep flammable materials away. Make sure that the air intake vents are not obstructed.

- Most interiors will be coated with non-stick material for easy cleaning. Avoid using metal cutleries when putting or taking out food. Opt for silicone-tipped tongs or wooden ladles instead.

- Never use abrasive scrubs or scouring pads when cleaning the accessories in order to preserve its coating.

- Clean the appliance after each use. Conduct deep cleaning periodically to remove any debris, especially on the heating elements.

- For baked-on food, simply soak the racks, trays, and pans in warm soapy water before washing. Dry all the components thoroughly.

- Keep electrical parts such as the body and power cords away from any liquids.

- Always unplug the unit after each use. Wait for the appliance to completely cool down before conducting any cleaning.

Chapter 2: Breakfast Recipes

Baked Apple Toast

Here's a simple breakfast that's sweet and delicious.
Prep Time and Cooking Time: 10 minutes | Serves: 2

Ingredients to Use:

- 2 slices bread
- 1 tablespoon butter, melted
- 1 teaspoon ground cinnamon
- 3 tablespoons apple, chopped
- 2 tablespoons honey

Step-by-Step Directions

1. Spread melted butter on top of bread slices.
2. Sprinkle with ground cinnamon.
3. Place the apples on the bread.
4. Drizzle with honey.
5. Slide into the air fryer oven.
6. Choose the toast setting.
7. Toast at 330 degrees F for 3 minutes.

Serving Suggestion:

Sprinkle with ground cinnamon before serving.

Tip:

Use whole wheat bread.

Apple Cider Donut

Serve with tasty donut with a cup of warm coffee.
Prep Time and Cooking Time: 30 minutes | Serves: 4

Ingredients to Use:

Donut
- 1-3/4 all-purpose flour
- 1 teaspoon baking soda
- 1 teaspoon baking powder
- 2 teaspoons ground cinnamon
- 1/3 brown sugar
- Pinch salt
- 1-1/2 cups apple cider
- 3 tablespoon butter, melted
- 1 egg, beaten
- Cooking spray

For serving
- 2 tablespoons butter, melted
- 2 teaspoons ground cinnamon
- 1/2 cup granulated sugar

Step-by-Step Directions

1. In a bowl, mix the all purpose flour, baking soda, baking powder, cinnamon, sugar and salt.
2. Add the apple cider to a pan over medium heat.
3. Simmer for 15 minutes.
4. Transfer to a bowl and let cool.
5. Add butter and eggs to the apple cider.
6. Add this mixture to the flour mixture.
7. Mix until fully combined.
8. Spray donut pan with oil.
9. Add the batter to the pan.
10. Place inside the air fryer oven.
11. Set the air fryer oven to bake.
12. Cook at 320 degrees F for 15 minutes.

Serving Suggestion:

Brush the donut with butter for coating. Sprinkle with cinnamon and sugar.

Tip:

Use olive oil cooking spray if available.

Breakfast Casserole

You'll love the flavors of this breakfast

casserole and the fact that it's easy to prepare.
Prep Time and Cooking Time: 20 minutes | Serves: 6

- 4 eggs, beaten
- 1 lb. Italian sausage, cooked and crumbled
- 1 cup tomato, diced
- 2 tablespoons heavy cream
- 2 teaspoons Italian seasoning
- 1/2 cup cheddar cheese, shredded

Step-by-Step Directions

1. Combine all the ingredients in a small baking pan, adding the cheese last on top.
2. Place inside the air fryer oven.
3. Choose air fry setting.
4. Air fry at 340 degrees F for 5 minutes.

Serving Suggestion:

Garnish with chopped parsley.

Tip:

Check to see if the eggs are done. If not, extend cooking time in the air fryer oven.

Toaster Strudel

You'll find this breakfast dish hard to resist.
Prep Time and Cooking Time: 10 minutes | Serves: 6

Ingredients to Use:

- 1 pack frozen toaster strudels

Step-by-Step Directions

1. Add the toaster straddles to the air crisper tray.
2. Select air fry function.
3. Cook at 350 degrees F for 5 minutes.

Serving Suggestion:

Let cool before serving.

Tip:

Air fry only what you'll eat for breakfast.

Baked Oatmeal with Blueberry

The ideal breakfast for busy mornings!
Prep Time and Cooking Time: 5 minutes | Serves: 4

Ingredients to Use:

- 1 egg
- 1 cup milk
- 1/2 teaspoon cinnamon
- 1 cup rolled oats
- 1/2 teaspoon baking powder
- 3/4 cup brown sugar
- 1/2 teaspoon nutmeg
- 1/4 cup blueberries, sliced

Step-by-Step Directions

1. Beat the egg and milk in a bowl.
2. Mix the remaining ingredients except blueberries in another bowl.
3. Pour mixture into a small baking pan.
4. Top with the egg mixture and with the sliced blueberries.
5. Set your air fryer oven to bake.
6. Bake at 320 degrees F for 10 to 15 minutes.

Serving Suggestion:

Garnish with blueberry slices.

Tip:

Check to see if the eggs are done. If not extend cooking time.

Cinnamon French Toast

This is bound to become a staple breakfast at your home.
Prep Time and Cooking Time: 15 minutes | Serves: 4

Ingredients to Use:

- Cooking spray

- 2 eggs, beaten
- 1 teaspoon vanilla extract
- 1/4 cup milk
- 1/2 teaspoon ground cinnamon
- 4 slices bread

1. Spray your baking pan with oil.
2. Mix all the ingredients except bread in a bowl.
3. Dip bread slices in the mixture.
4. Add to the baking pan.
5. Set your air fryer oven to toast function.
6. Set the temperature to 320 degrees F.
7. Cook for 3 minutes per side.

Serving Suggestion:

Drizzle with maple syrup before serving.

Tip:

Use day-old bread for best results.

Crispy Bacon

Who doesn't like bacon for breakfast?
Prep Time and Cooking Time: 15 minutes | Serves: 6

Ingredients to Use:

- 1 lb. bacon

Step-by-Step Directions

1. Preheat your air fryer to 400 degrees F.
2. Select air fry setting.
3. Add the bacon to the air fryer rack.
4. Cook at 400 degrees F for 10 minutes, flipping once or twice.

Serving Suggestion:

Serve with toasted bread and scrambled eggs.

Tip:

Use honey cured bacon.

Pancake

If you're running out of time to make breakfast, here's a recipe you can turn to.
Prep Time and Cooking Time: 5 minutes | Serves: 4

Ingredients to Use:

- 1 pack frozen pancakes
- Butter

Step-by-Step Directions

1. Add the frozen pancake to the air fryer oven.
2. Choose air fry function.
3. Cook at 330 degrees F for 5 minutes.
4. Top with butter.

Serving Suggestion:

Drizzle with pancake syrup.

Tip:

Do not overcrowd. Cook in batches.

Zucchini Bread

Start your day right with this high-fiber breakfast.
Prep Time and Cooking Time: 50 minutes | Serves: 4

Ingredients to Use:

Dry
- 3 cups all-purpose flour
- 1 teaspoon baking powder
- 1 teaspoon baking soda
- 1 teaspoon allspice
- 1 teaspoon ground nutmeg
- 1 teaspoon ground cinnamon
- Pinch salt

Wet
- 3 eggs, beaten
- 2-1/4 cup sugar
- 1 cup vegetable oil
- 2 cups zucchini, grated
- 1 teaspoon vanilla extract
- 1 cup walnuts, chopped

1. Mix the dry ingredients in a bowl.
2. Combine the wet ingredients in another bowl.
3. Blend the two together.
4. Pour mixture into a baking pan.
5. Add the baking pan to the air fryer oven.
6. Select bake function.
7. Bake at 320 degrees F for 30 to 40 minutes.

Serving Suggestion:

Serve with cream cheese.

Tip:

Use mini loaf pan.

Egg Cups

These egg cups are simple to make yet filling and satisfying.
Prep Time and Cooking Time: 10 minutes | Serves: 2

Ingredients to Use:

- Cooking spray
- 2 eggs, beaten
- 1/4 cup milk
- Salt and pepper to taste
- 2 slices bread
- 2 eggs
- 1/4 cup cheddar cheese, shredded

Step-by-Step Directions

1. Spray your ramekins with oil.
2. In a bowl, mix the beaten eggs and milk.
3. Season with salt and pepper.
4. Dip the bread in this mixture.
5. Press bread onto the ramekins.
6. Crack eggs on top of bread. Sprinkle with cheese.
7. Place the ramekins inside the air fryer oven.
8. Choose air fry function.
9. Air fry at 330 degrees F for 7 minutes.

Serving Suggestion:

Garnish with chopped parsley.

Tip:

Use whole-wheat bread.

Breakfast Potatoes

Potatoes sliced into cubes will come out nice and crispy from your air fryer.
Prep Time and Cooking Time: 20 minutes | Serves: 4

Ingredients to Use:

- 4 potatoes, sliced into cubes
- 1 onion, diced
- 1 clove garlic, minced
- 1 teaspoon onion powder
- 1 teaspoon garlic powder
- 1 teaspoon paprika

Step-by-Step Directions

1. Toss the potatoes, onion and garlic in a bowl.
2. Sprinkle with the spices.
3. Mix well.
4. Transfer to the air fryer tray.
5. Set your air fryer oven to air fry.
6. Cook at 350 degrees F for 10 minutes, stirring once.

Serving Suggestion:

Garnish with chopped parsley.

Tip:

Check the potatoes in the last 5 to 7 minutes of cooking to see if they are tender.

Peanut Butter Toast with Banana

You can't say no to this classic toast that you won't ever get tired of.
Prep Time and Cooking Time: 5 minutes | Serves: 2

Ingredients to Use:

- 2 slices bread

- 1/4 cup peanut butter
- 1 banana, sliced

1. Add the bread slices to your air fryer oven.
2. Set it to toast function.
3. Toast the bread at 365 degrees F for 3 minutes.
4. Transfer bread slices on a plate.
5. Spread with peanut butter.
6. Top with banana slices.
7. Put these back to the air fryer.
8. Select air fry setting.
9. Cook at 365 degrees F for 30 seconds.

Serving Suggestion:

Drizzle with honey.

Tip:

Use whole wheat bread and organic peanut butter.

Cheesy Hash Browns

Here's a simple and delicious way to make your own hash browns at home.
Prep Time and Cooking Time: 20 minutes | Serves: 4

Ingredients to Use:

- 4 potatoes, grated
- 1/2 cup onion, chopped
- 1/2 cup cheddar cheese, grated
- 1 egg, beaten
- 3 teaspoons garlic powder
- Salt and pepper to taste
- Cooking spray

Step-by-Step Directions

1. Mix the ingredients in a bowl.
2. Spray the air fryer tray with oil.
3. Add the mixture to the air crisper tray.
4. Choose air fry setting.
5. Air fry at 400 degrees F for 4 minutes.

6. Stir and cook for another 5 minutes.

Serving Suggestion:

Serve with eggs and sausages.

Tip:

You can also cook frozen pre-prepared hash brown in the air fryer oven.

German Pancakes

Also called Dutch Baby pancakes, German pancakes are typically baked in cast iron pan. But this one is made using the air fryer oven.
Prep Time and Cooking Time: 45 minutes | Serves: 2

Ingredients to Use:

- 1/4 cup all-purpose flour
- 1/2 cup milk
- 1 teaspoon sugar
- 1 teaspoon baking soda
- 2 eggs, beaten
- 1 teaspoon vanilla extract

Step-by-Step Directions

1. Mix all the ingredients in a bowl.
2. Add to a small baking pan.
3. Place the baking pan in the air crisper tray.
4. Select air fry function.
5. Cook at 350 degrees F for 12 to 15 minutes.

Serving Suggestion:

Serve with fruits and pancake syrup.

Tip:

You can also add butter to the mixture if you like.

Cinnamon Vanilla Toast

Here's a quick breakfast idea that you'd surely love.
Prep Time and Cooking Time: 15 minutes | Serves: 4

Ingredients to Use:

- 2 slices bread
- 2 teaspoons butter, softened
- 2 teaspoons sugar
- 1/2 teaspoon vanilla extract
- 1 teaspoon ground cinnamon

Step-by-Step Directions

1. Add the bread slices to a cutting board.
2. In a bowl, mix the remaining ingredients.
3. Add the butter mixture to the bread slices.
4. Place the bread to the air fryer tray.
5. Set it to toast.
6. Toast at 400 degrees F for 2 minutes.

Serving Suggestion:

Let cool and slice in half diagonally to create triangles.

Tip:

Use whole wheat bread slices.

English Muffin Sandwich

Create your own version of this famous breakfast sandwich using your air fryer.
Prep Time and Cooking Time: 20 minutes | Serves: 1

Ingredients to Use:

- Cooking spray
- 1 egg
- 1 English muffin, split in 2
- 2 slices bacon, cooked crispy

Step-by-Step Directions

1. Spray our ramekin with oil.
2. Crack the egg inside the ramekin.
3. Add the ramekin to the air fryer basket.
4. Place the muffin beside.
5. Choose air fry function.
6. Air fry at 330 degrees F for 4 minutes.
7. Top the muffin with bacon slices and egg.

8. Top with the other muffin slice.

Serving Suggestion:

Serve with milk or coffee.

Tip:

You can also use other types of bread for this recipe.

Avocado Toast

This breakfast toast is not only colorful, it's also delicious and nutritious!
Prep Time and Cooking Time: 10 minutes | Serves: 1

Ingredients to Use:

- 1 avocado, mashed
- 1 clove garlic, minced
- 1 teaspoon lemon juice
- Salt to taste
- 2 slices bread
- Chopped tomatoes

Step-by-Step Directions

1. Mix the mashed avocado, garlic, lemon juice, salt and pepper.
2. Spread avocado mixture on top of the bread slices.
3. Top with the tomatoes.
4. Choose air fry option.
5. Air fry at 330 degrees F for 3 minutes.

Serving Suggestion:

Sprinkle with pepper.

Tip:

Use whole wheat bread.

Baby Pancake with Raspberry

You'll have fun preparing these cute pancakes in your air fryer.
Prep Time and Cooking Time: 15 minutes | Serves: 2

- 1/2 cup all-purpose flour
- 1/2 cup milk
- 1/8 cup butter
- 3 eggs, beaten
- 1/2 teaspoon vanilla extract
- Cooking spray
- 1/2 cup raspberries

Step-by-Step Directions

1. Mix the flour, milk, butter, eggs and vanilla in a bowl.
2. Spray your muffin pan with oil.
3. Pour the batter into the muffin cups.
4. Place the muffin pan inside the air fryer oven.
5. Set your air fryer oven to air fry.
6. Cook at 320 degrees F for 5 minutes.
7. If not fully cooked, cook for 2 to 3 more minutes.
8. Top with raspberries.

Serving Suggestion:

Serve with maple syrup.

Tip:

You can also sprinkle with confectioners' sugar.

Pumpkin Pancake

Here's a different way of preparing your pancake in the air fryer.
Prep Time and Cooking Time: 10 minutes | Serves: 8

Ingredients to Use:

- 1 cup all-purpose flour
- 1/2 cup pumpkin puree
- 1/2 teaspoon baking soda
- 1 teaspoon baking powder
- 2 tablespoon brown sugar
- 1 teaspoon ground cinnamon
- 1/2 teaspoon ground nutmeg

- 2 tablespoons vegetable oil
- 1 egg, beaten
- 3/4 cup buttermilk
- 1 teaspoon vanilla extract
- Pinch salt

Step-by-Step Directions

1. Mix all the ingredients in a bowl.
2. Spray a small baking pan with oil.
3. Pour some of the batter into the pan.
4. Select air fry setting.
5. Cook at 300 degrees F for 3 minutes per side.
6. Do the same steps for the remaining batter.

Serving Suggestion:

Drizzle with melted butter before serving.

Tip:

You can use canned pumpkin puree.

Avocado Eggs

Mornings are healthier with breakfast dish like this one.
Prep Time and Cooking Time: 15 minutes | Serves: 2

Ingredients to Use:

- 1 avocado, sliced and pitted
- 2 eggs
- Salt and pepper to taste

Step-by-Step Directions

1. Crack the egg into the avocado hole.
2. Add the avocado halves to the air fryer tray.
3. Turn to air fry option.
4. Cook at 400 degrees for 10 minutes.
5. Sprinkle with the salt and pepper.

Serving Suggestion:

Serve with toasted whole wheat bread.

Tip:

You can also season with dried herbs.

Three-Cheese Quiche

Don't stress over breakfast. Make yourself this easy-to-cook quiche.
Prep Time and Cooking Time: 30 minutes | Serves: 6

Ingredients to Use:

- 1 package frozen pie crust
- 4 oz. mozzarella cheese, shredded
- 4 oz. Parmesan cheese, shredded
- 8 oz. cheddar cheese, grated and divided
- 6 eggs
- 1/2 cup milk
- 1/2 cup sour cream

Step-by-Step Directions

1. Add mozzarella and Parmesan cheese on top of the pie crust.
2. Top with half of the cheddar cheese.
3. In a bowl, beat the eggs.
4. Stir in the milk and cream.
5. Pour mixture on top of the cheese.
6. Place the crust in the air fryer tray.
7. Set it to bake function.
8. Cook at 300 degrees F for 12 to 15 minutes.
9. Sprinkle the remaining cheddar on top.
10. Cook for another 5 minutes.

Serving Suggestion:

Let cool before slicing.

Tip:

Use low-fat sour cream.

Spinach & Tomato Frittata

Full of color and nutrients—this frittata dish is sure to please.
Prep Time and Cooking Time: 15 minutes | Serves: 2

Ingredients to Use:

- 2 eggs
- 2 tablespoons milk
- 1 tablespoons Parmesan cheese, grated
- Salt and pepper to taste
- 1/4 cup spinach, sliced
- 1/4 cup tomatoes, chopped

Step-by-Step Directions

1. Beat the eggs in a bowl.
2. Stir in the milk, Parmesan cheese, salt and pepper.
3. Add the tomatoes and spinach.
4. Pour mixture into a baking pan.
5. Turn to air fry setting.
6. Air fry at 330 degrees F for 7 minutes.

Serving Suggestion:

Garnish with fresh basil leaves.

Tip:

You can also use non-dairy milk for this recipe.

Ham & Cheese Egg Cups

Quick and simple, these ham and cheese cups will fill you up and satisfy your cravings.
Prep Time and Cooking Time: 20 minutes | Serves: 6

Ingredients to Use:

- 4 eggs
- 1/4 cup ham, diced
- 1/4 cup cheddar cheese, shredded
- 4 tablespoons heavy cream
- Salt and pepper to taste
- Cooking spray

Step-by-Step Directions

1. Beat the eggs in a bowl.
2. Stir in the ham, cheese, cream, salt and pepper.
3. Spray your muffin pan with oil.
4. Pour mixture into the muffin cups.
5. Choose bake setting.
6. Cook at 350 degrees F for 10 minutes.

Garnish with chopped scallions.

Tip:

Use turkey ham.

Cheesy Egg Bites

You'll enjoy making these as much as eating these fabulous egg bites.
Prep Time and Cooking Time: 15 minutes | Serves: 6

Ingredients to Use:

- 4 eggs
- 4 teaspoons milk
- 1/4 cup cheddar cheese, shredded
- Salt and pepper to taste

Step-by-Step Directions

1. Mix the ingredients in a bowl.
2. Pour mixture into a muffin pan.
3. Slide the muffin pan inside the air fryer oven.
4. Select bake function.
5. Bake at 350 degrees F for 5 to 7 minutes.

Serving Suggestion:

Garnish with chopped chives.

Tip:

You can also add dried herbs to the mixture.

Bacon & Egg Cups

Bacon and eggs are a good combination for breakfast.
Prep Time and Cooking Time: 10 minutes | Serves: 4

Ingredients to Use:

- 4 pieces of Canadian bacon
- 4 eggs
- Salt and pepper to taste

Step-by-Step Directions

1. Line your muffin pan with bacon slices.

2. Crack eggs into each of the cups.
3. Add the muffin pan to the air fryer oven.
4. Set it to air fry.
5. Cook at 330 degrees F for 5 minutes.

Serving Suggestion:

Sprinkle with pepper before serving.

Tip:

Use Canadian bacon for this recipe.

Broccoli Quiche

High fiber and rich in nutrients, this broccoli quiche is always a good idea for breakfast.
Prep Time and Cooking Time: 30 minutes | Serves: 4

Ingredients to Use:

- 4 eggs
- 2 cups broccoli florets
- 1 cup cheddar cheese, shredded
- 1-1/2 cup milk
- Salt and pepper to taste
- 1 frozen pie crust

Step-by-Step Directions

1. Combine the eggs, broccoli, cheese, milk, salt and pepper in a bowl.
2. Pour the mixture on top of the pie crust.
3. Add the pie crust to the air fryer tray.
4. Choose air fry function.
5. Cook at 320 degrees F for 12 to 15 minutes.

Serving Suggestion:

Garnish with chopped parsley.

Tip:

If eggs are not fully cooked after 15 minutes, reduce temperature to 300 degrees F and cook for another 5 minutes.

Breakfast Bombs

Explode with satisfaction with these

breakfast bombs.

Prep Time and Cooking Time: 20 minutes | Serves: 6

- 1 cup scrambled eggs
- 1/2 cup cheddar cheese, shredded
- 1/2 cup bacon, cooked and crumbled
- 1 package refrigerator biscuits
- Salt and pepper to taste
- Cooking spray

Step-by-Step Directions

1. In a bowl, combine the eggs, cheese and bacon.
2. Place in the center of the biscuits.
3. Season with salt and pepper.
4. Roll and seal the edges.
5. Add to the air fryer oven.
6. Spray with oil.
7. Choose toast setting.
8. Toast at 330 degrees F for 5 minutes.

Serving Suggestion:

Serve with hot chocolate drink.

Tip:

You can also use mozzarella cheese for this recipe.

Vegetable Frittata

This vegetable frittata is loaded with flavors and textures that you love.

Prep Time and Cooking Time: 15 minutes | Serves: 6

Ingredients to Use:

- 4 eggs, beaten
- 1/4 cup leek, chopped
- 1 cup spinach, chopped
- 1 cup mushrooms, sliced
- 3 tablespoons heavy cream
- 1/2 cup cheddar cheese, shredded
- 1 teaspoon garlic salt
- Salt and pepper to taste

Step-by-Step Directions

1. Mix all the ingredients in a bowl.
2. Pour mixture into a small baking pan.
3. Slide the baking pan into the air fryer oven.
4. Opt for air fry setting.
5. Air fry at 300 degrees F for 10 minutes.

Serving Suggestion:

Garnish with chopped chives.

Tip:

You can also add other vegetables into the mix.

Sausage Patties

If you want something heavy for breakfast, try these delicious sausage patties.

Prep Time and Cooking Time: 15 minutes | Serves: 8

Ingredients to Use:

- 1 package thawed sausage patties

Step-by-Step Directions

1. Spread the sausage patties on the air fryer tray.
2. Set it to air fry.
3. Cook at 400 degrees F for 5 minutes.
4. Flip and cook for another 5 minutes.

Serving Suggestion:

Garnish with parsley.

Tip:

Thaw the sausages before air frying.

Breakfast Burrito

Enjoy Mexican flavors with this delicious breakfast burrito.

Prep Time and Cooking Time: 30 minutes | Serves: 4

Ingredients to Use:

- 4 scrambled eggs

- 1 lb. ground sausage, cooked and crumbled
- 1/2 cup red bell pepper, chopped
- 4 tortillas
- 1/2 cup salsa
- 1/2 cup cheese, shredded

Step-by-Step Directions

1. Mix the eggs, sausage and red bell pepper.
2. Add this mixture on top of the tortillas.
3. Sprinkle with cheese.
4. Roll up the tortillas.
5. Select air fry option.
6. Cook at 400 degrees F for 5 minutes.
7. Spread the salsa on top.

Serving Suggestion:

Garnish with basil leaves.

Tip:

Use Colby Jack cheese for this recipe.

Chocolate French Toast

A rich and delicious breakfast toast that only takes a few minutes to prepare.
Prep Time and Cooking Time: 20 minutes | Serves: 4

Ingredients to Use:

- 4 eggs, beaten
- 1 cup milk
- 1/4 cup cocoa powder
- 1/2 cup sugar
- 1/2 teaspoon baking powder
- Pinch salt
- 8 slices bread, cut into strips

Step-by-Step Directions

1. Mix the eggs, milk, cocoa powder, sugar, baking powder and salt in a bowl.
2. Dip the bread slices in the mixture.
3. Let it soak for 5 minutes.
4. Transfer to the air fryer oven.

5. Choose toast setting.
6. Cook at 350 degrees F for 5 minutes per side.

Serving Suggestion:

Dust with powdered sugar.

Tip:

Use unsweetened cocoa powder.

Sausage Muffin

Craving for your favorite fast food breakfast? Here's how to make your own at home.
Prep Time and Cooking Time: 15 minutes | Serves: 2

Ingredients to Use:

- 2 sausage patties
- 2 English muffins, split in half
- 2 tablespoons butter, softened
- 2 slices cheddar cheese

Step-by-Step Directions

1. Place the sausage patties in the air fryer oven.
2. Set it to toast.
3. Cook at 400 degrees F for 5 minutes per side.
4. Brush the muffins with the softened butter.
5. In the last 3 minutes of cooking the sausages, add the muffins.
6. Place the muffins on a plate.
7. Top with the cheese and sausages.
8. Top with the other muffin slice.

Serving Suggestion:

Serve with a cup of hot coffee.

Sweet Potato Hash

There's so much to love about this dish—its flavors and aroma are truly enticing.
Prep Time and Cooking Time: 25 minutes | Serves: 4

- 2 cups sweet potatoes, diced
- 3 slices bacon, chopped
- 3 tablespoons olive oil
- 1 teaspoon sweet paprika
- 1 teaspoon Italian seasoning
- Salt and pepper to taste

Step-by-Step Directions

1. Combine all the ingredients in a bowl.
2. Mix well.
3. Transfer to the air fryer oven.
4. Select roast setting.
5. Roast at 400 degrees F for 15 minutes, stirring twice.

Serving Suggestion:

Sprinkle with pepper.

Tip:

Spread the sweet potatoes in a single layer to cook evenly.

Egg in Hole Sandwich

Impress your family with this interesting yet easy to make breakfast dish.
Prep Time and Cooking Time: 15 minutes | Serves: 4

Ingredients to Use:

- 4 teaspoons butter, softened
- 4 slices bread
- 4 eggs
- Salt and pepper to taste

Step-by-Step Directions

1. Spread the butter on top of the breads slices.
2. Cut a hole in the center using a cookie or biscuit cutter.
3. Place the bread slices on the air crisper.
4. Crack the eggs into the holes of the bread.
5. Set your air fryer oven to toast.

6. Toast at 330 degrees F for 5 to 7 minutes.

Serving Suggestion:

Sprinkle with chopped green onion.

Tip:

Any type of bread can be used for this recipe.

Sausages

A classic breakfast dish that's perfect for busy mornings.
Prep Time and Cooking Time: 15 minutes | Serves: 10

Ingredients to Use:

- 1 package breakfast sausage

Step-by-Step Directions

1. Arrange the sausages on the air fryer tray.
2. Select air fry setting.
3. Cook at 400 degrees F for 5 minutes.
4. Flip and cook for another 5 minutes.

Serving Suggestion:

Serve with hash browns.

Tip:

Poke the sausages with a fork before air frying.

Hash Browns

Here's a quick and easy breakfast dish that would certainly fill you up.
Prep Time and Cooking Time: 15 minutes | Serves: 6

Ingredients to Use:

- Cooking spray
- 6 frozen hash browns

Step-by-Step Directions

1. Spray your air crisper tray with oil.
2. Arrange the hash browns in the air crisper tray.
3. Turn to air fry setting.

4. Cook at 400 degrees F for 5 minutes.
5. Flip and cook for another 5 minutes.

Serve with ketchup and mayo.

Do not overcrowd your air crisper tray.

Banana Bread

This banana bread comes out nice and fluffy when you cook it in your air fryer oven.
Prep Time and Cooking Time: 40 minutes | Serves: 4

Ingredients to Use:

- 2 cups flour
- 1 egg, beaten
- 1-1/4 cup sugar
- 1 teaspoon baking soda
- Pinch salt
- 2 tablespoons milk
- 1 teaspoon vanilla extract
- 1/2 cup vegetable oil
- 3 ripe bananas, mashed

Step-by-Step Directions

1. Combine flour, egg, sugar, baking soda and salt in a bowl.
2. Mix well.
3. Stir in the milk, vanilla extract and oil.
4. Mix until fully combined.
5. Add the mashed bananas and mix well.
6. Pour the batter into a small loaf pan.
7. Place the pan inside the air fryer oven.
8. Choose bake function.
9. Bake at 310 degrees F for 30 minutes.

Serving Suggestion:

Let cool for 5 to 10 minutes before slicing and serving.

Tip:

Check for doneness by inserting a toothpick into the bread. If it comes out clean, then it means that the bread is already cooked.

Strawberry Oatmeal

Make your oatmeal more flavorful by topping it with strawberries.
Prep Time and Cooking Time: 40 minutes | Serves: 2

Ingredients to Use:

- 2 cups strawberries, sliced and divided
- 1 cup milk
- 1 cup rolled oats
- 4 tablespoons brown sugar
- 1/2 teaspoon ground cinnamon
- 1/2 teaspoon baking powder
- 4 tablespoons almonds, slivered
- Pinch salt

Step-by-Step Directions

1. Combine half of the strawberries with the rest of the ingredients in a small baking pan.
2. Let sit for 10 minutes.
3. Sprinkle the remaining strawberries on top.
4. Place the pan inside the air fryer oven.
5. Turn to bake function.
6. Bake at 350 degrees F for 10 minutes, stirring once.

Serving Suggestion:

Sprinkle with nutmeg before serving.

Tip:

You can also add 1 egg into the mixture.

Buttered Bagel

Who can say no to buttered bagel in the morning?
Prep Time and Cooking Time: 10 minutes | Serves: 2

Ingredients to Use:

- 2 tablespoons butter, softened

- 2 bagels, sliced in half

1. Spread half of the butter on the bagels.
2. Place inside the air fryer oven.
3. Set your air fryer oven to toast.
4. Toast at 365 degrees F for 3 minutes.
5. Take the bagels out of the oven.
6. Spread remaining butter.
7. Toast for another 3 minutes.

Serving Suggestion:

Serve with coffee or hot chocolate drink.

Grilled Cheese Sandwich

This grilled cheese sandwich is always a good idea for breakfast!
Prep Time and Cooking Time: 10 minutes | Serves: 2

Ingredients to Use:

- 2 tablespoons butter, softened
- 4 slices bread
- 8 slices provolone cheese
- 2 eggs, fried

Step-by-Step Directions

1. Spread butter on the bread slices.
2. Add the cheese slices on top of the 2 bread slices.
3. Preheat your air fryer oven to 350 degrees F for 5 minutes.
4. Choose toast setting.
5. Toast all the bread slices inside the oven for 3 minutes.
6. Take the bread slices out of the oven.
7. Add the egg on top.
8. Top with the other bread slice.

Serving Suggestion:

Serve with hot drink.

Tip:

You can skip the egg to reduce calorie count if you like.

Chocolate Croissant

These chocolate drizzled croissants are perfect whether for breakfast or for snack.
Prep Time and Cooking Time: 15 minutes | Serves: 8

Ingredients to Use:

- 1 pack frozen croissant rolls
- 4 tablespoons chocolate syrup

Step-by-Step Directions

1. Add the croissant rolls to the air fryer oven.
2. Choose air fry setting.
3. Cook at 320 degrees F for 4 to 5 minutes per side or until golden.
4. Drizzle with the chocolate syrup and serve.

Serving Suggestion:

Sprinkle with chopped walnuts on top.

Tip:

You can also use canned croissant rolls.

Blueberry Buckle

Want something sweet but healthy for breakfast? Here's the perfect choice.
Prep Time and Cooking Time: 30 minutes | Serves: 6

Ingredients to Use:

- Cooking spray
- Cake
- 2 cups cake mix
- 3/4 cup butter, melted
- 14 oz. condensed milk
- 1-3/4 cup blueberries
- 1 teaspoon lemon zest
- Topping
- 1/2 cup cake mix
- 2 tablespoons butter, melted
- 1/2 cup brown sugar

1. Combine the cake ingredients in a bowl.
2. Mix well.
3. Spray a small cake pan with oil.
4. Pour the batter into the cake pan.
5. Blend the topping ingredients in another bowl.
6. Spread this mixture on top of the batter.
7. Place the pan inside the air fryer oven.
8. Turn to bake option.
9. Cook at 320 degrees F for 10 minutes.

Serving Suggestion:

Drizzle with syrup before serving.

Tip:

Check for doneness by inserting a toothpick into the bread. If it comes out clean, then it means that the bread is already cooked.

Cinnamon Roll French Toast

This can easily become a family favorite. It's very easy to make too.
Prep Time and Cooking Time: 15 minutes | Serves: 6

Ingredients to Use:

- Cooking spray
- 6 cinnamon rolls
- 3 eggs
- 1 teaspoon vanilla extract
- 1 cup milk

Step-by-Step Directions

1. Spray your baking pan with oil.
2. Add the cinnamon rolls to the air fryer oven.
3. Choose toast setting.
4. Toast at 350 degrees F for 7 minutes.
5. Take out of the oven.
6. Let cool for 10 minutes.
7. In a bowl, beat the eggs.
8. Stir in the vanilla extract and milk.
9. Soak the cinnamon rolls in the mixture.

10. Place these back to the air fryer.
11. Toast at 340 degrees F for 3 minutes per side.

Serving Suggestion:

Dust with confectioners' sugar.

Tip:

You can also make your own cinnamon rolls if you prefer but to save time, it would be a good idea to buy these pre-made.

Breakfast Pinwheels

You'll be delighted to learn how to make these awesome pinwheels for breakfast.
Prep Time and Cooking Time: 20 minutes | Serves: 6

Ingredients to Use:

- 1 pack crescent rounds
- 1/2 cup cheddar cheese, grated
- 3 slices bacon, cooked

Step-by-Step Directions

1. Unroll the crescent rounds.
2. Sprinkle the grated cheddar cheese on top.
3. Top with the bacon.
4. Roll up the crescent rounds.
5. Add to the air fryer oven.
6. Choose air fry setting.
7. Cook at 330 degrees F for 5 minutes.
8. Flip and cook for another 2 minutes.

Serving Suggestion:

Sprinkle with a little pepper.

Tip:

You can also brush the tops with melted butter before air frying.

Sugar Glazed Donuts

Glazed donuts are a sweet way to start your morning.
Prep Time and Cooking Time: 10 minutes |

Serves: 10

- 10 refrigerated biscuits
- 4 tablespoons butter, melted
- 1 cup powdered sugar
- 2 tablespoons milk

Step-by-Step Directions

1. Cut the middle part of the biscuit using a round cookie cutter.
2. Soak the biscuits in the butter.
3. Add to the air fryer.
4. Select bake setting.
5. Bake at 330 degrees F for 4 to 6 minutes or until golden.
6. Mix the milk and sugar in a bowl.
7. Dip the donuts in the mixture.

Serving Suggestion:

Let the milk mixture harden before serving.

Tip:

You can also sprinkle with ground cinnamon.

Lemon Poppy Seed Muffins

You're going to enjoy making these muffins and of course, eating them afterwards!
Prep Time and Cooking Time: 20 minutes | Serves: 12

Ingredients to Use:

- 1 cup all-purpose flour
- 1 tablespoon lemon juice
- 1 tablespoon lemon zest
- 1/4 teaspoon baking soda
- 1 teaspoon baking powder
- 1/4 cup sugar
- Pinch salt
- 1/4 cup sour cream
- 1/4 cup butter, melted
- 1 egg, beaten
- 1 teaspoon vanilla extract
- 1 tablespoons poppy seeds

- Cooking spray

Step-by-Step Directions

1. Mix flour, lemon juice, lemon zest, baking soda, baking powder, sugar and salt in a bowl.
2. In another bowl, blend sour cream, butter, egg and vanilla extract.
3. Add this mixture to the flour mixture.
4. Stir in the poppy seeds.
5. Spray your muffin pan with oil.
6. Pour the batter into the muffin cups.
7. Choose bake function.
8. Bake at 350 degrees F for 10 minutes.

Serving Suggestion:

Serve with hot chocolate drink.

Tip:

Insert a toothpick in the middle of the muffin. If it does not come out clean, air fry for a few more minutes.

Cheese Danish

Creamy and cheesy—this breakfast item does not fail to impress.
Prep Time and Cooking Time: 15 minutes | Serves: 4

Ingredients to Use:

- 1/2 cup sugar
- 8 oz. cream cheese
- 1 teaspoon vanilla extract
- 1 pack frozen crescent rolls

Step-by-Step Directions

1. In a bowl, mix the sugar, cream cheese and vanilla extract.
2. Spread the crescent rolls.
3. Slice into smaller portions.
4. Roll the sides but leave the center shallow.
5. Top the center with the cream cheese mixture.
6. Add to the air fryer oven.

7. Select air fry function.
8. Cook at 320 degrees F for 5 minutes.

Sprinkle with cinnamon.

You can freeze these, and air fry when ready to serve.

Apple Pie Biscuit

Here's something that you can enjoy in the morning or at anytime you feel like it.
Prep Time and Cooking Time: 20 minutes | Serves: 4

- 4 teaspoons butter, melted and divided
- 1 pack refrigerated biscuits, separated
- 1 teaspoon ground cinnamon
- 1/4 cup brown sugar
- 1 cup apple pie filling
- 2 tablespoons milk
- 1/2 cup powdered sugar

1. Combine half of the butter, cinnamon and sugar.
2. Dip the biscuits in this mixture.
3. Arrange in a small baking pan.
4. In another bowl, mix the remaining butter with the rest of the ingredients.
5. Pour the mixture on top of the biscuits.
6. Place inside the air fryer oven.
7. Select bake setting.
8. Bake at 330 degrees F for 8 minutes.
9. Check to see if done.
10. If not, cook for another 2 to 3 minutes.

Drizzle with syrup.

Loaded Omelette

This bright and colorful omelette will surely brighten up the rest of your day.
Prep Time and Cooking Time: 20 minutes | Serves: 2

- 2 eggs
- 1/4 cup milk
- Pinch salt
- 1 onion, chopped
- 1 red bell pepper, diced
- 1 green bell pepper, diced
- 1/4 cup cheddar cheese, shredded
- 1 ham, diced
- 1 teaspoon Italian seasoning

1. Beat the eggs and milk in a bowl.
2. Season with salt.
3. Stir in the rest of the ingredients.
4. Pour into a small baking pan.
5. Place inside the air fryer oven.
6. Set it to air fry.
7. Cook at 350 degrees F for 10 minutes.

Sprinkle chopped scallions on top.

You can also add mushrooms to the mixture.

Scrambled Eggs with Mushrooms

Make your scrambled eggs without any fuss using your air fryer.
Prep Time and Cooking Time: 15 minutes | Serves: 2

- 2 eggs, beaten
- 2 tablespoons milk
- 1/4 tablespoon butter, melted
- 1/8 cup cheddar cheese, shredded
- 1/4 cup mushrooms
- Salt and pepper to taste

Step-by-Step Directions

1. Add the eggs to a bowl.
2. Stir in the rest of the ingredients.
3. Add the mixture to a baking pan.
4. Place baking pan inside the air fryer oven.
5. Choose air fry setting.
6. Set temperature to 300 degrees F.
7. Cook for 3 minutes.
8. Stir and cook for another 3 minutes.
9. Stir again and cook until eggs are set.

Serving Suggestion:

Sprinkle with chopped green onions.

Tip:

Use sliced button mushrooms for this recipe.

Chapter 3: Beef Dishes

Steak with Olive Tapenade

This dish will make you go wow, not just once but several times!
Prep Time and Cooking Time: 30 minutes | Serves: 4

Ingredients to Use:

Steak
- 1-1/4 lb. sirloin steak
- 1 tablespoon olive oil
- Salt and pepper to taste

Tapenade
- 1/2 cup red onion, chopped
- 1 clove garlic, minced
- 1 green bell pepper, chopped
- 1 tablespoon fresh parsley, chopped
- 2 tablespoons capers
- 1 cup kalamata olives, pitted and sliced
- 2 tablespoons olive oil
- 3 tablespoons lemon juice
- Salt and pepper to taste

Step-by-Step Directions

1. Preheat your air fryer to 400 degrees F for 5 minutes.
2. Brush steaks with oil.
3. Season with salt and pepper.
4. Add to the air fryer oven.
5. Choose air fry option.
6. Cook the steaks for 5 to 6 minutes per side.
7. Mix the tapenade ingredients.
8. Serve steak with tapenade.

Serving Suggestion:

Serve with fresh green salad.

Tip:

Let steak come to room temperature for 30 minutes before seasoning.

Steak Salad

Top your leafy greens with steak strips for the ultimate salad you can't get over with.
Prep Time and Cooking Time: 1 hour and 30 minutes | Serves: 4

Ingredients to Use:

Steak
- 2 rib eye steaks, sliced into strips
- 2 teaspoons garlic, minced
- 1/4 cup soy sauce
- 1/4 cup honey
- 1/4 cup bourbon
- 1/4 cup Worcestershire sauce
- 1/4 cup brown sugar
- 1/2 teaspoon red pepper flakes

Salad
- 4 cups Romaine lettuce
- 1/4 cup red onions, sliced
- 1/2 cucumber, diced
- 1 cup cherry tomatoes, sliced in half
- 1/2 mozzarella cheese, shredded

Step-by-Step Directions

1. Add the steaks to a bowl.
2. In another bowl, mix the steak ingredients.
3. Pour mixture into the steak strips.
4. Cover and marinate in the refrigerator for 1 hour.
5. Preheat your air fryer at 400 degrees F for 5 minutes.
6. Select air fry option.
7. Cook the steak strips for 5 minutes per side.
8. Toss the salad ingredients in a large

bowl.
9. Top with the steak strips.

Serving Suggestion:

Serve with vinaigrette.

Tip:

You can also use sirloin steak for this recipe.

Meatballs

Meatballs can be used to top your pasta dish or serve with brown rice.
Prep Time and Cooking Time: 15 minutes | Serves: 4

Ingredients to Use:

- 1/2 lb. ground beef
- 1/2 cup ground pork
- 1 onion, chopped
- 2 cloves garlic, minced
- 2 teaspoons dried basil
- 2 teaspoons dried oregano
- 2 teaspoons dried parsley
- 1 cup breadcrumbs
- 1 egg, beaten
- 1/2 cup Parmesan cheese
- Salt and pepper to taste
- Cooking spray

Step-by-Step Directions

1. Combine all the ingredients in a large bowl.
2. Mix well.
3. Form balls from the mixture.
4. Spray with oil.
5. Add the meatballs to the air fryer oven.
6. Choose air fry option.
7. Cook at 350 degrees F for 4 minutes per side.

Serving Suggestion:

Garnish with chopped green onions.

Tip:

Use lean ground beef and lean ground pork.

Beef Enchilada

Here's a simple beef enchilada recipe if you're craving for Mexican flavors.
Prep Time and Cooking Time: 20 minutes | Serves: 2

Ingredients to Use:

- 1 cup lean ground beef, cooked
- 2 teaspoons taco seasoning
- 1/4 cup tomatoes, chopped
- 1/4 cup black beans
- 1/4 cup enchilada sauce
- 2 tortillas

Step-by-Step Directions

1. Season the ground beef with taco seasoning.
2. Mix with the tomatoes and black beans.
3. Top the tortillas with the beef mixture.
4. Sprinkle cheese on top.
5. Roll up the tortillas.
6. Place in the air fryer.
7. Brush with the enchilada sauce.
8. Select air fry setting.
9. Cook at 350 degrees F for 5 minutes per side.

Serving Suggestion:

Serve with sour cream and Mexican cheese.

Tip:

You can make this ahead of time and freeze. Air fry when you're ready to serve it.

Rib Eye Steak

Give yourself a treat with this delicious rib eye steak that's a cinch to make in the air fryer.
Prep Time and Cooking Time: 20 minutes | Serves: 2

Ingredients to Use:

- 2 rib eye steaks
- 2 tablespoons butter, melted

- Salt and pepper to taste

Step-by-Step Directions

1. Brush steaks with melted butter.
2. Season with salt and pepper.
3. Preheat your air fryer oven to 400 degrees F.
4. Add the steaks to the air fryer oven.
5. Set it to air fry.
6. Cook at 5 minutes per side.

Serving Suggestion:

Let steak rest for 10 minutes before serving.

Tip:

Let steaks sit at room temperature for 30 minutes before seasoning.

Beef Teriyaki

Enjoy this beef teriyaki that only takes a few minutes to prepare.
Prep Time and Cooking Time: 20 minutes | Serves: 2

Ingredients to Use:

- 1 tablespoon soy sauce
- 2 tablespoons olive oil
- Pepper to taste
- 1 lb. sirloin steak, sliced into strips
- 1 onion, sliced
- 1 red bell pepper, sliced into strips
- 1 green bell pepper, sliced into strips
- 1 yellow bell pepper, sliced into strips
- 1 cup teriyaki sauce

Step-by-Step Directions

1. Mix the soy sauce, olive oil and pepper in a bowl.
2. Pour half of the mixture into another bowl.
3. Stir in the steak strips into the first bowl.
4. Add the onion and peppers to the other bowl.
5. Preheat your air fryer to 400 degrees F.

6. Add the steak and vegetables to the air fryer tray.
7. Select roasting setting.
8. Cook for 5 to 7 minutes.
9. Stir in the teriyaki sauce.
10. Cook for another 2 minutes.

Serving Suggestion:

Garnish with chopped scallions and sesame seeds.

Tip:

You can also use other types of steak for this recipe.

New York Strip Steak

Don't worry about the complexity of preparing steak. It's easy if you have the air fryer.
Prep Time and Cooking Time: 20 minutes | Serves: 2

Ingredients to Use:

- 2 New York strip steaks
- Salt and pepper
- 2 tablespoons olive oil
- Herbed butter
- 1/2 cup butter
- 1 teaspoon garlic, minced
- 1 teaspoon lemon juice
- 1 tablespoon rosemary, chopped
- 1 tablespoon parsley, chopped
- 1 teaspoon thyme, chopped
- Salt and pepper to taste

Step-by-Step Directions

1. Combine the herbed butter ingredients in a bowl.
2. Form a log from the mixture. Wrap with plastic.
3. Refrigerate for 1 hour.
4. Sprinkle both sides of steaks with salt and pepper.

5. Preheat your air fryer to 400 degrees F for 5 minutes.
6. Choose air fry setting.
7. Cook the steaks for 5 minutes per side.
8. Top with the butter log and let butter melt before serving.

Serving Suggestion:

Let steak rest for 10 minutes before serving.

Steak Bites

Slice your steak into cubes and season with steak rub before air frying.
Prep Time and Cooking Time: 15 minutes | Serves: 4

Ingredients to Use:
- 1 lb. steak, sliced into cubes
- Steak rub
- 1 tablespoon olive oil
- 1 teaspoon onion powder
- 1 teaspoon garlic powder
- 1 teaspoon Montreal steak seasoning
- 1/2 teaspoon cayenne pepper
- Salt and pepper to taste

Step-by-Step Directions
1. Select roast setting in your air fryer oven.
2. Preheat your air fryer oven to 400 degrees F.
3. Mix the olive oil, onion powder, garlic powder, steak seasoning, cayenne pepper, salt and pepper.
4. Rub the steak with the mixture.
5. Add the steaks to the air fryer oven.
6. Cook for 5 minutes.
7. Turn and cook for another 3 minutes.

Serving Suggestion:

Serve with mashed potatoes.

Tip:

Use rib eye steak for this recipe.

Meatloaf

This meatloaf is a simple yet filling dish that will only take 30 minutes to prepare using the air fryer.
Prep Time and Cooking Time: 30 minutes | Serves: 6

Ingredients to Use:
- 2 tablespoons butter
- 1/2 cup onions
- 1/2 cup green bell peppers, chopped
- 1 lb. ground pork
- 1 lb. ground beef, lean
- 1 tablespoon soy sauce
- 2 eggs, beaten
- 1 tablespoon Worcestershire sauce
- 1 cup breadcrumbs
- 1/4 cup ketchup

Step-by-Step Directions
1. Add the butter to a pan over medium heat.
2. Sauté the onion and bell peppers for 2 minutes.
3. Mix the rest of the ingredients along with the cooked onion and bell peppers.
4. Press mixture into a small loaf pan.
5. Choose bake function.
6. Cook at 350 degrees F for 15 minutes.

Serving Suggestion:

Let cool for 10 minutes before slicing and serving.

Tip:

Internal temperature should be 160 degrees F.

Steak with Basil & Garlic Butter

Your mouth will water once the aroma of this steak fill up your kitchen.
Prep Time and Cooking Time: 30 minutes | Serves: 2

Ingredients to Use:

- 2 rib eye steaks
- 2 tablespoons olive oil
- Salt and pepper to taste
- 3 rosemary sprigs
- Garlic Basil Butter:
- 1/2 teaspoon garlic powder
- 4 teaspoons fresh basil, chopped
- 1/2 cup butter
- 1 teaspoon fresh parsley, chopped

Step-by-Step Directions

1. Brush both sides of steaks with oil.
2. Season with salt and pepper.
3. Add the steak to the air fryer oven.
4. Top with the rosemary sprigs.
5. Add to the air fryer oven.
6. Choose air fry setting.
7. Cook at 400 degrees F for 5 minutes per side.
8. Mix the garlic basil butter ingredients.
9. Spread mixture on top of the steaks before serving.

Serving Suggestion:

Serve with mashed potatoes and gravy.

Tip:

Let steak sit at room temperature for 30 minutes before seasoning.

Steak with Chimichurri

Homemade chimichurri certainly ups the ante of your favorite flank steak.
Prep Time and Cooking Time: 20 minutes | Serves: 4

Ingredients to Use:

- 2 lb. flank steak
- 2 tablespoons butter
- Salt and pepper to taste
- Chimichurri Sauce
- 1/4 cup olive oil
- 2 tablespoons red wine vinegar

- 1/2 cup cilantro, chopped
- 1/2 cup parsley, chopped
- 1/2 onion, sliced
- 1 clove garlic
- 1/2 teaspoon red pepper flakes
- Salt and pepper to taste

Step-by-Step Directions

1. Preheat your air fryer oven to 400 degrees F.
2. Select air fry option.
3. Coat your flank steak with butter.
4. Season with salt and pepper.
5. Place inside the air fryer oven.
6. Cook for 6 minutes per side.
7. Add the chimichurri ingredients to the food processor.
8. Pulse until smooth.
9. Spread steak with the chimichurri and serve.

Serving Suggestion:

Serve with your favorite salad.

Tip:

Let steak rest for 30 minutes at room temperature before rubbing with butter.

Beef & Bean Rolls

Perfect for parties or at anytime you're craving for beef and bean taquitos!
Prep Time and Cooking Time: 20 minutes | Serves: 4

Ingredients to Use:

- 1 lb. ground beef, cooked
- 1/2 cup refried beans
- 2 teaspoons taco seasoning
- 4 corn tortillas
- 1/4 cup tomatoes, chopped
- 1/2 cup Mexican cheese, shredded

Step-by-Step Directions

1. Mix beef and beans in a bowl.

2. Season with taco seasoning.
3. Top the tortillas with the beef mixture.
4. Sprinkle tomatoes and cheese on top.
5. Roll up the tortillas.
6. Add the rolls to the air fryer tray.
7. Select air fry setting.
8. Cook at 340 degrees F for 4 minutes per side.

Serve with sour cream.

Tip:

You can make these in advance and freeze until ready to air fry.

Beef Kebab

With simple marinade, you can transform beef kebab into something spectacular.
Prep Time and Cooking Time: 2 hours and 30 minutes | Serves: 8

Ingredients to Use:

- 2 cups teriyaki sauce, divided
- 1-1/2 lb. sirloin steak, sliced into cubes
- 1 onion, diced
- 1 green bell pepper, sliced

Step-by-Step Directions

1. Add half of the teriyaki sauce to a sealable plastic bag.
2. Add steak cubes to the bag.
3. Turn to coat evenly.
4. Refrigerate for 2 hours.
5. Thread steak cubes and vegetables onto skewers.
6. Brush with the remaining sauce.
7. Place in the air fryer oven.
8. Choose grill or roast option.
9. Cook at 400 degrees F for 5 minutes per side.

Serving Suggestion:

Serve with remaining teriyaki sauce.

Tip:

You can also use rib eye steak sliced into cubes.

Barbecue Meatballs

Give your taste buds a treat with these amazing barbecue meatballs.
Prep Time and Cooking Time: 15 minutes | Serves: 6

Ingredients to Use:

- 1 pack frozen meatballs
- 1 cup barbecue sauce

Step-by-Step Directions

1. Spread meatballs onto the air fryer tray.
2. Turn to air fry setting.
3. Cook at 350 degrees F for 5 minutes.
4. Pour the barbecue sauce into a pan over medium heat.
5. Heat the sauce for 5 minutes.
6. Toss meatballs in the sauce and serve.

Serving Suggestion:

Garnish with chopped scallions.

Tip:

You can also make your own meatballs if you like. Simply mix ground beef, breadcrumbs, egg and chopped onions.

Roast Beef

You don't have to wait for a special occasion to enjoy this delightful dish.
Prep Time and Cooking Time: 40 minutes | Serves: 6

Ingredients to Use:

- 2 tablespoons olive oil
- 1 tablespoon fresh oregano, minced
- Salt and pepper to taste
- 2 lb. roast beef

Step-by-Step Directions

1. Mix olive oil, oregano, salt and pepper in

a bowl.
2. Rub mixture all over the roast beef.
3. Preheat your air fryer oven to 400 degrees F.
4. Choose roast setting.
5. Add the roast beef to the air fryer.
6. Roast for 12 to 15 minutes per side.

Let roast beef rest for 5 minutes before slicing and serving.

Tip:

Internal temperature should be 160 degrees F for well done.

Beef Burger with Bacon

There's no need to go to a fast food when you can you're your own burger at home.
Prep Time and Cooking Time: 20 minutes | Serves: 4

Ingredients to Use:

Patty
- 1/2 cup onion, chopped
- 1-1/2 lb. lean ground beef
- 1 teaspoon Worcestershire sauce
- 1 teaspoon soy sauce
- 1 teaspoon dried parsley
- 1 teaspoon garlic powder

Burger
- 4 slices bacon, cooked
- 4 burger rolls

Step-by-Step Directions

1. In a bowl, combine the patty ingredients.
2. Form patties from the mixture.
3. Place the patties inside the air fryer oven.
4. Select grill setting.
5. Cook at 400 degrees F for 8 minutes.
6. Flip and cook for another 3 minutes.
7. Serve in burger buns with bacon.

Serving Suggestion:

Serve with ketchup and mayo.

Tip:

You can also add cheese to your burger.

Steak with Rosemary Butter

You'll feel like you're in a fancy restaurant when you make this steak in your air fryer.
Prep Time and Cooking Time: 1 hour and 20 minutes | Serves: 2

Ingredients to Use:
- 2 rib eye or t-bone steaks
- Salt and pepper to taste
- 1/4 cup butter
- 1 tablespoon rosemary, chopped

Step-by-Step Directions

1. Preheat your air fryer oven to 400 degrees F for 5 minutes.
2. Choose air fry setting.
3. Season steaks with salt and pepper.
4. In a bowl, mix butter and rosemary.
5. Form round shapes from the mixture.
6. Wrap with plastic.
7. Refrigerate for 1 hour.
8. Cook the steaks in the air fryer oven for 6 minutes per side.
9. Top with the herbed butter before serving.

Serving Suggestion:

Serve with mashed potatoes and gravy.

Tip:

Let beef rest for 30 minutes at room temperature before seasoning.

Sirloin Steak with Mustard Butter

This is one quick and simple dish that you can't get enough.

Prep Time and Cooking Time: 20 minutes | Serves: 2

Ingredients to Use:

- 2 sirloin steaks
- 2 tablespoons olive oil
- Salt and pepper to taste
- Mustard butter
- 2 tablespoons butter
- 1 tablespoon scallion, chopped
- 1 teaspoon mustard
- Salt and pepper to taste

Step-by-Step Directions

1. Preheat your air fryer to 400 degrees F for 5 minutes.
2. Brush steaks with oil.
3. Season with salt and pepper.
4. Choose air fry setting in your air fryer oven.
5. Cook the steaks for 6 minutes per side.
6. Mix the mustard butter ingredients in a bowl.
7. Press onto a small circular dish.
8. Cover and refrigerate for 1 hour.
9. Top the steaks with the mustard butter and serve.

Serving Suggestion:

Serve with steamed or grilled asparagus.

Tip:

Use Dijon style mustard.

Bourbon Steaks

Add bourbon to your steaks and you'll be surprised with the outcome.
Prep Time and Cooking Time: 1 hour and 20 minutes | Serves: 4

Ingredients to Use:

- 1 lb. steak, sliced into cubes

Marinade
- 1/2 cup vegetable oil
- 1/2 cup bourbon
- 1/2 cup Worcestershire sauce
- 1/2 cup mustard
- 1/2 cup brown sugar

Step-by-Step Directions

1. Mix the marinade ingredients in a bowl.
2. Add the steak cubes to the marinade.
3. Cover and marinate for 1 hour in the refrigerator.
4. Transfer steak cubes to the air fryer tray.
5. Select grill setting.
6. Set it to 400 degrees F.
7. Cook for 5 minutes.
8. Turn and cook for another 5 minutes.

Serving Suggestion:

Serve with vegetable side dish.

Tip:

You can also use honey instead of brown sugar.

Rib Eye Steak with Buttered Garlic & Chives

Make your herbed butter with garlic and chives for incredible flavors you'd love.
Prep Time and Cooking Time: 1 hour and 20 minutes | Serves: 2

Ingredients to Use:

- 2 rib eye steaks
- Olive oil
- Salt and pepper to taste
- Garlic & chive butter
- 1/2 cup butter
- 1 clove garlic, minced
- 1 tablespoon chives, chopped

Step-by-Step Directions

1. Combine the butter ingredients in a bowl.
2. Refrigerate for 1 hour.
3. Preheat your air fryer to 400 degrees F

for 5 minutes.

4. Rub steaks with oil and season with salt and pepper.
5. Place inside the air fryer oven.
6. Choose air fry option.
7. Air fry the steaks for 6 minutes.
8. Turn and cook for another 6 minutes.
9. Top the steaks with the butter compound and serve.

Serving Suggestion:

Serve with gravy.

Tip:

You can also use other types of steaks for this recipe.

Sesame Beef Stir Fry

There's no need for Chinese takeout when you can make this fantastic dish at home.
Prep Time and Cooking Time: 15 minutes | Serves: 2

Ingredients to Use:

Stir Fry
- 1 lb. flank steak, sliced into strips
- 1/2 cup red onions, sliced
- 1/2 cup carrots, shredded
- 1/2 cup snow peas
- 1/2 cup broccoli florets

Sauce
- 2 cloves garlic, minced
- 1/4 cup hoisin sauce
- 1 tablespoon soy sauce
- 1 teaspoon ground ginger
- 1 teaspoon sesame oil
- 1/4 cup water

Step-by-Step Directions

1. Preheat your air fryer to 400 degrees F for 5 minutes.
2. Choose grill setting.
3. Mix the sauce ingredients in a bowl. Set aside.

4. Add the steaks to the air fryer tray.
5. Cook for 5 minutes per side.
6. Stir in the rest of the stir fry ingredients.
7. Cook for 3 minutes.
8. Add the sauce and stir.
9. Cook for 7 minutes, stirring once or twice.

Serving Suggestion:

Garnish with sesame seeds.

Tip:

Stir to make sure that the steak and veggies do not stick to the air fryer basket.

Steak with Pastrami Butter

Making steak has never been this easy!
Prep Time and Cooking Time: 20 minutes | Serves: 2

Ingredients to Use:

- 2 sirloin steaks
- 2 tablespoons butter
- Salt and pepper to taste
- 1/4 cup butter
- 2 teaspoons pastrami spice blend

Step-by-Step Directions

- Preheat your air fryer oven to 400 degrees F for 5 minutes.
- Spread 2 tablespoons butter on both sides of steaks.
- Sprinkle with salt and pepper.
- Place the steaks inside the air fryer oven.
- Turn to air fry setting.
- Cook steaks for 6 minutes per side.
- Mix the butter and pastrami spice blend.
- Serve on top of the steaks.

Serving Suggestion:

Serve with green leafy salad.

Tip:

Let steak rest for 10 minutes at room temperature before seasoning.

Garlic Steak with Creamy Horseradish

This is a no-fuss steak dish that you can cook quickly in the air fryer.
Prep Time and Cooking Time: 30 minutes | Serves: 2

- 2 sirloin steaks
- 2 tablespoons olive oil
- 2 cloves garlic, minced
- Salt and pepper to taste

Creamy horseradish

- 2 tablespoons horseradish
- 1 cup sour cream
- 1 teaspoon dill
- Salt and pepper to taste

1. Brush both sides of steak with oil.
2. Sprinkle with garlic, salt and pepper.
3. Select roast setting.
4. Place the steaks inside the air fryer oven.
5. Cook the steaks for 6 minutes per side.
6. In a bowl, mix the creamy horseradish ingredients.
7. Spread on top of steaks and serve.

Serve on top of sautéed spinach.

You can also use prime rib for this recipe.

Beef Taco

Enjoy Mexican flavors with this easy to make beef taco recipe.
Prep Time and Cooking Time: 20 minutes | Serves: 4

- 1 lb. ground beef
- 1 tablespoon taco seasoning
- 4 corn tortillas
- Cilantro slaw
- 1 red onion, chopped
- 1 clove garlic, minced
- 2 tablespoons fresh cilantro, chopped
- 1 cup cabbage, shredded
- 1 tablespoon olive oil
- 2 teaspoons lime juice

1. Add the ground beef to a small baking pan.
2. Sprinkle with taco seasoning and mix.
3. Place inside the air fryer oven.
4. Choose air fry setting.
5. Air fry at 400 degrees F for 5 minutes.
6. Stir and cook for another 5 minutes.
7. Toss the cilantro slaw in a bowl.
8. Top the tortilla with the beef mixture and cilantro slaw.
9. Fold and serve.

Serve with sour cream.

You can also use flour tortilla for this recipe.

Strip Steak with Boursin Cheese

Your house will seem like a fancy restaurant once you make this awesome steak dish.
Prep Time and Cooking Time: 20 minutes | Serves: 2

- 2 strip steaks
- Olive oil
- Salt and pepper to taste
- Boursin Cheese
- 12 oz. cream cheese
- 1 clove garlic, minced
- 1 teaspoon parsley, chopped
- 1 teaspoon dried marjoram
- 1 teaspoon dried basil

- 1 teaspoon dried oregano
- 1 teaspoon dried sage
- 1 teaspoon dried chives

1. Coat steaks with oil.
2. Season with salt and pepper.
3. Add to the air fryer oven.
4. Set it to grill or roast.
5. Cook at 400 degrees F for 6 minutes per side.
6. Mix boursin cheese ingredients in a bowl.
7. Serve steak with the boursin cheese on top.

Serving Suggestion:

Serve with roasted baby potatoes.

Tip:

Use New York strip steaks if available.

Baked Meatballs

You and your family will surely be delighted with this amazing dish.
Prep Time and Cooking Time: 15 minutes | Serves: 4

Ingredients to Use:

- 16 oz. frozen meatballs
- 14 oz. marinara sauce
- 1/2 cup mozzarella cheese

Step-by-Step Directions

1. Spread marinara sauce on top of a baking pan.
2. Add meatballs on top.
3. Place the pan inside the air fryer oven.
4. Choose bake function.
5. Set it to 340 degrees F.
6. Cook for 10 minutes.
7. Sprinkle mozzarella cheese over the meatballs.
8. Cook for another 5 minutes.

Serving Suggestion:

Garnish with fresh basil leaves.

Tip:

Use low-sodium marinara sauce.

Pepper Kebabs

Here's a delicious twist to your favorite beef kebab.
Prep Time and Cooking Time: 2 hour and 30 minutes | Serves: 4

Ingredients to Use:

- 1 lb. sirloin steak, sliced into cubes
- 1 bell pepper, sliced
- 1 onion, sliced

Marinade

- 1 clove garlic, minced
- 1/4 cup soy sauce
- 2 tablespoons olive oil
- 2 tablespoons vinegar
- 1 teaspoon ginger, grated
- Pepper to taste

Step-by-Step Directions

1. Mix the marinade ingredients in a bowl.
2. Transfer half of the mixture to another bowl.
3. Marinate steak slices in the first bowl and the veggies in the second bowl for 2 hours.
4. Thread beef and veggies onto skewers.
5. Place inside the air fryer oven.
6. Choose air fry setting.
7. Cook at 350 degrees F for 5 minutes per side.

Serving Suggestion:

Serve with grilled vegetables.

Tip:

Use red wine vinegar if available.

Garlic Parmesan Strip Steak

Make your compound butter with garlic and Parmesan for unforgettable steak.
Prep Time and Cooking Time: 20 minutes | Serves: 2

Ingredients to Use:

- Steaks
- 2 strip steaks
- 1 teaspoon olive oil
- Salt and pepper to taste
- Garlic Parmesan butter
- 2 teaspoons garlic, minced
- 1/2 cup butter
- 1/4 cup Parmesan cheese, grated

Step-by-Step Directions

1. Brush both sides of steaks with olive oil.
2. Place inside the air fryer oven.
3. Select air fry option.
4. Air fry for 5 minutes per side.
5. Mix garlic, butter and cheese in a bowl.
6. Form butter mixture into a round shape.
7. Refrigerate until firm.
8. Top steaks with the butter.

Serving Suggestion:

Let rest for 5 minutes before serving.

Tip:

Use New York strip steaks.

T-Bone Steak with Gorgonzola Butter

Top your steak with a mixture of butter, herbs and Gorgonzola cheese.
Prep Time and Cooking Time: 1 hour and 15 minutes | Serves: 2

Ingredients to Use:

- Steaks
- 2 t-bone steaks
- Olive oil
- Salt and pepper to taste
- Gorgonzola butter
- 1/2 cup butter
- 2 oz. Gorgonzola cheese

Step-by-Step Directions

1. Rub steaks with oil.
2. Sprinkle with salt and pepper.
3. Transfer to the air fryer oven.
4. Choose air fry setting.
5. Cook at 400 degrees F for 5 minutes.
6. Turn and cook for another 5 minutes.
7. Mix butter and cheese in a bowl.
8. Place on top of a plastic sheet.
9. Roll it up to form a log.
10. Freeze for 1 hour.
11. Slice and top steaks with butter.

Serving Suggestion:

Sprinkle with dried herbs before serving.

Tip:

Reduce cooking time to 3 minutes per side if you want your steaks medium well instead of well done.

Parmesan Crusted Steak

You're going to enjoy every bite into this Parmesan crusted steak.
Prep Time and Cooking Time: 15 minutes | Serves: 4

Ingredients to Use:

- 4 flank steaks
- 2 tablespoons olive oil
- 3 tablespoons Parmesan cheese, grated
- Salt and pepper to taste

Step-by-Step Directions

1. Rub steaks with olive oil.
2. Sprinkle both sides with Parmesan cheese, salt and pepper.
3. Add steaks to the air crisper tray.
4. Set your air fryer oven to air fry.

5. Cook for 6 minutes per side.

Garnish with parsley.

Tip:

You can also add dried herbs to the Parmesan mixture.

Seared Sirloin Steak

This will fill you up and satisfy you both at the same time!
Prep Time and Cooking Time: 15 minutes | Serves: 2

Ingredients to Use:

- 2 sirloin steaks
- 2 tablespoons olive oil
- Salt and pepper to taste

Step-by-Step Directions

1. Preheat your air fryer oven to 400 degrees F for 5 minutes.
2. Select air fry setting.
3. Coat steaks with olive oil.
4. Sprinkle with salt and pepper.
5. Place steaks in the air crisper tray.
6. Cook for 6 minutes per side.

Serving Suggestion:

Serve with roasted baby potatoes.

Tip:

You can also season with dried rosemary.

Cranberry Meatballs

Whether you serve it for appetizer or as main course, these meatballs are sure to please.
Prep Time and Cooking Time: 20 minutes | Serves: 6

Ingredients to Use:

- 28 oz. frozen meatballs
- 12 oz. chili sauce
- 14 oz. cranberry sauce

Step-by-Step Directions

1. Select air fry setting in your air fryer oven.
2. Cook meatballs at 350 degrees F for 5 minutes, turning once.
3. In a bowl, mix chili sauce and cranberry sauce.
4. Pour sauce into a pan over medium heat.
5. Heat for 10 minutes.
6. Toss meatballs in sauce and serve.

Serving Suggestion:

Garnish with chopped scallions.

Tip:

Insert toothpicks if serving as appetizer.

Beef Tenderloin with Garlic Butter Sauce

This is the kind of dish you'd want to eat over and over.
Prep Time and Cooking Time: 20 minutes | Serves: 4

Ingredients to Use:

- 4 beef tenderloin fillets
- 4 tablespoons olive oil
- Salt and pepper to taste
- 2 teaspoons fresh rosemary, chopped

Garlic butter sauce

- 1/4 cup butter
- 4 cloves garlic, minced
- Salt to taste
- 1 teaspoon fresh dill, minced
- 1 tablespoon lemon juice

Step-by-Step Directions

1. Preheat your air fryer oven to 400 degrees F for 5 minutes.
2. Coat beef with oil.
3. Sprinkle with salt, pepper and rosemary.
4. Choose air fry setting.
5. Air fry for 6 minutes per side.

6. Add butter to a pan over medium heat.
7. Add garlic and salt.
8. Cook for 1 minute, stirring.
9. Stir in dill and lemon juice.
10. Pour sauce over the beef and serve.

Serving Suggestion:

Garnish with rosemary sprig.

Tip:

Use freshly squeezed lemon juice.

Pepper Steak with Veggies

This is as delicious as it is colorful!
Prep Time and Cooking Time: 1 hour and 15 minutes | Serves: 4

Ingredients to Use:

- 1 tablespoon olive oil
- 1/4 cup soy sauce
- 1 lb. flank steak, sliced into strips
- 2 cloves garlic, minced
- 1 teaspoon ground ginger
- Salt and pepper to taste
- 1 red bell pepper, sliced into strips
- 1 green bell pepper, sliced into strips
- 1 yellow bell pepper, sliced into strips

Step-by-Step Directions

1. Combine all ingredients except bell peppers in a sealable plastic bag.
2. Seal and refrigerate for 1 hour.
3. Add beef to the air crisper tray.
4. Select roast setting.
5. Cook at 400 degrees F for 10 minutes.
6. Stir and add the bell peppers.
7. Cook for another 5 minutes.

Serving Suggestion:

Serve on top of white rice.

Tip:

Slice steak against the grain.

Pepper & Thyme Steak

Flavor up your flank steak with thyme and pepper.
Prep Time and Cooking Time: 10 minutes | Serves: 4

Ingredients to Use:

- 2 tablespoons olive oil
- 1 teaspoon thyme, chopped
- 1 tablespoon lemon zest
- 4 tablespoons soy sauce
- Salt and pepper to taste
- 1 lb. flank steak

Step-by-Step Directions

1. Combine all the ingredients except flank steak in a bowl.
2. Brush both sides of steaks with this mixture.
3. Place steaks inside the air fryer oven.
4. Select roast function.
5. Cook at 400 degrees F for 7 to 10 minutes per side.

Serving Suggestion:

Serve with salad.

Tip:

Add 2 more minutes cooking time for well done.

Greek Burger

Take a trip to Greece when you make this burger at your home.
Prep Time and Cooking Time: 20 minutes | Serves: 4

Ingredients to Use:

- 1-1/2 lb. ground beef
- 1 clove garlic, minced
- 1 tablespoon fresh oregano, chopped
- 1/2 cup feta cheese
- 1 tablespoon lemon juice

Step-by-Step Directions

1. Combine all ingredients in a bowl.
2. Form patties from the mixture.
3. Add these to the air fryer oven.
4. Choose air fry setting.
5. Cook at 380 degrees F for 5 minutes per side.

Serving Suggestion:

Serve in burger buns with lettuce and tomatoes.

Tip:

You can swap garlic with garlic powder.

Bacon Wrapped Beef Tenderloin

You don't have to be a kitchen pro to make this amazing dish.
Prep Time and Cooking Time: 20 minutes | Serves: 2

Ingredients to Use:

- 2 beef tenderloin fillets
- Salt and pepper to taste
- 2 slices bacon

Step-by-Step Directions

1. Season beef with salt and pepper.
2. Wrap bacon around the beef.
3. Set your air fryer oven to air fry.
4. Cook at 400 degrees F for 6 minutes per side.

Serving Suggestion:

Drizzle with steak sauce before serving.

Tip:

Use a toothpick to secure the bacon.

Blue Cheese Burger

This is a surprisingly easy burger dish that you'd enjoy making.
Prep Time and Cooking Time: 20 minutes | Serves: 15

Ingredients to Use:

- 3 lb. lean ground beef
- 1/8 cup chives, minced
- 4 oz. blue cheese
- 1 teaspoon Worcestershire sauce
- 1/4 teaspoon hot pepper sauce
- Salt and pepper to taste

Step-by-Step Directions

1. Combine all the ingredients in a bowl.
2. Form patties from the mixture.
3. Add patties to the air fryer oven.
4. Cook the patties at 360 degrees F for 6 minutes.
5. Flip and cook for another 5 to 7 minutes.

Serving Suggestion:

Serve in burger buns with lettuce and tomatoes.

Tip:

Make sure burger patty is fully cooked. Extend cooking time if necessary.

Carne Asada

This isn't like any other dish you've ever taste.
Prep Time and Cooking Time: 30 minutes | Serves: 6

Ingredients to Use:

- 1/4 cup olive oil
- 1/4 cup lime juice
- 1/2 cup cilantro, chopped
- 4 cloves garlic, minced
- 1 teaspoon cumin powder
- 1 teaspoon chili powder
- Salt and pepper to taste
- 1-1/2 lb. flank steak

Step-by-Step Directions

1. Combine all the ingredients except flank steak in a bowl.
2. Mix well.

3. Add the flank steak to the bowl.
4. Coat evenly with the marinade.
5. Cover and marinate for 1 hour in the refrigerator.
6. Transfer the steak to the air fryer oven.
7. Choose roast setting.
8. Cook at 400 degrees F for 7 minutes per side.

Serving Suggestion:

Serve with salad.

Tip:

Internal temperature should be 145 degrees F.

Hoisin Meatballs

These meatballs are bursting with so much flavor.
Prep Time and Cooking Time: 20 minutes | Serves: 6

Ingredients to Use:

- 1 lb. lean ground beef
- 2 tablespoons scallions, chopped
- 2 tablespoons ginger, minced
- 1 teaspoon sugar
- 2 teaspoons garlic powder
- 1 egg, beaten
- 1/2 cup breadcrumbs
- 1/2 cup hoisin sauce
- Cooking spray

Step-by-Step Directions

1. Mix all the ingredients except hoisin sauce in a bowl.
2. Form meatballs from the mixture.
3. Spray with oil.
4. Transfer to the air fryer oven.
5. Select roast setting.
6. Cook at 350 degrees F for 6 minutes per side.
7. Toss in hoisin sauce and serve.

Serving Suggestion:

Garnish with toasted sesame seeds.

Tip:

Use lean ground beef.

Fried Steak

Want crispy steak? Here's how to do it right.
Prep Time and Cooking Time: 30 minutes | Serves: 4

Ingredients to Use:

- 4 steaks
- Salt and pepper to taste
- 1 cup flour
- 1 egg, beaten
- 1/4 cup milk
- 1 cup breadcrumbs
- Cooking spray

Step-by-Step Directions

1. Season steaks with salt and pepper.
2. Cover with flour.
3. Dip in egg mixed with milk.
4. Dredge with breadcrumbs.
5. Spray with oil.
6. Place steaks in the air fryer tray.
7. Choose air fry setting.
8. Cook at 400 degrees F for 5 minutes per side.

Serving Suggestion:

Serve with mashed potatoes and gravy.

Tip:

Use prime rib or rib eye steaks.

Steak Fajitas

This dish is overflowing with color and flavor.
Prep Time and Cooking Time: 3 hours and 30 minutes | Serves: 4

Ingredients to Use:

- 1 lb. flank steak, sliced into strips

Marinade

- 4 cloves garlic, minced
- 2 tablespoons olive oil
- 1/4 cup lime juice
- 2 teaspoons soy sauce
- 1/4 cup water
- 1/2 teaspoon cayenne pepper
- 1/2 teaspoon liquid smoke flavoring
- Salt and pepper to taste

Vegetables

- 1 red bell pepper, sliced into strips
- 1 orange bell pepper, sliced into strips
- 1 yellow bell pepper, sliced into strips
- 1 sweet onion, sliced into strips

1. Combine marinade ingredients in a bowl.
2. Stir in the beef strips.
3. Cover and marinate for 3 hours.
4. Add steak and vegetables to the air fryer oven.
5. Select bake setting.
6. Cook at 400 degrees F for 10 minutes.
7. Stir and cook for another 10 minutes.

Serving Suggestion:

Serve on top of tortillas.

Tip:

Slice beef against the grain.

Steak Tips

Tender fall-off-the-bone steak tips—something you'd love to have for dinner.
Prep Time and Cooking Time: 2 hours and 15 minutes | Serves: 4

Ingredients to Use:

- 2 lb. rib eye steak, sliced into cubes
- Marinade
- 1 tablespoon olive oil
- 1 teaspoon onion powder

- 1 teaspoon garlic powder
- 2 teaspoons steak seasoning
- Salt and pepper to taste

Step-by-Step Directions

1. Combine marinade ingredients in a bowl.
2. Marinate beef for 2 hours.
3. Transfer beef to the air fryer tray.
4. Turn to air fry setting.
5. Cook at 400 degrees F for 4 minutes.
6. Turn the beef and cook for another 3 minutes.

Serving Suggestion:

Serve with mashed potatoes and gravy.

Tip:

You can also use butter instead of olive oil.

Korean Short Ribs

Take your taste buds to a trip to Korea with this amazing recipe.
Prep Time and Cooking Time: 1 hour and 10 minutes | Serves: 4

Ingredients to Use:

- 2 lb. beef short ribs
- 1 teaspoon garlic, minced
- 1/2 teaspoon red pepper flakes
- 1 tablespoon ground ginger
- 1/2 cup brown sugar
- 1/2 cup soy sauce

Step-by-Step Directions

1. Combine all the ingredients in a bowl.
2. Cover and marinate for 1 hour.
3. Add to the air fryer oven.
4. Select air fry option.
5. Cook at 400 degrees F for 5 minutes.
6. Brush with marinade and flip.
7. Cook for another 5 minutes.

Serving Suggestion:

Garnish with chopped scallions.

You can also use honey instead of sugar.

Cheese Stuffed Meatloaf

This meatloaf gives you cheesy surprise you'd love.

Prep Time and Cooking Time: 20 minutes | Serves: 4

Ingredients to Use:

- 2 lb. ground beef
- 1 teaspoon Italian seasonings
- Salt and pepper to taste
- 1/2 cup mozzarella cheese
- 1 cup marinara sauce

Step-by-Step Directions

1. Mix ground beef, Italian seasoning, salt and pepper in a bowl.
2. Press mixture onto a loaf pan.
3. Squeeze in the cheese inside the meatloaf.
4. Brush the top with marinara sauce.
5. Press bake setting in your air fryer oven.
6. Place the meatloaf inside the air fryer oven.
7. Bake at 350 degrees F for 10 to 15 minutes.

Serving Suggestion:

Serve with caramelized onions.

Tip:

You can also add ground turkey to the mixture.

Lettuce Cups with Beef

Add more veggies to your dishes. Here's one way to do this.

Prep Time and Cooking Time: 30 minutes | Serves: 4

Ingredients to Use:

- 1 lb. beef, sliced

- 2 tablespoons ginger, minced
- 2 tablespoons garlic, minced
- 4 tablespoons rice vinegar
- 2 tablespoons sesame oil
- 2 tablespoons soy sauce
- Salt and pepper to taste
- 1 cucumber, chopped
- 4 cups lettuce, chopped

Step-by-Step Directions

1. Combine all ingredients except cucumber and lettuce in a bowl.
2. Transfer to the air fryer oven.
3. Choose air fry setting.
4. Cook at 400 degrees F for 5 minutes.
5. Add mixture on top of the lettuce leaves.
6. Stir in the cucumber.

Serving Suggestion:

Garnish with white and black sesame seeds.

Tip:

Use large Romaine lettuce leaves.

Steak with Bourbon & Peppercorn Sauce

You'll definitely be impressed with this spectacular peppercorn steak dish.

Prep Time and Cooking Time: 20 minutes | Serves: 4

Ingredients to Use:

- Steaks
- 4 sirloin steaks
- Salt and pepper to taste
- Sauce
- 2 tablespoons olive oil
- 1 shallot, chopped
- 1 clove garlic, minced
- 2 tablespoons peppercorn, crushed
- 2 cups beef broth
- 1/4 cup bourbon
- 2 tablespoons butter
- 1/2 cup heavy cream

- 1 tablespoon sugar

1. Season steaks with salt and pepper.
2. Place in the air fryer oven.
3. Choose air fry setting.
4. Cook at 400 degrees F for 5 to 7 minutes per side.
5. Pour olive oil into a pan over medium heat.
6. Cook the shallots and garlic for 2 minutes.
7. Stir in the rest of the ingredients.
8. Simmer for 10 minutes.
9. Pour sauce over the steaks and serve.

Serving Suggestion:

Garnish with peppercorns.

Tip:

Use low-sodium beef broth.

Steak Cubes with Barbecue Sauce

You'll love the sweet and savory flavors of these steak cubes.
Prep Time and Cooking Time: 10 minutes | Serves: 4

Ingredients to Use:

- 1 lb. steak, sliced into cubes
- 1 cup barbecue sauce

Step-by-Step Directions

1. Toss the steak cubes in the sauce.
2. Spread in the air fryer tray.
3. Choose air fry setting.
4. Cook at 400 degrees F for 5 minutes per side.
5. Set oven to broil.
6. Increase temperature to 450 degrees F.
7. Cook for 2 minutes.

Serving Suggestion:

Season with pepper before serving.

Tip:

Spread steak cubes in a single layer.

Flank Steak with Roasted Garlic Sauce

Roasted garlic lends incredible flavor to your steak.
Prep Time and Cooking Time: 20 minutes | Serves: 2

Ingredients to Use:

- 2 flank steaks
- 1 tablespoon olive oil
- Salt and pepper to taste
- Sauce
- 1/2 cups demi-glace sauce
- 5 cloves garlic, roasted and crushed
- 1 teaspoon chives, minced
- 1/4 cup water

Step-by-Step Directions

1. Brush steaks with oil.
2. Season with salt and pepper.
3. Place the steaks inside the air fryer oven.
4. Choose roast function.
5. Cook at 400 degrees F for 3 to 5 minutes per side.
6. Add sauce ingredients to a pan over medium heat.
7. Bring to a boil.
8. Reduce heat and simmer for 10 minutes.
9. Pour the sauce over the steak and serve.

Serving Suggestion:

Garnish with chopped scallions.

Tip:

You can also serve with grilled asparagus.

Beef & Spinach Rolls

It takes quite some effort to make these beef and spinach rolls, but they are surely worth it.

Prep Time and Cooking Time: 20 minutes | Serves: 2

Ingredients to Use:

- 2 beef tenderloin fillets
- Salt and pepper to taste
- 1 cup spinach, sliced
- 1/2 cup garlic herb cream cheese

Step-by-Step Directions

1. Season beef with salt and pepper.
2. In a bowl, mix spinach and garlic herb cream cheese.
3. Spread mixture on top of the beef.
4. Roll up the beef.
5. Place in the air fryer tray.
6. Choose air fry setting.
7. Set it to 400 degrees F.
8. Cook for 6 minutes per side.

Serving Suggestion:

Serve with green salad.

Tip:

Flatten beef with meat mallet.

Chapter 4: Pork Dishes

Pork Teriyaki

With this quick and simple recipe, dinner is no-stress.

Prep Time and Cooking Time: 6 hours and 30 minutes | Serves: 4

Ingredients to Use:

- 1 tablespoon garlic, minced
- 1 teaspoon ginger, grated
- 1 tablespoon vegetable oil
- 2 tablespoons soy sauce
- 1 tablespoon vinegar
- 1 tablespoon dry sherry
- 1 tablespoon brown sugar
- Salt and pepper to taste
- 1 lb. pork tenderloin

Step-by-Step Directions

1. Combine all the ingredients except pork in a large bowl.
2. Mix well.
3. Add the pork to the marinade.
4. Cover and marinate for 6 hours.
5. Preheat your air fryer to 400°F for 5 minutes.
6. Add pork to the air fryer tray.
7. Cook for 25 to 30 minutes.

Serving Suggestion:

Garnish with sesame seeds or chopped scallions.

Tip:

Use rice vinegar if available.

Bratwursts

You can't go wrong with bratwursts! They're surprisingly easy to prepare using the air fryer.

Prep Time and Cooking Time: 20 minutes | Serves: 4

Ingredients to Use:

- 1 pack bratwursts

Step-by-Step Directions

1. Preheat your air fryer to 350°F.
2. Add sausages to the air fryer oven.
3. Cook for 10 minutes, turning once.

Serving Suggestion:

Serve with mustard and hot pepper sauce.

Tip:

Internal temperature should be 145°F.

Honey Glazed Ham

It'd certainly feel like Thanksgiving or Christmas when you serve this delicious ham on an ordinary night.

Prep Time and Cooking Time: 1 hour | Serves: 6

Ingredients to Use:

- 1 cup brown sugar
- 1 cup honey
- 2 lb. ham, cooked

Step-by-Step Directions

1. Combine sugar and honey in a pan over medium heat.
2. Simmer while stirring for 10 minutes.
3. Add the ham to a baking pan.
4. Pour half of the mixture over ham.
5. Place in the air fryer oven.
6. Cook at 310°F for 20 minutes.
7. Pour the remaining mixture.
8. Cook for another 20 minutes.

Serve with toasted bread.

You can also use maple syrup if honey is not available.

Barbecue Pork Tenderloin

You'll love the fusion of sweet and savory flavors in this barbecue pork tenderloin dish.
Prep Time and Cooking Time: 8 hours and 30 minutes | Serves: 2

Ingredients to Use:

- 10 oz. pork tenderloin

Sauce

- 1/2 cup vinegar
- 2/3 cup ketchup
- 1 teaspoon ground cumin
- 1 teaspoon paprika
- 1/4 cup brown sugar
- Salt and pepper to taste

Step-by-Step Directions

1. Combine all sauce ingredients in a bowl.
2. Simmer for 7 minutes.
3. Let cool.
4. Marinate the pork tenderloin in the sauce for 8 hours.
5. Transfer pork to the air fryer oven.
6. Cook at 400°F for 10 to 15 minutes.

Serving Suggestion:

Serve with green salad.

Tip:

Use cider vinegar.

Apricot Pork Chops

Drizzle pork chops with apricot sauce for a delicious lunch or dinner.
Prep Time and Cooking Time: 30 minutes | Serves: 2

Ingredients to Use:

- 2 pork chops
- Salt and pepper to taste
- 1 tablespoon olive oil
- 1 clove garlic, minced
- 1/2 cup apricot jam
- 1 teaspoon soy sauce
- 1/4 cup water

Step-by-Step Directions

1. Season pork chops with salt and pepper.
2. Spray your air fryer tray with oil.
3. Add pork chops to the tray.
4. Cook at 320°F for 5 to 8 minutes.
5. In a pan over medium heat, add olive oil and cook garlic for 1 minute.
6. Stir in the remaining ingredients.
7. Pour sauce over the pork chops and serve.

Serving Suggestion:

Serve with roasted carrots.

Tip:

Flatten the pork chops with a meat mallet before seasoning.

Breaded Pork Chops

Crispy breaded pork chops air fried to a golden crisp.
Prep Time and Cooking Time: 20 minutes | Serves: 4

Ingredients to Use:

- 4 pork chops
- Salt and pepper to taste
- 1 egg, beaten
- 1/2 cup cornflake crumbs
- 1 cup breadcrumbs
- 1 teaspoon chili powder
- 2 teaspoons sweet paprika
- 1 teaspoon onion powder
- 1 teaspoon garlic powder

1. Season pork chops with salt and pepper.
2. Dip in egg.
3. In a bowl, mi the remaining ingredients.
4. Dredge pork chops with breadcrumb mixture.
5. Air fry at 400°F for 10 minutes.

Serving Suggestion:

Serve with garlic mustard dip.

Tip:

Use boneless pork chops.

Crispy Pork Belly

Forget your diet plan for a while and enjoy these delicious crispy pork belly slices.
Prep Time and Cooking Time: 40 minutes | Serves: 4

Ingredients to Use:

- 1 lb. pork belly, sliced into 3
- 2 tablespoons olive oil
- Salt to taste

Step-by-Step Directions

1. Coat pork belly with oil.
2. Season with salt.
3. Place in the air fryer tray.
4. Cook at 350°F for 20 minutes.
5. Increase temperature to 400°F.
6. Cook for 10 minutes.

Serving Suggestion:

Garnish with basil leaves.

Tip:

You can also slice the pork belly into smaller portions.

Chili Cheese Dog

This chili cheese dog is great either for snack or dinner.
Prep Time and Cooking Time: 30 minutes |

Serves: 4

Ingredients to Use:

- 4 hotdogs
- 4 hotdog rolls
- 1 cup chili
- 1/2 cup cheddar cheese, shredded

Step-by-Step Directions

1. Air fry the hot dogs at 370°F for 5 minutes.
2. Place the hot dogs in the buns.
3. Pour chili on top of the hot dogs.
4. Sprinkle cheese on top.
5. Air fry at 300°F for 5 minutes or until cheese has melted.

Serving Suggestion:

Sprinkle with pepper before serving.

Tip:

You can also use cheese dogs.

Sausage & Cheese Egg Scramble

Combine your sausage and cheese in this baked egg dish that you can eat for breakfast or lunch.
Prep Time and Cooking Time: 15 minutes | Serves: 4

Ingredients to Use:

- 6 eggs
- 3/4 cup milk
- 6 sausages, cooked and crumbled
- 1 cup cheddar cheese, shredded
- Cooking spray

Step-by-Step Directions

1. In a bowl, beat the eggs and stir in the milk, sausages and cheese.
2. Spray your air fryer tray with oil.
3. Pour the mixture into the ramekins.
4. Add ramekins to the air fryer tray.
5. Cook at 320°F for 8 minutes.
6. Check if the eggs are done.

7. Cook for another 5 minutes.

Serving Suggestion:

Sprinkle chopped scallions on top.

Tip:

You can also add herbs to the mixture.

Thyme Pork Chops

You'll love how thyme boosts the flavor of pork chops.
Prep Time and Cooking Time: 15 minutes | Serves: 4

Ingredients to Use:

- 4 pork chops
- 4 teaspoons dried thyme
- Salt and pepper to taste
- 2 eggs, beaten
- 1 cup cornstarch
- Cooking spray

Step-by-Step Directions

1. Season pork chops with thyme, salt and pepper.
2. Dip pork chops in eggs.
3. Cover with cornstarch.
4. Spray with oil.
5. Add to the air fryer tray.
6. Cook at 360°F for 6 minutes per side.

Serving Suggestion:

Serve with salad made of shredded purple cabbage.

Tip:

You can also use other herbs to season the pork chops.

Honey Garlic Pork Chops

This nice and flavorful pork chop dish is bound to impress.
Prep Time and Cooking Time: 20 minutes | Serves: 4

Ingredients to Use:

- 4 pork chops
- Salt and pepper to taste
- 4 tablespoons olive oil
- 4 cloves garlic, minced
- 1/2 cup honey
- 2 tablespoons sweet chili sauce
- 4 tablespoons lemon juice

Step-by-Step Directions

1. Season pork chops with salt and pepper.
2. Add to the air fryer tray.
3. Cook at 400°F for 7 minutes per side.
4. Pour olive oil into a pan over medium heat.
5. Cook garlic for 1 minute, stirring often.
6. Stir in the remaining ingredients.
7. Simmer for 10 minutes.
8. Pour sauce over the pork chops and serve.

Serving Suggestion:

Sprinkle with pepper.

Tip:

Use bone-in pork chops.

Ham with Apricot Sauce

Here's a fun and easy way to cook ham in the air fryer.
Prep Time and Cooking Time: 20 minutes | Serves: 2

Ingredients to Use:

- 1/4 cup apricot jam
- 1 teaspoon mustard
- 1 teaspoon lemon juice
- 1/2 teaspoon ground cinnamon
- 2 ham steaks

Step-by-Step Directions

1. Combine apricot jam, mustard, lemon juice and cinnamon in a bowl.
2. Brush sauce on both sides of ham.

3. Place the ham on the air fryer tray.
4. Cook at 350°F for 5 minutes.
5. Flip and brush with the remaining sauce.
6. Cook for another 5 minutes.

Serving Suggestion:

Garnish with lemon wedges.

Tip:

Use Dijon mustard.

Baby Back Ribs

You don't have to eat in a fancy restaurant to enjoy this amazing dish.
Prep Time and Cooking Time: 35 minutes | Serves: 4

Ingredients to Use:

- 1 rack baby back ribs

Dry rub

- 2 tablespoons olive oil
- 1/2 teaspoon ground paprika
- 1 tablespoon brown sugar
- 1 tablespoon ground cumin
- 1 teaspoon chili powder
- 1/2 teaspoon garlic powder
- 2 teaspoons liquid smoke
- Salt and pepper to taste

Step-by-Step Directions

1. Mix the dry rub ingredients.
2. Rub it on all sides of ribs.
3. Add the ribs to the air fryer.
4. Cook at 400°F for 20 minutes.
5. Flip and cook for another 10 minutes.

Serving Suggestion:

Serve with ketchup and mustard.

Tip:

Extend cooking time if not fully done after 30 minutes.

Homemade Shake & Bake Pork Chops

Make your own version of shake and bake seasoning for your pork chops.
Prep Time and Cooking Time: 15 minutes | Serves: 4

Ingredients to Use:

- 4 bone-in pork chops
- 1/4 cup vegetable oil

Herb & spice mixture

- 3 cups breadcrumbs
- 1 tablespoon dried onion flakes
- 3 teaspoons paprika
- 2 teaspoons sugar
- 1 teaspoon garlic powder
- 1 teaspoon black pepper
- 1/2 teaspoon cayenne pepper
- 1/2 teaspoon dried parsley
- 1/2 teaspoon dried basil
- 1/2 teaspoon dried oregano
- Salt to taste

Step-by-Step Directions

1. Coat pork chops with oil.
2. In a bowl, mix the herbs and spice mixture ingredients.
3. Dredge pork chops with this mixture.
4. Add pork chops to the air fryer tray.
5. Cook at 400°F for 7 minutes.

Serving Suggestion:

Serve with mac and cheese, and arugula salad.

Tip:

Internal temperature should be 160°F.

Sausages, Onions & Peppers

Delicious and colorful—this dish is surely impressive.
Prep Time and Cooking Time: 15 minutes |

Serves: 4

- 1 onion, sliced
- 2 red bell peppers, sliced
- 2 tablespoons olive oil
- 1 tablespoon Italian seasoning
- 1 lb. Italian sausages

Step-by-Step Directions

1. Combine all the ingredients except sausages in a bowl.
2. Add mixture to the air fryer tray.
3. Add sausages on top of the vegetables.
4. Cook at 400°F for 5 minutes.
5. Turn sausages and cook for another 3 minutes.

Serving Suggestion:

Serve with mustard.

Tip:

You can also add green bell pepper and yellow bell pepper.

Pork, Cabbage & Mushrooms

Add veggies to your pork dish with this recipe.
Prep Time and Cooking Time: 30 minutes | Serves: 4

Ingredients to Use:

- 1 lb. pork tenderloin
- 1 tablespoon Cajun seasoning
- Salt and pepper to taste
- 1/2 cup onion, chopped
- 10 oz. Cremini mushrooms, diced
- 2 red bell peppers, diced
- 1 lb. cabbage, shredded
- 2 tablespoons olive oil

Step-by-Step Directions

1. Season pork with Cajun seasoning, salt and pepper.
2. Add to the air fryer tray.

3. Cook at 350°F for 5 minutes per side.
4. Toss veggies in oil.
5. Add to the air fryer tray along with the pork.
6. Cook for another 5 minutes.

Serving Suggestion:

Drizzle with cooking liquid.

Tip:

You can also add garlic powder to the seasoning mixture.

Paprika Pork Chops

You're going to love how juicy and tender these pork chops are.
Prep Time and Cooking Time: 20 minutes | Serves: 4

Ingredients to Use:

- 4 pork chops
- 2 tablespoons olive oil
- 2 tablespoon garlic salt
- 1 teaspoon smoked paprika
- Salt and pepper to taste

Step-by-Step Directions

1. Brush pork chops with oil.
2. Sprinkle with garlic salt, paprika, salt and pepper.
3. Air fry the pork at 380°F for 7 minutes.
4. Turn and cook for another 7 minutes.

Serving Suggestion:

Serve with herbed boiled potatoes.

Tip:

Internal temperature should be 145°F.

Country Style Crispy Pork Chops

You're going to love every bite of these golden crispy pork chops.
Prep Time and Cooking Time: 20 minutes | Serves: 6

Ingredients to Use:

- 6 pork chops
- 1 teaspoon dried rosemary
- 1 teaspoon dried tarragon
- Salt and pepper to taste
- 2 eggs, beaten
- 1 tablespoon almond milk
- 1 cup breadcrumbs
- Cooking spray

Step-by-Step Directions

1. Season pork chops with herbs, salt and pepper.
2. Coat pork chops with flour and then dip in eggs.
3. Cover with breadcrumbs.
4. Spray with oil.
5. Add to the air fryer oven.
6. Cook at 400°F for 6 minutes.
7. Turn and cook for another 3 minutes.
8. Turn once more and cook for 3 more minutes.

Serving Suggestion:

Garnish with chopped parsley.

Tip:

Dry the pork chops with paper towels before seasoning with salt and pepper.

Blackened Pork Loin

This comes out with intense flavors you'd definitely love.
Prep Time and Cooking Time: 20 minutes | Serves: 4

Ingredients to Use:

- 1 lb. pork loin

Dry rub

- 1 teaspoon sugar
- 1 teaspoon chili powder
- 1 teaspoon paprika
- 1 teaspoon dried thyme
- 1 teaspoon cayenne pepper
- 1 teaspoon garlic powder
- Salt and pepper to taste

Step-by-Step Directions

1. Mix dry rub ingredients.
2. Season pork loin with dry rub.
3. Place in the air fryer tray.
4. Cook at 360°F for 7 minutes per side.

Serving Suggestion:

Serve with pasta or vegetables.

Tip:

Use thick-cut pork loin.

Pork Chops with Broccoli

This complete meal is ready in only 15 minutes.
Prep Time and Cooking Time: 15 minutes | Serves: 2

Ingredients to Use:

- 2 pork chops
- 2 tablespoons avocado oil, divided
- 1/2 teaspoon onion powder
- 1/2 teaspoon garlic powder
- 1/2 teaspoon paprika
- 2 cups broccoli florets
- 2 cloves garlic, minced
- Salt to taste

Step-by-Step Directions

1. Preheat your air fryer to 350°F.
2. Spray your air fryer tray with oil.
3. Drizzle pork chops with oil.
4. Season with onion powder, garlic powder and paprika.
5. Cook in the air fryer for 5 minutes per side.
6. Toss broccoli in avocado oil, garlic and salt.
7. Cook the broccoli in the air fryer for 3 minutes per side.

Sprinkle with pepper.

You can use avocado oil instead of olive oil.

Pepper Pork Chops

Enjoy these succulent pork chops dotted with pepper.
Prep Time and Cooking Time: 10 minutes | Serves: 4

Ingredients to Use:

- 4 pork chops
- 2 to 3 teaspoons black pepper
- Cooking spray

Step-by-Step Directions

1. Start by flattening your pork on a cutting board.
2. Season with salt and pepper.
3. Cook at 320°F for 5 minutes per side.

Serving Suggestion:

Garnish with fresh herbs.

Tip:

Flatten pork chops with meat mallet before seasoning.

Parmesan Pork Fillet with Herbs

You'll love how Parmesan cheese and herbs come together to flavor up juicy pork fillet.
Prep Time and Cooking Time: 30 minutes | Serves: 4

Ingredients to Use:

- 4 pork chops
- Salt and pepper to taste
- 1/2 cup all-purpose flour
- 2 eggs
- 1/4 cup breadcrumbs
- 1/2 teaspoon garlic powder
- 1/4 cup Parmesan cheese, grated

- 1/2 teaspoon thyme
- 1/2 teaspoon oregano
- 1/2 teaspoon basil
- Cooking spray

Step-by-Step Directions

1. Sprinkle pork chops with salt and pepper.
2. Cover with flour.
3. Dip in eggs.
4. In a bowl, mix the remaining ingredients.
5. Dredge with breadcrumbs.
6. Spray with oil.
7. Cook at 360°F for 8 minutes
8. Turn and cook for another 8 minutes.

Serving Suggestion:

Serve with brown rice.

Tip

Add a teaspoon of sugar to the herb mixture.

Crispy Pork Strips

Enjoy these golden crunchy pork strips seasoned with paprika and garlic.
Prep Time and Cooking Time: 20 minutes | Serves: 3

Ingredients to Use:

- 3 pork fillets, sliced into strips
- 2 teaspoons olive oil
- 1 teaspoon garlic powder
- 1 teaspoon paprika
- Salt and pepper to taste
- 1 egg
- 1 cup breadcrumbs

Step-by-Step Directions

1. Coat pork strips with oil.
2. Season with garlic powder, paprika, salt and pepper.
3. Dip in eggs.
4. Cover with breadcrumbs.
5. Cook at 350°F for 5 minutes per side.

Serving Suggestion:

Serve with dip of choice.

Tip:

Cook in batches so as not to overcrowd the air fryer.

Pork & Green Beans

Serve your crispy pork fillet with steamed green beans for a satisfying meal.
Prep Time and Cooking Time: 30 minutes | Serves: 4

Ingredients to Use:

- 1/4 cup almond flour
- 1 teaspoon Creole seasoning
- 1/4 cup Parmesan cheese, grated
- 1 teaspoon paprika
- 1 teaspoon garlic powder
- 4 pork chops
- 4 cups green beans, trimmed and steamed
- Cooking spray

Step-by-Step Directions

1. Preheat your air fryer to 375°F.
2. Spray your air fryer tray with oil.
3. In a bowl, mix all the ingredients except pork chops and green beans.
4. Spray pork chops with oil.
5. Coat with spice mixture.
6. Air fry for 15 minutes, turning once.

Serving Suggestion:

Serve with ketchup and hot sauce.

Tip:

You can also sprinkle green beans with Parmesan cheese before serving.

Pork & Potatoes

For sure, you're going to enjoy this beautiful pairing.
Prep Time and Cooking Time: 20 minutes |

Ingredients to Use:

- 2 pork chops
- 1 tablespoons oil
- 1 tablespoons steak seasoning
- 1 teaspoon paprika
- 2 cups French fries, cooked

Step-by-Step Directions

1. Preheat your air fryer to 400°F for 5 minutes.
2. Brush pork chops with oil.
3. Season with steak seasoning and paprika.
4. Air fry for 6 to 8 minutes per side.
5. Serve with French fries.

Serving Suggestion:

Garnish with lemon wedges and chopped scallions.

Tip:

Use pork chops that are at least 1 ½ inch thick.

Pork & Mushroom Bites

Delicious and easy to make—these pork and mushroom bites will be the star on the dinner table.
Prep Time and Cooking Time: 30 minutes | Serves: 4

Ingredients to Use:

- 1 lb. pork fillet, sliced into cubes
- 8 oz. mushrooms
- 1 teaspoon Worcestershire sauce
- 2 tablespoons butter, melted
- 1/2 teaspoon garlic powder
- Salt and pepper to taste

Step-by-Step Directions

1. Preheat your air fryer to 400°F for 5 minutes.
2. Toss all the ingredients in a bowl.

3. Transfer to the air fryer tray.
4. Cook at 400°F for 20 minutes, turning twice.

Serving Suggestion:

Serve with dip of choice.

Tip:

Extend cooking time if you want your pork more well done.

Pork & Brussels Sprouts

Serve your beautifully cooked with roasted Brussels sprouts.
Prep Time and Cooking Time: 30 minutes | Serves: 8

Ingredients to Use:

- 8 pork chops
- Cooking spray
- Salt and pepper to taste
- 1 teaspoon olive oil
- 1 teaspoon mustard
- 1 teaspoon maple syrup
- 6 oz. Brussels sprouts, sliced

Step-by-Step Directions

1. Spray your pork chops with oil.
2. Season with salt and pepper.
3. In a bowl, mix the remaining ingredients.
4. Add pork chops to the air fryer.
5. Cook for 5 minutes per side.
6. Transfer to a plate.
7. Add Brussels sprouts to the air fryer.
8. Cook for 3 minutes.

Serving Suggestion:

Season with pepper before serving.

Tip:

Use Dijon style mustard.

Pork with Mashed Potatoes

This dish will make you feel like you're in a top-rated restaurant.
Prep Time and Cooking Time: 25 minutes | Serves: 4

Ingredients to Use:

- 4 pork chops
- Salt to taste
- 1 tablespoons mustard
- 1 egg, beaten
- 1 cup breadcrumbs
- 1/2 teaspoon onion powder
- 1/2 teaspoon garlic powder
- 1/4 cup Parmesan cheese, grated
- Cooking spray
- Cooked mashed potatoes

Step-by-Step Directions

1. Preheat your air fryer to 400°F for 10 minutes.
2. Season your pork chops with salt.
3. Mix the mustard and egg.
4. Dip pork chops in mustard mixture.
5. In another bowl, mix the remaining ingredients.
6. Dredge pork chops with breadcrumb mixture.
7. Spray with oil.
8. Cook in the air fryer for 6 minutes per side.
9. Serve with mashed potatoes.

Serving Suggestion:

Serve with steamed green beans.

Tip:

Season pork and mashed potatoes with pepper.

Honey Barbecue Pork

Pork chops glazed with honey barbecue sauce is surely enticing.
Prep Time and Cooking Time: 20 minutes | Serves: 4

- 4 pork loin steaks
- Salt and pepper to taste
- 2 teaspoons honey
- 4 tablespoons barbecue sauce
- 1 teaspoon paprika powder
- 1 teaspoon celery salt

Step-by-Step Directions

1. Season pork chops with salt and pepper.
2. In a bowl, mix the remaining ingredients.
3. Brush pork chops with the mixture.
4. Cook at 395°F for 10 minutes, turning once.
5. Brush with the remaining sauce.
6. Cook for another 5 minutes.

Serving Suggestion:

Serve with steamed greens.

Tip:

Adjust cooking time if you have thick pork chops.

Maple Pork Chops

Add sweet flavor to your pork chops using this recipe.
Prep Time and Cooking Time: 30 minutes | Serves: 4

Ingredients to Use:

- 4 pork chops
- Vegetable oil
- 1 tablespoon grill seasoning
- 1/4 cup maple syrup
- 2 teaspoons lemon juice
- 2 tablespoons Dijon mustard
- Salt to taste

Step-by-Step Directions

1. Brush your pork chops with oil.
2. Sprinkle with grill seasoning.
3. Air fry at 375°F for 15 minutes, and flip

once.
4. Mix the remaining ingredients.
5. Pour the sauce over the pork chops and serve.

Serving Suggestion:

Let pork chops rest for 3 minutes.

Tip:

Use freshly squeezed lemon juice.

Savory Crispy Pork Chops

With the air fryer, you don' need lots of oil to create the deep-fried crispy effect.
Prep Time and Cooking Time: 30 minutes | Serves: 2

Ingredients to Use:

- 1/2 cup breadcrumbs
- 1/4 teaspoon onion powder
- 1/4 teaspoon garlic powder
- 1 teaspoon paprika
- 2 pork chops
- Cooking spray
- Salt to taste

Step-by-Step Directions

1. Put the breadcrumbs, onion powder, garlic powder and paprika in a bowl.
2. Stir in the pork.
3. Coat evenly with the breading.
4. Spray both sides with oil.
5. Arrange in a single layer in the air crisper tray.
6. Set the air fryer oven to air fry.
7. Cook at 360°F for 15 minutes or until golden and crispy.

Serving Suggestion:

Serve on top of leafy greens and garnish with lemon wedges.

Tip:

Use boneless pork chops and trim the fat.

Baked Pork Chops

Extremely juicy and full of flavor, these pork chops are sure to impress.
Prep Time and Cooking Time: 20 minutes | Serves: 4

- 1 teaspoon dried oregano
- 2 teaspoons onion powder
- 2 teaspoons garlic powder
- 1 tablespoon paprika
- Salt and pepper to taste
- 2 tablespoons olive oil
- 4 pork chops

Step-by-Step Directions

1. Combine oregano, onion powder, garlic powder, paprika, salt and pepper in a bowl.
2. Drizzle both sides of pork chops with oil.
3. Season with the spice mixture.
4. Place the pork chops inside the oven.
5. Choose bake function.
6. Cook at 400°F for 18 to 20 minutes.

Serving Suggestion:

Serve with mashed potatoes and gravy.

Tip:

Use boneless pork chops that are 1-1/4 inch thick.

Marinated Pork Chops

Here's a tasty weekday lunch or dinner that you and your family will enjoy.
Prep Time and Cooking Time: 1 hour | Serves: 6

Ingredients to Use:

- 1 tablespoon soy sauce
- 2 tablespoons vegetable oil
- 1 tablespoon Worcestershire sauce
- 1 teaspoon lemon juice

- 2 tablespoons brown sugar
- 2 tablespoons ketchup
- 6 pork chops, fat trimmed

Step-by-Step Directions

1. Preheat your air fryer oven to 350°F.
2. Set it to bake.
3. In a bowl, mix all the ingredients except pork chops.
4. Marinate the pork chops for 30 minutes.
5. Add the pork chops to the air fryer oven.
6. Bake in the oven for 30 minutes per side.

Serving Suggestion:

Serve with sautéed vegetables.

Tip:

Internal temperature should reach 145°F.

Garlic Butter Thyme Pork

These pork chops are super tender and juicy. You're going to enjoy every bite.
Prep Time and Cooking Time: 30 minutes | Serves: 2

Ingredients to Use:

- 2 pork chops
- Salt and pepper to taste
- 2 cloves garlic, minced
- 1 tablespoon fresh thyme, chopped
- 4 tablespoons butter, melted
- 1 tablespoon olive oil

Step-by-Step Directions

1. Set your air fryer oven to bake.
2. Preheat it to 375°F.
3. Season pork chops with salt and pepper.
4. In a bowl, combine the garlic, thyme and butter.
5. Add the oil to a pan over medium heat.
6. Brown the pork chops for 2 to 3 minutes per side.
7. Add the pork chops to the air fryer oven.
8. Pour the butter thyme mixture over the

pork.

9. Bake in the oven for 15 minutes.

Serving Suggestion:

Drizzle pork chops with butter sauce and serve.

Tip:

You can also add more herbs to the mixture if you like.

Rosemary Garlic Pork Roast

You'll feel like there's a special occasion when you cook this amazing dish at your home.
Prep Time and Cooking Time: 1 hour and 30 minutes | Serves: 8

Ingredients to Use:

- 1/4 cup olive oil
- 4 cloves garlic, minced
- 1 tablespoon rosemary, chopped
- 1 tablespoon thyme, chopped
- 2 tablespoons parsley, chopped
- 1/2 teaspoon red pepper flakes
- Salt and pepper to taste
- 4 lb. pork loin
- 2 bulbs garlic, sliced in half
- Cooking spray

Step-by-Step Directions

1. Set your air fryer oven to roast.
2. Preheat it to 375°F.
3. In a bowl, mix all the ingredients except pork and garlic bulbs.
4. Spray pork with oil.
5. Rub with the herb mixture.
6. Add the pork and garlic bulbs to a pan over high heat.
7. Sear for 3 minutes per side.
8. Transfer to the air fryer oven.
9. Roast for 80 minutes.

Serving Suggestion:

Slice and serve with gravy.

Tip:

Internal temperature should be at least 145° F.

Roasted Pork with White Wine

The combination of roasted pork and white wine can give you a refreshing taste.
Prep Time and Cooking Time: 1 hour and 20 minutes | Serves: 8

Ingredients to Use:

- 2 lb. pork loin roast
- 1/4 cup olive oil
- 3 cloves garlic, minced
- 1 tablespoon dried rosemary
- Salt and pepper to taste
- 1/2 cup white wine

Step-by-Step Directions

1. Set your air fryer to roast.
2. Preheat it to 350°F.
3. Make slits all over the pork.
4. In a bowl, mix the olive oil, garlic, rosemary, salt and pepper.
5. Rub mixture all over the pork.
6. Place the pork inside the air fryer oven.
7. Roast for 1 hour.
8. Add the cooking liquid and wine into a pan over medium heat.
9. Heat for 5 minutes.
10. Pour the sauce over the pork and serve.

Serving Suggestion:

Let rest for 5 minutes before slicing.

Tip:

Use boneless pork loin roast for this recipe.

Chinese Pork Roast

You don't have to go to a Chinese restaurant to enjoy this succulent pork dish.
Prep Time and Cooking Time: 2 hours and 10 minutes | Serves: 6

- 2 lb. pork belly
- 6 cloves garlic
- 1 teaspoon five spice powder
- Salt to taste

Step-by-Step Directions

1. Set your air fryer oven to roast.
2. Preheat it to 350°F.
3. Make slits all over the pork belly.
4. Insert garlic cloves in the slits.
5. Season all sides with five spice powder and salt.
6. Add the pork belly to the air fryer oven.
7. Roast for 1 hour.
8. Increase temperature to 400°F.
9. Roast for another 40 minutes.

Serving Suggestion:

Serve with hoisin sauce and chili garlic sauce.

Tip:

Dry the pork thoroughly before seasoning it.

Honey Soy Pork Chops

You're going to enjoy every bite of this honey soy pork chops.
Prep Time and Cooking Time: 2 hours and 20 minutes | Serves: 4

Ingredients to Use:

- 1/2 cup soy sauce
- 1/4 cup honey
- Red pepper flakes
- 2 cloves garlic, minced
- 4 pork chops

Step-by-Step Directions

1. Combine soy sauce, honey, red pepper flakes and garlic in a bowl.
2. Soak the pork chops in the marinade.
3. Cover and refrigerate for 2 hours.

4. Choose grill setting in your air fryer oven.
5. Set it to medium high heat.
6. Cook for 8 to 10 minutes per side.

Serving Suggestion:

Let rest for 5 minutes before serving.

Tip:

Use low-sodium soy sauce.

Lemon Pepper Pork Chops

Serve delicious and juicy pork chops marinated in sauce with lemon pepper and garlic.
Prep Time and Cooking Time: 2 hours and 15 minutes | Serves: 6

Ingredients to Use:

- 2 cloves garlic, minced
- 1/4 cup soy sauce
- 1/2 cup water
- 3 tablespoons lemon pepper seasoning
- 1/4 cup vegetable oil
- 6 pork chops, fat trimmed

Step-by-Step Directions

1. Mix the garlic, soy sauce, water, lemon pepper seasoning and vegetable oil in a bowl.
2. Coat the pork chops with the sauce.
3. Marinate the pork chops in the sauce for 2 hours.
4. Choose grill setting in the air fryer oven.
5. Add the pork chops inside the air fryer oven.
6. Grill the pork chops for 6 minutes per side.

Serving Suggestion:

Serve with roasted vegetables.

Tip:

Internal temperature should be 145°F.

Pork with Honey & Cumin

Flavor up your pork chops with honey, cumin and other spices.
Prep Time and Cooking Time: 1 hour and 20 minutes | Serves: 4

- 2 tablespoons vegetable oil
- 1 tablespoon apple cider vinegar
- 1/4 cup honey
- 1/2 teaspoon red pepper flakes
- 1 teaspoon ground cumin
- Salt and pepper to taste
- 8 pork chops

Step-by-Step Directions

1. Combine all the ingredients except pork chops in a bowl.
2. Add the pork chops to the bowl.
3. Cover and marinate in the refrigerator for 1 hour.
4. Preheat your air fryer oven to medium.
5. Set it to grill.
6. Cook the pork chops for 4 to 5 minutes per side.

Serving Suggestion:

Serve with tomato and cucumber salad.

Tip:

You can also increase temperature to sear the pork and give it grill marks.

Baked Pork & Veggies in Packets

Bake pork chops and vegetables in foil packets in the air fryer oven.
Prep Time and Cooking Time: 30 minutes | Serves: 4

Ingredients to Use:

- 4 pork chops
- Salt and pepper to taste
- 2 tablespoons canola oil
- 1 lb. potatoes, sliced into cubes
- 1 lb. asparagus, trimmed
- 1/2 lb. carrots, sliced into strips

Marinade

- 1 clove garlic, minced
- 1-1/2 teaspoons thyme, minced
- 1 tablespoon Creole seasoning
- 1 teaspoon Worcestershire sauce
- 3 tablespoons brown sugar
- 1/2 tablespoon Dijon-style mustard

Step-by-Step Directions

1. Select bake setting in your air fryer oven.
2. Season pork chops with salt and pepper.
3. In a bowl, mix the marinade ingredients.
4. Soak the pork chops in the marinade.
5. Cover and marinate for 2 hours.
6. In another bowl, toss the veggies in oil, salt and pepper.
7. Add the pork and veggies on top of a foil sheet.
8. Fold to make a packet.
9. Add to the air fryer oven.
10. Cook for 30 to 40 minutes.

Serving Suggestion:

Garnish with chopped parsley.

Tip:

Use bone-in pork chops that are at least ¾ inch thick.

Pork Rolls

Pork rolls are versatile enough to be served as a main course, appetizer or snack.
Prep Time and Cooking Time: 30 minutes | Serves: 6

Ingredients to Use:

- 1 onion, chopped
- 1 carrot, grated
- 1 green onion, minced
- 2 lb. ground pork
- 1 egg, beaten
- 12 egg roll wrappers

- Cooking spray

1. Mix all the ingredients in a bowl except wrappers.
2. Top the wrappers with the pork mixture.
3. Roll and seal the wrappers.
4. Spray your rolls with oil.
5. Place the rolls in the air fryer oven.
6. Set it to air fry.
7. Cook at 370°F for 5 minutes.
8. Flip and cook for another 5 minutes.

Serving Suggestion:

Serve with sweet chili sauce.

Tip:

Use lean ground pork.

Mustard Pork Chop

Flavor up your pork chops with mustard and spices.
Prep Time and Cooking Time: 10 minutes | Serves: 4

Ingredients to Use:

- 4 pork chops
- 4 tablespoons mustard
- 1 teaspoon dried sage
- Salt and pepper to taste

Step-by-Step Directions

1. Spread mustard on both sides of pork chops.
2. Sprinkle with sage, salt and pepper.
3. Place the pork chops in the air fryer oven.
4. Set it to grill.
5. Cook at 320°F for 5 to 7 minutes per side.

Serving Suggestion:

Garnish with lemon wedges.

Tip:

Make sure that the pork's internal temperature is 145°F.

Maple Pork Sausage

These are savory and with just the right amount of sweet. For sure, you'll be delighted with this maple pork sausage recipe.
Prep Time and Cooking Time: 20 minutes | Serves: 6

Ingredients to Use:

- 2 lb. pork sausages
- 1/2 cup maple syrup
- 1 teaspoon dried sage
- 1 teaspoon dried thyme
- Salt and pepper to taste

Step-by-Step Directions

1. Coat the pork sausages with maple syrup.
2. Sprinkle with sage, thyme, salt and pepper.
3. Transfer to the air fryer oven.
4. Choose bake setting.
5. Cook at 400°F for 5 minutes.
6. Turn and cook for another 5 minutes.

Serving Suggestion:

Sprinkle with chopped parsley.

Tip:

Cook longer to make sure sausages are fully cooked.

Country-Style Fried Pork

This is the comfort food that you'll never get tired of.
Prep Time and Cooking Time: 15 minutes | Serves: 6

Ingredients to Use:

- 6 pork chops
- Salt and pepper to taste
- 1 teaspoon dried thyme
- 1 teaspoon dried oregano
- 1 cup flour

- 1 egg, beaten
- 1 cup bread crumbs
- Cooking spray

Step-by-Step Directions

1. Season pork with salt and pepper.
2. Sprinkle with thyme and oregano.
3. Cover with flour.
4. Dip in egg.
5. Dredge with breadcrumbs.
6. Spray with oil.
7. Place the pork chops in the air crisper tray.
8. Set the air fryer oven to air fry.
9. Cook at 400°F for 3 to 4 minutes per side.

Serving Suggestion:

Serve with fries.

Tip:

Dry the pork with paper towel before seasoning.

Italian Sausage Bites

You will fall in love with this crispy snack with origin Italian flavor.
Prep Time and Cooking Time: 15 minutes | Serves: 4

Ingredients to Use:

- 1 lb. Italian sausage, sliced in 2 to 3
- 2 tablespoons olive oil
- Pinch Italian seasoning

Step-by-Step Directions

1. Insert toothpicks into the sausages.
2. Drizzle with oil.
3. Sprinkle with Italian seasoning.
4. Add to the air crisper tray.
5. Set the air fryer oven to roast.
6. Roast at 400°F for 5 minutes.
7. Flip and cook for another 2 to 3 minutes until sausages are fully cooked.

Serving Suggestion:

Serve with marinara dip.

Tip:

You can also use other sausages for this recipe.

Baked Pork with Potatoes

Whether it's a special occasion or just an ordinary day at home, this pork with potatoes will surely delight everyone.
Prep Time and Cooking Time: 40 minutes | Serves: 4

Ingredients to Use:

Rub
- 1 tablespoon olive oil
- 2 teaspoons vinegar
- 1 clove garlic, minced
- 2 tablespoons ketchup
- 1 teaspoon Worcestershire Sauce
- 2 tablespoons brown sugar
- 1 tablespoon soy sauce
- Pork & potatoes
- 4 pork chops
- 1 tablespoon olive oil
- Salt and pepper to taste

Step-by-Step Directions

1. Set your air fryer oven to bake.
2. Preheat it to 430°F.
3. Mix the rub ingredients.
4. Coat the pork with the rub.
5. Marinate for 30 minutes.
6. Toss the potatoes in the oil.
7. Season with salt and pepper.
8. Spread in the air fryer oven.
9. Place the pork on one side.
10. Cook for 15 minutes.
11. Set the oven to broil.
12. Cook for 10 minutes.

Garnish with chopped parsley.

Tip:

Use cider vinegar.

Grilled Pork Belly

Yes, you can make delicious grilled pork belly using air fryer oven. Here's how.
Prep Time and Cooking Time: 4 hours |
Serves: 6

Ingredients to Use:

- 3 lb. pork belly, sliced
- Marinade
- 1 clove garlic, minced
- 1 tablespoon lemon juice
- 1/2 cup soy sauce
- 1/2 cup ketchup
- Pepper to taste

Step-by-Step Directions

1. Mix the marinade ingredients in a bowl.
2. Coat the pork belly with the marinade.
3. Soak in the marinade for 3 hours, covered in the refrigerator.
4. Add the pork belly to the air fryer oven.
5. Set it to grill.
6. Cook at 370°F for 15 minutes per side, basting with the marinade every few minutes.
7. Choose roast setting in your air fryer oven.
8. Increase temperature to 430°F.
9. Cook for 10 minutes.

Serving Suggestion:

Serve with pickled onion or cucumber.

Tip:

Use thick-cut pork belly.

Herb Roasted Pork & Veggies

Here's a quick recipe for a simple but hearty lunch or dinner.
Prep Time and Cooking Time: 50 minutes |
Serves: 4

Ingredients to Use:

- Salt and pepper to taste
- 3/4 teaspoon Italian seasoning
- 1 onion, sliced into wedges
- 8 potatoes, sliced into wedges
- 2 lb. carrots, sliced
- 1 tablespoon olive oil, divided
- 4 pork chops

Step-by-Step Directions

1. Set your air fryer oven to roast.
2. In a bowl, mix the salt, pepper and Italian seasoning.
3. Toss the onion, potatoes and carrots in half of olive oil.
4. Sprinkle with half of seasoning mixture.
5. Add to the air fryer oven.
6. Set it to 350°F.
7. Roast for 20 minutes.
8. Transfer to a serving plate.
9. Drizzle pork chops with remaining oil.
10. Sprinkle with remaining seasoning mixture.
11. Add to the air fryer oven.
12. Select bake setting.
13. Cook at 375°F for 10 minutes per side.

Serving Suggestion:

Serve pork chops with veggies.

Tip:

You can also use baby carrots for this recipe.

Sweet Bacon Knots

Here's a different way of preparing your bacon.

Prep Time and Cooking Time: 15 minutes |
Serves: 4

Ingredients to Use:

- 1 lb. bacon
- 1/4 cup maple syrup
- 1/4 cup brown sugar

Step-by-Step Directions

1. Tie the bacon into a knot.
2. Place in the air fryer oven.
3. Brush with the maple syrup and sprinkle with the brown sugar.
4. Choose air fry setting.
5. Cook at 350°F for 10 minutes, flipping once or twice.

Serving Suggestion:

Garnish with chopped parsley.

Tip:

You can also use honey instead of maple syrup.

Chapter 5: Lamb & Goat Dishes

Roasted Lamb Chops with Garlic & Rosemary

This is a traditional lamb dish that you will surely fall in love with over and over again.
Prep Time and Cooking Time: 45 minutes | Serves: 4

Ingredients to Use:

- 2 tablespoons olive oil
- 1 tablespoon fresh rosemary, chopped
- 4 cloves garlic, minced
- Pepper to taste
- 8 lamb chops
- Salt to taste

Step-by-Step Directions

1. Combine olive oil, rosemary, garlic, and pepper in a bowl.
2. Coat lamb chops with mixture.
3. Marinate for 30 minutes at room temperature.
4. Line your baking sheet with foil.
5. Season lamb chops with salt.
6. Place the baking pan inside the air fryer oven.
7. Choose bake function.
8. Bake at 425°F for 15 minutes.

Serving Suggestion:

Garnish with rosemary sprigs.

Tip:

You can also marinate lamb chops overnight.

Lamb chops with Fennel& Orange Salad

A dish made of tender lamb bursting with fresh citrus flavors that's perfect for the summer season.
Prep Time and Cooking Time: 45 minutes | Serves: 4

Ingredients to Use:

- 6 garlic cloves, minced
- 2 garlic heads, sliced crosswise
- 1 teaspoon orange zest, grated
- 1 teaspoon red pepper flakes
- 1 cup white wine
- 2 tablespoons rosemary, finely chopped
- 2 tablespoons lemon juice
- 2 tablespoons olive oil
- 1 cup orange, sliced
- 6 to 8 lamb chops
- 1 fennel bulb, thinly sliced
- Salt and pepper to taste

Step-by-Step Directions

1. Score lamb with a sharp knife.
2. Season with salt and pepper.
3. Mix minced garlic, zest, olive oil, rosemary, and pepper flakes in a bowl.
4. Coat lamb with the mixture.
5. Place lamb in the baking pan together with garlic heads and wine. Cover with foil
6. Select the roast function.
7. Roast at 300°F for 30 minutes or until tender.
8. Mix fennel, orange slices, salt, and lemon juice in a bowl.
9. Serve with lamb chops.

Serving Suggestion:

Top lamb with rosemary.

Tip:

Drizzle leftover juices over meat and salad.

Lamb Chops in Dijon Garlic

This dish is perfect for a laid-back evening. It can be marinated in advance and stored in the fridge.

Prep Time and Cooking Time: 47 minutes | Serves: 2

Ingredients to Use:

- 8 pieces lamb chops
- 2 teaspoons Dijon mustard
- 1 teaspoon soy sauce
- 2 teaspoons olive oil
- 1 teaspoon cumin powder
- 1 teaspoon minced garlic
- 1 teaspoon cayenne powder
- Salt to taste

Step-by-Step Directions

1. Combine Dijon mustard, olive oil, cumin and cayenne powder, soy sauce, and garlic in a bowl.
2. Place lamb chops in a Ziploc bag together with the mixture.
3. Marinate for 30 minutes in the fridge.
4. Choose bake function.
5. Cook for 17 minutes at 350°F.

Serving Suggestion:

Add 3 minutes to the cooking time to make lamb chops well done.

Tip:

You can also marinate the lamb chops overnight to save time.

Braised Lamb Shanks

A flavorful lamb dish that is roasted and slow-cooked in an air fryer.

Prep Time and Cooking Time: 2 hours and 25 minutes | Serves: 4

Ingredients to Use:

- 4 garlic cloves, crushed
- 1-1/2 teaspoon kosher salt
- 3 cups beef broth
- 4 sprigs of fresh rosemary
- 4 lamb shanks
- 2 tablespoons balsamic vinegar
- Salt and pepper to taste

Step-by-Step Directions

1. Rub lamb with salt, pepper, garlic, and olive oil.
2. Place in baking pan with rosemary.
3. Select roast function.
4. Roast for 20 minutes at 425°F.
5. Turn lamb halfway while roasting.
6. Add the vinegar and 2 cups of broth and switch to slow cook.
7. Slow cook at 250°F for 1 hour.
8. Add remaining cup of broth and slow cook for another hour.

Serving Suggestion:

Garnish with fresh rosemary sprigs.

Tip:

Lamb is ready when the meat easily pulls from the bone.

Roasted Lamb with Cumin& Lemon Crust

This luscious-looking dish is so easy to make, and people won't believe you cooked it in an air fryer.

Prep Time and Cooking Time: 40 minutes | Serves: 3

Ingredients to Use:

- 1/2 cup breadcrumbs
- 1 egg, beaten
- 1 cloves garlic, grated
- 1 teaspoon cumin seeds
- 1/4 lemon rind, grated
- 1 teaspoon oil
- 1 teaspoon ground cumin
- 1.7 lb. rack of lamb, frenched

- Salt and freshly ground black pepper to taste

1. Season lamb rack with salt and pepper.
2. Combine breadcrumbs, cumin seeds, garlic, ground cumin, oil, ½ teaspoon of salt, and lemon rind in a large bowl.
3. Dip the lamb in the egg then coat with the breadcrumb mixture until a crust is formed.
4. Arrange the lamb in the frying basket.
5. Choose the bake function.
6. Bake at 100°F for 25 minutes.
7. Switch to roast function.
8. Roast at 200°F for 5 minutes.
9. Remove from air fryer and cover with foil.
10. Let it rest for 10 minutes before carving.

Serving Suggestion:

Serve with a fresh salad or roasted vegetables.

Tip:

You can substitute Dijon mustard for the egg.

Spiced Lamb Pizza with Red Onion& Parsley Salad

The fresh onion and parsley in this pizza complement the crispy crust and spicy lamb.
Prep Time and Cooking Time: 35 minutes | Serves: 4

Ingredients to Use:

- 12 oz. ground lamb
- 2 garlic cloves, finely grated
- 3/4 teaspoon smoked paprika
- 3/4 teaspoon ground cinnamon
- 1 cup parsley leaves with tender stems
- 3/4 teaspoon ground cumin
- 8 oz. pizza dough, divided into 2
- 1 tablespoon fresh lemon juice
- 1/2 red onion, thinly sliced
- 2 tablespoons olive oil
- 1/4 cup tomato paste
- All-purpose flour
- Red pepper flakes, crushed
- Salt to taste

Step-by-Step Directions

1. In a bowl, combine lamb, garlic, paprika, cumin, tomato paste, cinnamon, and salt.
2. Put parchment paper on a baking tray and lightly dust with flour.
3. Stretch the dough until it fits the tray. Cover and let dough rest if it springs back.
4. Spread half of the lamb mixture over the dough and brush the edges with oil.
5. Do the same with the other dough.
6. Select the bake or air fry function.
7. Cook for 7 minutes at 375°F.
8. Transfer to a wire rack and drizzle with oil.

Serving Suggestion:

Combine onion, lemon juice, parsley, and salt in a bowl. Toss and sprinkle on top of the pizza. Scatter red pepper flakes for a dash of spice.

Tip:

You can also add fresh herbs like sweet basil as toppings.

Lamb Rack with Potatoes &Yogurt Mint Sauce

An entire lamb meal that can be made in less than an hour.
Prep Time and Cooking Time: 30 minutes | Serves: 2

Ingredients to Use:

- 2 teaspoons fresh rosemary, chopped

- 1 teaspoon paprika
- 1 bunch asparagus
- 1-1/2 tablespoon olive oil
- 1 red bell pepper, cut into strips
- 1/2 lb. potatoes, cut into wedges
- 1 lb. lamb rack
- Salt and pepper to taste
- 1/2 bunch mint, finely chopped
- 2/3 cup Greek yogurt

Step-by-Step Directions

1. Season lamb with salt, pepper, and rosemary.
2. Coat potatoes with 1 tablespoon oil, paprika, and pepper.
3. Arrange lamb and potatoes in the pan.
4. Select roast function.
5. Roast for 15 minutes at 400°F.
6. Remove lamb and potatoes from air fryer and cover with foil for 10 minutes before carving.
7. Mix bell pepper and asparagus with the remaining oil.
8. Roast for 6 minutes at 300°F.
9. Mix yogurt with mint.

Serving Suggestion:

Serve lamb and vegetables with yogurt sauce.

Tip:

You can also add Dijon mustard as seasoning before roasting.

Lamb Kebabs

Try the rotisserie function on your air fryer oven with this tasty lamb recipe.
Prep Time and Cooking Time: 10 minutes | Serves: 3

Ingredients to Use:

- 1 tablespoon extra-virgin olive oil
- 2 teaspoons cumin powder

- 1 lb. lamb fillet, cut into 1-inch pieces
- Salt and fresh ground pepper to taste

Step-by-Step Directions

1. Combine all the ingredients in a bowl.
2. Put 2 pieces of lamb onto 6-inch skewers.
3. Choose the air fry option.
4. Cook for 8 minutes at 400°F.
5. Flip halfway through the cooking time.

Serving Suggestion:

Serve with yogurt and mint sauce as finger food.

Tip:

You can cook the lamb without the skewers and serve with pitta bread.

Spiced Lamb Chops with Garlic Yogurt sauce

A luxurious-looking meal that takes so little effort to cook.
Prep Time and Cooking Time: 40 minutes | Serves: 4

Ingredients to Use:

- 1/4 teaspoon allspice powder
- 1 teaspoon coriander, ground
- 2 teaspoons cumin, ground
- 2 cloves garlic, grated
- 3/4 teaspoon turmeric, ground
- 1/2 lemon, squeezed
- 1-1/2 cups Greek yogurt
- Salt and pepper to taste
- Cooking oil
- 8 lamb chops

Step-by-Step Directions

1. Whisk together yogurt, garlic, lemon, salt, and pepper in a bowl.
2. Transfer 1/2 of the yogurt mixture to a small bowl and set aside.

3. Add the cumin, allspice, coriander, and turmeric to the yogurt mixture and set aside.
4. Season lamb chops with salt and pepper.
5. Coat lamb with spiced yogurt.
6. Leave at room temperature for 30 minutes.
7. Choose the air fry option.
8. Lightly spray the pan with oil and put lamb.
9. Air fry at 400°F for 3 minutes on each side.
10. Serve with the garlic yogurt mixture.

Serving Suggestion:

Serve with a fresh salad or herbed mashed potatoes.

Tip:

Spray a light coating of oil halfway through or after flipping the lamb.

Air Fried Lamb Meatballs with Pesto

Spicy air-fried meatballs with a hint of sweetness from the raisin pesto.
Prep Time and Cooking Time: 25 minutes | Serves: 4

Ingredients to Use:

- 1 lb. lamb, ground
- 2 cloves of garlic, 1 grated 1 whole
- 2 cups mint leaves
- 3 tablespoons raisins
- 1/4 teaspoon turmeric powder
- 1/2 teaspoon cumin, ground
- 1/2 cup Japanese breadcrumbs
- 1/4 teaspoon red pepper flakes, crushed
- 1 large egg
- 1/4 cup finely chopped parsley, plus 1/2 cup parsley with soft stems
- 2 tablespoons, plus ½ cup of olive oil
- 1/2 cup Greek yogurt
- Kosher salt to taste

Step-by-Step Directions

1. In a large bowl, combine breadcrumbs, egg, red pepper flakes, cumin, finely chopped parsley, grated garlic, turmeric, 2 tablespoons of oil, and salt.
2. Add lamb to the mixture and combine using your hand.
3. Form and shape into meatballs (about the size of a golf ball).
4. Arrange meatballs with even spaces in between.
5. Choose the air fry function.
6. Air fry for 8 minutes at 400°F.
7. Turn meatballs halfway through for even browning.
8. In a blender, puree raisin, mint, parsley with stems, 1/2 cup of oil, 1 garlic clove, and salt to taste.

Serving Suggestion:

Spread yogurt on the plate first, then the pesto. Add the meatballs on top.

Tip:

The pesto can be made ahead of time and stored in the fridge.

Lamb & Plantain Casserole

This lovely recipe from New Orleans is a new take on the shepherd's pie.
Prep Time and Cooking Time: 55 minutes | Serves: 8

Ingredients to Use:

- 2 lb. Lamb, ground
- 3 garlic cloves, finely chopped
- 1 teaspoon annatto powder
- 8 green olives, thinly sliced
- 2 teaspoon garlic powder
- 2 teaspoon chili powder

- 2 teaspoon cumin, ground
- 2 teaspoon dried oregano
- 2 teaspoon coriander, ground
- 2 teaspoon thyme, finely chopped
- 1 green bell pepper, finely chopped
- 1 large onion, finely chopped
- 4 plantains, cut lengthwise into 4 pieces each
- 1/2 cup raisins, chopped
- 2 cups white cheddar, grated
- 1 cup tomato sauce
- 3 large eggs
- 2 tablespoons whole milk
- Salt to taste
- Oil

Step-by-Step Directions

1. Lightly coat pan with oil.
2. Select the air fry option and set the temperature at 350°F.
3. Air fry the plantains for 3 minutes on each side until golden brown.
4. Season plantains with salt while hot.
5. Put the lamb in a baking pan.
6. Bake for 3 minutes at 350°F until brown.
7. Occasionally break lamb apart for even cooking.
8. Transfer lamb to a bowl once cooked.
9. Combine garlic, onion, and bell pepper in the pan.
10. Air fry for 8 minutes at 350°F.
11. Add the lamb together with garlic powder, annatto powder, thyme, cumin, oregano, coriander, and chili powder.
12. Stir occasionally for 20 seconds until fragrant.
13. Add tomato sauce, olives, and raisins and cook for 4 minutes.
14. Transfer lamb to a bowl and season with salt to taste.
15. Arrange the plantains on the bottom of the baking pan.
16. Pour lamb mixture over the plantains and top with cheese.
17. Cover the top with remaining plantains.
18. In a bowl, whisk egg, milk, and salt.
19. Pour mixture on the baking pan pressing it down lightly.
20. Cover with foil and select the bake option.
21. Bake at 300°F for 10 minutes until cheese melts.
22. Remove foil and continue to bake for 20 minutes or until the top becomes a rich golden brown color.

Serving Suggestion:

Let the casserole rest for 10 minutes before serving.

Tip:

you can arrange and cook the casserole a day ahead to save time.

Spiced Lamb with Sweet Potato & Mushrooms

This recipe makes for a lovely dinner for you and your significant other.
Prep Time and Cooking Time: 40 minutes | Serves: 2

Ingredients to Use:

- 1/2 fennel bulb, thinly sliced
- 1/4 cup apple cider vinegar
- 1/2 lb. lamb, ground
- 1 large sweet potato, halved lengthwise
- 1/2 red onion, thinly sliced
- 3 tablespoons olive oil
- 1/2 teaspoon cinnamon, ground
- 8 oz. mushrooms, sliced
- 2 tablespoons fresh lemon juice
- 1/2 cup plain yogurt
- 1/4 cup mint leaves
- 1 teaspoon cumin, ground

- 1 teaspoon Aleppo-style pepper
- Salt to taste

1. Using a fork, poke holes in the potatoes.
2. Coat with olive oil and season with salt.
3. Select the bake option.
4. Bake at 400°F for 20 minutes until fork tender.
5. In a bowl, combine vinegar, onion, fennel, and salt. Toss occasionally and set aside.
6. Remove potatoes and transfer to a plate.
7. Coat baking pan with oil.
8. Put in lamb, pepper, cumin, cinnamon, and salt.
9. Select the air fry option.
10. Air fry for 4 minutes at 350°F or until brown.
11. Push lamb on one side and add mushrooms.
12. Season with salt and cook for 2 minutes until brown and soft.
13. Mix mushrooms together with lamb.
14. Cook for 1 more minute.
15. Whisk together yogurt, 1 tablespoon oil, salt, and lemon juice to create the sauce.

Serving Suggestion:

Place the potato on a bowl and lightly mash with a fork. Put yogurt and lamb mixture on top. Discard the vinegar in the fennel bowl and scatter fennel on top of the lamb mixture. Garnish with mint leaves.

Tip:

You can also substitute coconut or unseasoned rice vinegar for apple cider.

Air Fryer Feta& Lamb Frittata

This lamb recipe is easy and quick to make, have a try to make it a perfect weekday meal.
Prep Time and Cooking Time: 20 minutes |

Serves: 4

Ingredients to Use:

- 8 large eggs
- 1 garlic clove, grated
- 1 teaspoon lemon zest, grated
- 1/4 cup plain yogurt
- 4 oz. lamb, ground
- 1 teaspoon fresh lemon juice
- 2 scallions, thinly sliced
- 1/4 cup feta, crumbled
- 1 tablespoon tarragon leaves
- 2 cups baby kale
- 1 tablespoon za'atar
- 1/2 cup cilantro leaves
- 1/4 cup basil leaves, torn
- Mild red pepper flakes
- 3 tablespoons olive oil
- Salt and freshly ground black pepper to taste

Step-by-Step Directions

1. In a bowl, mix 1 tablespoon oil, za'atar, garlic, 1/2 teaspoon lemon zest, lemon juice, and lamb. Season with salt and pepper.
2. Combine yogurt, eggs, scallions, feta, basil, tarragon, cilantro, and kale.
3. Whisk mixture and season with salt and pepper.
4. Select the air fry option in your air fryer oven.
5. Lightly coat pan with oil and add lamb mixture.
6. Set temperature to 350°F and cook for at least 2 minutes or until golden brown.
7. Pour in the egg mixture.
8. With a rubber spatula, pull in the sides until it has set evenly.
9. Switch to bake function.
10. Bake at 300°F F for 10 minutes.

Top with yogurt and garnish with lemon zest, pepper, and herbs.

Tip:

Frittata is ready when the center wobbles when shaken.

Lamb Shanks with Walnuts and Pomegranate

A lamb recipe that's perfect to make on the weekends.

Prep Time and Cooking Time: 2 hours 35 minutes | Serves: 6

Ingredients to Use:

- 1-1/2 teaspoons cinnamon, ground
- 1/2 teaspoon cardamom, ground
- 1/2 teaspoon cumin, ground
- 1-1/2 teaspoons turmeric, ground
- 2 bay leaves
- 6 thyme sprigs
- 1/2 cup olive oil
- 4 garlic cloves, crushed
- 1 cup pomegranate juice
- 1/2 cup dry red wine
- 2 tablespoons all-purpose flour
- 2 medium onions, thinly sliced
- 4 cups chicken broth
- 3 strips lemon zest, thinly sliced
- 3 tablespoons unsalted butter
- 1/2 pomegranate molasses
- 6 lamb shanks
- 2 cups walnuts, rinsed
- Kosher salt and pepper to taste
- Cooked polenta

Step-by-Step Directions

1. Season lamb with salt and pepper.
2. Combine cumin, turmeric, cinnamon, and cardamom.
3. Massage mixture into the lamb.
4. Let rest at room temperature for 1 hour.
5. Coat baking sheet with oil.
6. Select roast function in your air fryer oven.
7. Roast shanks at 400°F for 10-15 minutes.
8. Coat baking pot with oil.
9. Cook onions until soft for 6 minutes.
10. Add garlic, thyme, and bay leaves. Cook for 2 minutes.
11. Slowly add pomegranate molasses, broth, and pomegranate juice and stir.
12. Cook for 5 minutes.
13. Arrange shanks in roasting pan.
14. Pour spiced mixture over shanks and cover with foil.
15. Cook for 1 hour.
16. Transfer lamb to a plate.
17. Strain liquid and skim off fat.
18. Select the bake function and set the temperature at 350°F.
19. Cook liquid until it is reduced and is velvety.
20. Add butter and stir until the mixture becomes glossy.
21. Add the lamb back and coat with the mixture.

Serving Suggestion:

Place lamb over polenta and drizzle sauce and walnuts on top. Garnish with lemon zest.

Tip:

Shanks can be braised one day in advance to save time.

Lamb Burgers with Fennel Slaw and Lemon-Caper Aioli

A seriously juicy burger with tangy slaw and anchovies.

Prep Time and Cooking Time: 60 minutes | Serves: 4

Ingredients to Use:

- 1-1/2 lamb, ground
- 6 tablespoons olive oil
- 1 cup mayonnaise
- 2 garlic cloves, finely grated
- 1/4 large sweet onion, thinly sliced
- 4 potato or ciabatta rolls, toasted
- 2 teaspoons dried mint, crushed
- 6 tablespoons fresh lemon juice
- 3 celery stalks, thinly sliced
- 1/2 fennel bulb, thinly sliced
- 1/4 cup salt-packed capers, rinsed
- 1 teaspoon lemon zest, finely grated
- 1 teaspoon Dijon mustard
- Boquerones or marinated white anchovies
- Salt and pepper to taste

Step-by-Step Directions

1. To make aioli, soak capers in a bowl with warm water for 20 minutes.
2. Drain, rinse, dry, and chop capers coarsely.
3. In a bowl, whisk together garlic, mustard, lemon juice, lemon zest, capers, and mayonnaise. Season with salt and pepper.
4. To make patties, season lamb with salt and divide into 4.
5. Shape into 1-inch think patties.
6. Rest patties for 30 minutes at room temperature.
7. Choose the air fry function.
8. Air fry lamb patties for 5 minutes (medium-rare) in olive oil.
9. Toss fennel, onions, celery, lemon juice, mint, and 2 tablespoons olive oil in a bowl. Season with salt and pepper.

Serving Suggestion:

Spread aioli on cut sides of the bread. Put the burger, then boquerones, and top with slaw.

Tip:

Aioli can be made in advance and chilled in the fridge.

Grilled Rosemary Jerk Lamb Chops

An easy lamb recipe oozing with umami flavors.

Prep Time and Cooking Time: 4 hours 30 minutes | Serves: 6-8

Ingredients to Use:

- 2 lb. lamb loin chops
- 1-1/2 tablespoons soy sauce
- 7 cloves garlic
- 1/3 cup scallions
- 1 sprig rosemary
- 1/2 Scotch bonnet chili
- 1/2 teaspoon allspice
- 1 medium yellow onion, chopped
- Salt and pepper to taste

Step-by-Step Directions

1. To make the marinade, blend soy sauce, garlic, onion, scallions, rosemary, chili, and allspice until smooth.
2. Coat and massage lamb chops with marinade.
3. Cover and chill for 4 hours.
4. Choose the grill option.

Grill lamb at 400°F for 11 to 14 minutes.

Serving Suggestion:

Garnish with rosemary sprigs.

Tip:

Lamb can be marinated overnight.

Grilled Lamb Chops with Tzatziki Sauce

Garlicky lamb paired with a refreshing yogurt and dill sauce.

Prep Time and Cooking Time: 1 hour 6

minutes | Serves: 2

Ingredients to Use:

- 4 lamb loin chops
- 3 tablespoons olive oil
- 1/2 teaspoon red chili flakes
- 2 teaspoons, plus 1 tablespoon fresh lemon juice
- 2 teaspoons dried dill
- 8 cloves garlic, minced
- 3/4 cup plain Greek yogurt
- 1/2 cup cucumber, minced
- Kosher salt and pepper to taste

Step-by-Step Directions

1. To create tzatziki sauce, whisk yogurt, 2 cloves minced garlic, 1 teaspoon dill, 1 tablespoon lemon juice, cucumber, salt, and pepper. Cover and chill.
2. Combine the remaining dill, garlic, lemon juice, chili flakes, and oil in a bowl to create the marinade.
3. Season lamb with salt and pepper and place in a baking tray.
4. Coat lamb with the marinade and leave at room temperature for 1 hour.
5. Choose the grill function in your air fryer.
6. Grill lamb at 350°F for 4 to 6 minutes (medium-rare).

Serving Suggestion:

Spread tzatziki sauce on a platter and lay lamb chops on top.

Tip:

A simple fresh green salad goes well with this dish.

Spiced Lamb Chops with Ginger Soy Sauce

A fragrant lamb recipe with a delicious dipping sauce.
Prep Time and Cooking Time: 2 hours 45

Ingredients to Use:

- 8 lamb rib chops
- 1/3 cup scallions, finely chopped
- 3 tablespoons shallot, minced
- 2 tablespoons cilantro, minced
- 2 tablespoons ginger, minced
- 2 tablespoons garlic, minced
- 3 tablespoons oyster sauce
- 1 tablespoon sugar
- 2 tablespoons light soy sauce
- Steamed Bok choy
- Salt and pepper to taste
- Red and yellow bell peppers, julienned
- Scallions, julienned

Step-by-Step Directions

1. Combine oyster sauce, soy sauce, oil, cilantro, sugar, garlic, shallot, and ginger.
2. Add lamb chops and marinate for 2 hours at room temperature.
3. Choose grill function in your air fryer.
4. Place lamb in tray and season with salt and pepper.
5. Grill chops at 400°F for 6 minutes.
6. Transfer to a platter and cover with foil.
7. Let sit for 10 minutes.
8. Pour marinade into the pan and cook for 8 minutes or until it is reduced to create the sauce.

Serving Suggestion:

Arrange steamed Bok choy in the plate and put lamb over together with julienned peppers and scallion. Serve with the sauce from the marinade.

Tip:

To reduce preparation time, marinate the lamb overnight, and keep in the fridge.

Spicy Lamb with Lentils & Herbs

Easy to make and wonderfully fragrant, you'll find this to be one of your go-to lamb recipes.
Prep Time and Cooking Time: 35 minutes | Serves: 4

Ingredients to Use:

- 1/2 lb. ground lamb
- 2 garlic cloves, thinly sliced
- 1/2 teaspoon cumin seeds
- 3/4 cup plain Greek yogurt
- 1 teaspoon crushed red pepper flakes
- 1/2 cucumber, chopped
- 1/4 cup fresh parsley
- 1/2 cup fresh cilantro, chopped
- 1-1/2 cups French green lentils
- 1 tablespoon vegetable oil
- Kosher salt and pepper to taste
- Flatbread and lemon wedges

Step-by-Step Directions

1. Season lamb with salt and pepper.
2. Place lamb on the baking sheet.
3. Choose the air fry option.
4. Air fry for 350°F for 5 minutes.
5. Break apart lamb and add red pepper flakes, cumin, and garlic.
6. Cook for 2 more minutes and set aside.
7. Season lentils with salt and pepper.
8. Put lentils in the baking pan and cook until brown for 6 minutes.
9. Add the lamb back and mix well.
10. Remove from heat and add parsley, cucumber, and cilantro.

Serving Suggestion:

Spread yogurt on the plate and put the lamb on top. Serve with the flatbread and lemon wedges.

Tip:

Garnish with fresh parsley and cilantro leaves.

Salt & Pepper Lamb

Simple yet delectable, this lamb recipe is also great as an appetizer.
Prep Time and Cooking Time: 45 minutes | Serves: 4

Ingredients to Use:

- 1-1/2 lb. lamb rump
- 4 oz. rice flour
- 3-1/2 oz. plain flour
- 3 egg whites
- 2 zucchinis, thinly sliced
- 1 red capsicum, sliced into strips
- 1 green capsicum, sliced into strips

Step-by-Step Directions

1. Cut lamb across the grain into thin strips.
2. Combine flours in a bowl and season with salt and pepper.
3. Whisk eggs in a separate bowl.
4. Dip strips of lamb in the egg then onto the flour individually.
5. Lightly coat a baking tray with oil.
6. Select the air fry option.
7. Air fry lamb for 3 to 4 minutes at 350°F.
8. Set aside lamb.
9. In the same tray, arrange the capsicums and zucchinis.
10. Air fry for 2 to 3 minutes until tender and has light charring.

Serving Suggestion:

Serve lamb with charred vegetables, lime wedges, and mayonnaise

Tip:

You can also add freshly chopped onions as garnish.

Barbecue Lamb Cutlets

Try this easy air fryer barbecue at your next family dinner.
Prep Time and Cooking Time: 1 hour 10

minutes | Serves: 4

Ingredients to Use:

- 2 cups tomato ketchup
- 1/2 cup white vinegar
- 2 teaspoons Tabasco sauce
- 3 teaspoons Worcestershire sauce
- 1/2 cup brown sugar
- 1 onion, finely chopped
- 2 teaspoons mild mustard
- 4 large potatoes, cut into wedges
- 3-1/2 oz. sour cream
- 3 tablespoons vegetable oil
- 2 tablespoons mint, chopped
- Salt and pepper to taste
- 16 small lamb chops

Step-by-Step Directions

1. To make the marinade, combine onion, ketchup, vinegar, Worcestershire sauce, tabasco sauce, and sugar.
2. Soak lamb cuts in the marinade for 1 hour in the refrigerator.
3. Mix oil with salt and pepper.
4. Coat potatoes with the oil mixture.
5. Choose the air fry option.
6. Air fry at 400°F for 25 minutes until crispy.
7. Set aside potatoes once cooked.
8. Take out lamb and place it in the baking tray.
9. Air fry for 15 minutes at 350°F.

Serving Suggestion:

Place 4 pieces of lamb on each plate. Serve with potato wedged topped with sour cream and garnished with mint leaves.

Tip:

You can marinate the lamb overnight to save time.

Lamb Chops with Fresh Tomato Salad

A flavorful and well-balanced lamb dish that takes less than 20 minutes to make.
Prep Time and Cooking Time: 18 minutes | Serves: 1

Ingredients to Use:

- 1/4 teaspoon cinnamon, ground
- 2 tablespoons olive oil
- 2 lamb loin chops
- 1 tablespoon roasted pistachios, powdered
- 1 tablespoon white sesame seeds, toasted
- 1/2 lemon
- 4 scallions, thinly sliced
- 2 medium heirloom tomatoes, coarsely chopped
- 1 head little gem lettuce
- Kosher salt and pepper to taste

Step-by-Step Directions

1. Season lamb with salt then with cinnamon.
2. Lightly coat a baking tray with oil.
3. Select the air fry function.
4. Air fry lamb at 350°F for 3 minutes per side until brown.
5. Remove from heat and let rest for 5 minutes.
6. Set aside 2 tablespoons of pan drippings.
7. Pour the remaining drippings over the lamb.
8. In a bowl, toss together 1 pinch of pistachio powder, sesame seeds, pepper, lemon zest, lemon juice, lettuce, tomatoes, and salt.

Serving Suggestion:

Arrange salad beside the lamb chops and sprinkle a generous amount of pistachio powder.

Tip:

You can substitute endive for the little gem lettuce. Adjust the cooking time if you like a little more done chop.

Air Fryer Marinated Lamb Chops

The wonderfully rendered fat and the spice marinade enhances the flavors in this must-try lamb dish.

Prep Time and Cooking Time: 3 hours 20 minutes | Serves: 4

Ingredients to Use:

- 12 lamb rib chops, frenched
- 1 teaspoon dried fenugreek leaves
- 1/2 teaspoon nutmeg, finely grated
- 1 teaspoon paprika
- 1/4 cup sour cream
- 1 serrano chile, finely grated
- 4 garlic cloves, finely grated
- 1 2-inch ginger, peeled and grated
- 1/2 teaspoon fennel seeds, toasted and ground
- 2 tablespoons fresh lime juice
- 2 tablespoons vegetable oil
- Kosher salt and pepper to taste

Step-by-Step Directions

1. In a bowl, combine sour cream, fennel powder, garlic, ginger, chile, fenugreek leaves, lime juice, pepper, nutmeg, paprika, and vegetable oil. Mix well.
2. Season lamb with salt and coat with spiced marinade.
3. Cover and chill in the refrigerator for 2 hours.
4. Remove from the refrigerator and let sit at room temperature at least 1 hour before grilling.
5. Lightly coat a baking tray with oil.
6. Select the grill function in your air fryer oven.
7. Grill each side for 3 minutes at 350°F for medium-rare.
8. Transfer to a plate and let rest for 10 minutes before serving.

Serving Suggestion:

Place 3 pieces of lamb chops on each plate. Dust chili or paprika powder over the lamb and serve with lemon wedges. Garnish with mint and cilantro.

Tip:

Adjust grilling time for the desired doneness. To cut on the preparation time, marinate the lamb overnight, and keep in the fridge.

Braised Lamb with Orange& Fennel

A lovely Mediterranean-inspired lamb dish that has exquisite flavors.

Prep Time and Cooking Time: 2 hours 7 minutes | Serves: 8

Ingredients to Use:

- 2 bay leaves
- 2 tablespoons olive oil
- 3 lb. boneless lamb shoulder, divided into 8 pieces
- 1 garlic head, cut crosswise
- 1 medium onion, coarsely chopped
- 1 cinnamon stick
- 1 fennel bulb, coarsely chopped
- 1 can (14.5 oz.) peeled whole tomatoes
- 3 cups low-sodium chicken broth
- 1 cup dry white wine
- 1 whole orange, cut into pieces with the skin on

Step-by-Step Directions

1. Dry lamb pieces with paper towels.
2. Season with salt and pepper.
3. Lightly coat pot with oil.
4. Choose the grill function in your air fryer.

5. Grill lamb at 325°F for 6-8 minutes turning occasionally.
6. Transfer lamb to a plate.
7. Put garlic, onion, and fennel in the same pot and use the same settings.
8. Stir occasionally until golden brown for 6 minutes.
9. Deglaze the pot by adding wine.
10. Decrease temperature to 280°F.
11. Add cinnamon stick, orange, bay leaves, broth, tomatoes, and lamb.
12. Switch to bake function.
13. Cover with foil and bake for 1-1/2 hours at 280°F or until lamb is tender.
14. Transfer lamb to a plate and strain liquid through a sieve.
15. Pour the strained liquid back into the cooking pot and cook for 20 minutes until it achieves a velvety texture.
16. Put the lamb back in the cooking pot and coat lamb pieces with the sauce thoroughly.

Serving Suggestion:

This dish goes well with three-herb and onion salad, cucumber-dill tzatziki, or westward pita bread.

Tip:

You can add 2 tablespoons of pomegranate molasses towards the end.

Air Fryer Spiced Lamb Burger

This is a new take on an old favorite. This unique burger has a crunchy crust and is filled with vibrant flavors and aroma.
Prep Time and Cooking Time: 1 hour 15 minutes | Serves: 8

Ingredients to Use:
- 8 thick pita breads, with pockets
- 1/2 teaspoon ground cinnamon
- 1 tablespoon ground coriander
- 1 medium onion, finely chopped
- 3/4 cup fresh parsley, chopped
- 3/4 teaspoon ground cumin
- 1/4 cup olive oil
- 2-1/2 lb. ground lamb
- Kosher salt and pepper to taste

Step-by-Step Directions
1. In a large bowl, combine olive oil, lamb, pepper, parsley, salt, coriander, cinnamon, cumin, and onion.
2. Mix well using a fork.
3. Cover and chill for 1 hour.
4. Cut an opening on each pita bread and insert the lamb mixture.
5. Lightly press down along the opening of the pita to seal.
6. Lightly coat tray with oil.
7. Select the Air fry function in your air fryer oven.
8. Set temperature at 350°F.
9. Air fry pita bread for 5 minutes on each side.

Serving Suggestion:

Cut pita into halves or quarters.

Tip:

The filling can be made in advance and chilled in the fridge for 8 hours. You can also add cheese to the filling.

Air Fryer Barbecue Goat with Aubergine Sauce

The barbecued goat, tangy fresh dressing, and creamy sauce strikes the balance for a delish meal.
Prep Time and Cooking Time: 50 minutes | Serves: 2

Ingredients to Use:
- 1/2 teaspoon cinnamon powder
- 1 tablespoon cumin powder

- 1/2 tablespoon fennel seeds, ground
- 1/2 teaspoon of clove powder
- 1/4 teaspoon cardamom powder
- 1 tablespoon coriander powder
- 8 goat chops
- 4 tablespoons yogurt
- 1/4 cup lemon juice
- 2 aubergines
- 1 garlic head
- 1 teaspoon grape vinegar
- 1 teaspoon sumac
- 1 teaspoon pomegranate molasses
- Salt and pepper to taste

Step-by-Step Directions

1. Combine salt, pepper, fennel, cumin, coriander, cardamom, cinnamon, and clove powder in a bowl.
2. Massage the spice mixture to the goat meat and leave at room temperature for 30 minutes.
3. Choose the grill function.
4. Grill aubergines at 400°F for 10 minutes until the skin turns black and starts to break.
5. Add the whole head of garlic halfway.
6. Set aside aubergines and garlic to cool.
7. Once cool, peel off the skin and combine the aubergine and garlic in a bowl together with the lemon juice, yogurt, and salt. Mix well.
8. In a separate bowl, mix the grape vinegar, sumac, and pomegranate molasses with a teaspoon of boiling water.
9. Cook the goat chops using the same settings for 5 minutes on each side.

Serving Suggestion:

Serve goat on top of the flatbread with the aubergine sauce as a side dish. Drizzle the pomegranate dressing over the meat and aubergines.

Tip:

This dish goes well with a simple fresh herb salad.

Goat Ragu with Vegetables & Red Wine

The inclusion of bone in this slow-cooked goat recipe adds wonderful flavors.
Prep Time and Cooking Time: 2 hours 15 minutes | Serves: 4

Ingredients to Use:

- 2 tablespoon olive oil
- 2 carrots, sliced
- 2 celery stalks, finely sliced
- 2 garlic cloves, finely sliced
- 2 onions, sliced
- 300 ml or 1 cup red wine
- 2 tablespoon tomato paste
- 1 teaspoon sugar
- 400 g canned tomatoes
- 300 ml stock or water
- 1 tablespoon thyme or rosemary, chopped
- 1 teaspoon dried oregano
- 3 bay leaves
- 1/4 teaspoon dried chili flakes
- 3 lb. goat meat with bone, chopped into chunks
- Salt and pepper to taste

Step-by-Step Directions

1. Rinse the goat meat and dry thoroughly.
2. Season generously with salt and pepper.
3. Choose the grill or roast function in your air fryer.
4. Set temperature to 400°F.
5. Cook goat meat for 5 minutes until brown.
6. Remove goat and transfer to a plate.
7. Put garlic, onion, celery, and carrot in the same pot and cook for 10 minutes.

8. Add red wine, stock, tomato paste, tomatoes, and sugar.
9. Add the goat back together with the oregano, chili flakes, thyme, bay leaves, salt, and pepper.
10. Choose the bake function.
11. Reduce the temperature to 320°F and cover the pan with foil.
12. Cook for 1-1/2—2 hours until meat becomes fork-tender.

Serving Suggestion:

Serve with toasted bread or rice and top with herbs and melty cheese.

Tip:

Skin off any excess fat in the surface before serving.

Kerala-Style Goat Ishtu

Tender goat meat cooked with spices and coconut milk.
Prep Time and Cooking Time: 3 hours 45 minutes | Serves: 4

Ingredients to Use:

- 4 green cardamom pods
- 1 tablespoon ghee
- 1 knob ginger, julienned
- 3 cassia sticks
- 1 tablespoon cashew nuts, halved
- 2 sprigs fresh curry leaves
- 2 bay leaves
- 1/2 teaspoon fennel seeds
- 3 green chilis, split
- pint coconut milk
- 2 tablespoons white wine vinegar
- 2 tablespoons cold-pressed coconut oil
- 6-3/4 fl. chicken or lamb stock
- 6 cloves
- 2 shallots, sliced
- 2-1/2 lb. goat shoulder, cubed
- 1 tablespoon ginger paste

- 2 medium potatoes, peeled and cut into chunks
- 1 teaspoon Telicherry whole peppercorns
- Salt and white pepper to taste

Step-by-Step Directions

1. Mix vinegar, ginger paste, and salt. Massage mixture into goat meat.
2. Cover and chill for 2 hours.
3. Choose the air fry function in your air fryer oven.
4. Lightly coat the bottom of the pot with coconut oil.
5. Add the cassia sticks, cardamom pods, cloves, fennel seeds, bay leaves, and peppercorns.
6. Cook for 1 minute at 400°F.
7. Add the ginger and onions, setting aside 1 tablespoon of onion for later.
8. Cook until onions are soft.
9. Add the goat meat and cook until brown for 5 minutes.
10. Add the stock, green chilis, and some white pepper and salt to taste.
11. Reduce temperature to 180°F and cook for 70 minutes until meat is fork-tender.
12. Add the potatoes and cook for 20 minutes.
13. In a separate pan, put ghee and remaining onions.
14. Cook at 400°F for a few seconds until brown.
15. Add cashew nuts and curry leaves.

Serving Suggestion:

Serve while hot. Stir in the coconut oil a few minutes before serving.

Tip:

Goes well with a hot bowl of rice or appam.

Goat Meat Caldereta with

Peanut Butter

This is a delicious dish to give you a whole new appreciation for goat meat.

Prep Time and Cooking Time: 2 hours 10 minutes | Serves: 8

Ingredients to Use:

- 3/4 cup green peas
- 4 cloves garlic, crushed
- 1 medium onion, chopped
- 3 tablespoons cooking oil
- 4 lb. goat meat, chopped
- 1 red bell pepper, sliced into squares
- 8 oz. can of tomato sauce
- 1 green bell pepper, sliced into squares
- 6 oz. can of tomato paste
- 2 cups beef broth
- 8 pieces Thai chili pepper
- 10 tablespoons peanut butter
- Salt and pepper to taste

Step-by-Step Directions

1. Lightly coat a baking tray with oil.
2. Select the air fry option.
3. Air fry garlic, onions, and chili for 3 minutes at 400°F.
4. Set aside.
5. Lightly coat pot with oil.
6. Air fry goat until evenly brown for 8 minutes.
7. Add garlic, onion, chili, tomato paste, and tomato sauce to the pot.
8. Add beef broth and mix ingredients well.
9. Cover with foil.
10. Set temperature to 350°F and cook until the goat is tender for 1-1/2 hours. Stir occasionally.
11. Add peanut butter, green peas, bell peppers, salt, and pepper.
12. Cook for another 8 minutes.

Serving Suggestion:

Serve with a steaming bowl of rice.

Tip:

You can adjust how spicy you want by putting more or less of the Thai chili pepper.

Grilled Goat Meat with Carrots & Peppers

This goat recipe is super easy to prepare and is beautifully seasoned.

Prep Time and Cooking Time: 45 minutes | Serves: 4

Ingredients to Use:

- 2 cloves garlic, crushed
- 2 medium onions, chopped
- 2 medium tomatoes, diced
- 1 medium carrot, chopped
- 2 tablespoons cooking oil
- 2 lb. goat meat, chopped into 2-inch pieces
- 1 green pepper, chopped
- 1/4 cup lemon juice
- Chili pepper (optional)
- Salt to taste

Step-by-Step Directions

1. Place goat in baking tray.
2. Rub goat with salt, lemon juice, and oil.
3. Add tomatoes and carrots.
4. Choose the grill option in your air fryer oven.
5. Grill goat at 400°F for 35 minutes with occasional turning.
6. Add garlic, onion, green pepper, and chili pepper.
7. Grill for 5 more minutes.

Serving Suggestion:

Drizzle with some lemon juice before serving.

Tip:

Garnish with herbs.

Brewmaster-Style Goat

A goat recipe that takes a day ahead to prepare but yields tender and delicious meat thanks to the beer marinade.
Prep Time and Cooking Time: 26 hours 10 minutes | Serves: 4

Ingredients to Use:

- 1 garlic clove, finely chopped
- 2 shallots, chopped
- 2 oz. pancetta, cubed
- 1 small onion, chopped
- 1/4 cup parsley, finely chopped
- 1/4 cup cilantro, finely chopped
- 1 sprig fresh thyme
- 6 button mushrooms, quartered
- 1 small jalapeno, seeded and chopped
- 1 medium carrot, chopped
- 2 lb. goat stew meat, cubed
- 2 cans of cold dark beer
- 2 bay leaves
- 1/4 green onion, finely chopped
- Olive oil

Step-by-Step Directions

1. Combine carrots, bay leaves, onions, thyme, parsley, chili, and beer.
2. Add goat meat and coat with the mixture.
3. Cover and refrigerate for 24 hours.
4. Pour half of the marinade on a pan.
5. Add garlic and pancetta.
6. Choose the bake function and set the temperature at 400°F.
7. Cook until reduced by half for 1 ½ hours and set aside.
8. Select the air fry function.
9. Lightly coat a baking tray with oil and air fry goat meat for 8 minutes at 400°F until brown.
10. Add the goat, shallots, and mushrooms to the pan with sauce.
11. Cover with foil and cook for 30 minutes.

Serving Suggestion:

Serve immediately while hot. Sprinkle with chopped cilantro and green onion. Goes well with mashed potatoes or white rice.

Tip:

To reduce preparation time, you can marinate the goat in advance.

Coconut Chevon (Goat)

Kid goat meat simmered in coconut milk that best pairs with a steaming bowl of coconut rice.
Prep Time and Cooking Time: 40 minutes | Serves: 3

Ingredients to Use:

- 4 tablespoons water
- 2 onions, chopped
- 3 garlic cloves, chopped
- 2 tomatoes, chopped
- 2 tablespoons cooking oil
- 1 bunch coriander
- 1.7 oz. coconut milk
- 9 oz. kid goat meat, cubed
- Salt to taste

Step-by-Step Directions

1. Select the air fry function.
2. Coat pan with oil.
3. Air fry onions at 400°F for 8 minutes until soft, then add garlic.
4. Add goat and cover with foil.
5. Cook for 20 minutes.
6. Add tomatoes and coriander.
7. Add coconut milk and water.
8. Cook for 10 minutes or until the goat is tender.

Serving Suggestion:

Serve in coconut shells if available. Goes well with a bowl of hot coconut rice.

Garnish with grated coconut and herbs.

Curried Chevon Stew

A scrumptious African and Caribbean dish that's perfectly spiced.

Prep Time and Cooking Time: 1 hour 45 minutes | Serves: 5

Ingredients to Use:

- 1 teaspoon garlic, minced
- 1 medium onion, sliced
- 2 tablespoons parsley, chopped
- 1 teaspoon smoked paprika
- 1 teaspoon ginger, minced
- 1 tablespoon bullion
- 1 teaspoon fresh thyme, chopped
- 2-1/2 lb. goat meat, cubed
- 1/2 cup cooking oil
- 3 teaspoons curry powder
- 2 green onions, sliced
- 4 tomatoes, diced
- 1 scotch bonnet pepper, chopped
- 2 cups stock
- Salt and pepper to taste

Step-by-Step Directions

1. Put goat meat in a pot.
2. Add water, salt, pepper, and some of the chopped onions
3. Choose the bake function.
4. Cook at 400°F for 1 hour until the goat is tender.
5. Remove the liquid and add oil.
6. Fry meat for 8 minutes until brown.
7. Add garlic, ginger, and the remaining onions and cook for 2 minutes.
8. Next add the paprika, parsley, curry powder, thyme, hot pepper, and diced tomatoes.
9. Stir frequently to prevent sticking.
10. Add stock, bullion, salt, and pepper. Mix.

11. Cover pot with foil and cook for 30 minutes. Add more water as needed to achieve the desired consistency.

Serving Suggestion:

Serve while hot together with white rice.

Tip:

Add green onions a few minutes before serving.

Spicy Roast Goat

A Nigerian goat dish filled with bold, smoky, and spicy flavors.

Prep Time and Cooking Time: 1 hour 30 minutes | Serves: 5

Ingredients to Use:

- 1 cup of onion, chopped
- 2 green onions, chopped
- 1 teaspoon ginger, minced
- 2 large tomatoes, chopped
- 2-1/2 lb. goat meat, cubed
- 3 cups or more water
- 1-1/2 tablespoons beef or chicken bouillon powder
- 3 tablespoons cooking oil
- 1 teaspoon smoked paprika
- 1/2 teaspoon curry powder
- 1 red or green bell pepper, chopped
- 2 or more scotch bonnet pepper
- 2 teaspoons garlic, minced
- Salt and white pepper to taste

Step-by-Step Directions

1. In a pot, mix goat, water, 1/2 tablespoon bouillon powder, salt, pepper, and some chopped onions.
2. Select the bake function and set the temperature to 400°F.
3. Cook goat meat until tender for 1 hour.
4. With a slotted spoon, transfer goat meat to a baking tray lined with foil.

5. Select the broil function.
6. Broil goat for 10 minutes turning halfway until brown. Set aside.
7. Add some cooking oil to the tray.
8. Put remaining chopped onion, ginger, and garlic.
9. After 1 minute, add green onion, paprika, curry powder, tomatoes, scotch bonnet, white pepper, and 1 tablespoon bouillon powder.
10. Cook for 7 minutes.
11. Add broiled goat and bell peppers and cook for 3 more minutes. Stirring occasionally.

Serving Suggestion:

Serve immediately after cooking.

Tip:

Can be paired with white rice or fried plantains.

Merguez Goat Meatballs

This easy to make North-African dish can be a wonderful appetizer as well as a delicious main course.

Prep Time and Cooking Time: 45 minutes | Serves: 3

Ingredients to Use:

- 1/2 teaspoon coriander, ground
- 1 teaspoon paprika
- 1/2 cup onion, finely chopped
- 1/4 teaspoon cayenne
- 1/4 teaspoon fennel, ground
- 1/2 teaspoon cumin, ground
- 2 cloves garlic, minced
- 1 lb. ground goat meat
- 1 tablespoon harissa paste (Moroccan red pepper sauce)
- 1/2 cup plain Greek yogurt
- 1 tablespoon fresh basil, finely chopped
- 1/4 cup feta cheese, crumbled

- Kosher salt and ground black pepper to taste

Step-by-Step Directions

1. In a bowl, combine ground goat, onion, garlic, coriander, paprika, cayenne, fennel, cumin, salt, and pepper.
2. With clean hands, mix all the ingredients until spices are evenly distributed.
3. Line baking tray with parchment paper.
4. Roll goat meat into 3-inch long meatballs and arrange in the tray.
5. Select the bake function in your air fryer oven.
6. Bake meatballs at 400°F for 30 minutes until brown.
7. In a bowl, mix yogurt, basil, feta, salt, and pepper to create the yogurt sauce. Set aside.

Serving Suggestion:

Serve meatballs immediately and add a dollop of yogurt sauce on top.

Tip:

Remember to not overmix the ground meat since it can become tough. Can be served on top of couscous as a main dish or as party appetizers.

Goat in Creole Sauce

A popular Haitian dish that could be your new comfort food.

Prep Time and Cooking Time: 3 hours 35 minutes | Serves: 6-8

Ingredients to Use:

- 4 garlic cloves, grated
- 1 medium white onion, sliced
- 1/3 cup tomatoes, chopped
- 1 sprig fresh thyme, finely chopped
- 1/4 cup fresh parsley, finely chopped
- 1 tablespoon olive oil
- 3 whole cloves

- 2 scallions, chopped
- 1/2 green bell pepper, sliced
- 3 lb. goat meat, cubed
- 1 cup white vinegar or lemon juice
- 1/3 cup unsweetened orange juice
- 1 tablespoon tomato paste
- Salt and black pepper to taste

Step-by-Step Directions

1. Pour lemon juice or vinegar on goat meat and massage.
2. Rinse with cold water and drain.
3. In a bowl, combine all spices, orange juice, and goat meat.
4. Cover and chill for at least 2 hours.
5. Allow meat to attain room temperature before cooking.
6. Put goat meat in a pot and add water until the meat is covered.
7. Choose bake function.
8. Cook meat at 400°F for 1 hour or until tender.
9. Add water as needed.
10. With a slotted spoon, transfer meat to a plate and set aside.
11. Strain liquid and set aside.
12. Choose roast function and set to 350°F.
13. Add oil and tomato paste to the pot.
14. Add meat and cook for 5 minutes.
15. Add chopped tomatoes and cook for 2 minutes.
16. Add sauce gradually until desired consistency.
17. Add onion, bell pepper, salt, and pepper.
18. Cook for 7 minutes.

Serving Suggestion:

Serve with rice or any root vegetables.

Tip:

When adding water, use hot water. Cold water tends to make the meat taste bland.

Air Fryer Goat Steak

A garlic-infused goat steak recipe you can easily make in your air fryer at home.
Prep Time and Cooking Time: 2 hours 10 minutes | Serves: 2

Ingredients to Use:

- 4 garlic cloves, minced
- 2 tablespoons fresh oregano, chopped
- 1 cup sheep's milk yogurt
- Salt and pepper to taste
- 2 tablespoons oil
- 2 1-inch thick goat steaks

Step-by-Step Directions

1. Rub goat generously with salt and pepper.
2. Combine yogurt, oregano, and garlic in a small bowl.
3. Massage the yogurt mixture into the goat.
4. Cover and chill for 2 hours.
5. Lightly coat tray with oil.
6. Choose the air fry option.
7. Air fry goat steaks at 350°F for 2 minutes on each side.

Serving Suggestion:

Tent with foil for 5 minutes after cooking.

Tip:

Carefully watch the goat meat when frying, as it can dry out quickly. Goat steaks taste better when allowed to marinate at least overnight. Do this in advance to save time.

Ground Goat Tacos with Blackened Tomatoes

A wonderful recipe choice if you're having friends over.
Prep Time and Cooking Time: 1 hour 18 minutes | Serves: 20

Ingredients to Use:

- 4 garlic cloves
- 1 large onion, diced
- 8 oz. can chipotle peppers in adobo, pureed
- 2 medium red vine tomatoes, diced
- 2 medium tomatillos, diced
- 1 oz. cilantro, chopped
- 2 jalapenos, diced
- 4 lb. ground goat meat
- 1 oz. grapeseed oil
- 4 oz. sour cream
- 4 oz. queso fresco cheese, crumbled
- Avocado and lime for serving

Step-by-Step Directions

1. Choose air fry option.
2. Coat pot with oil.
3. Air fry 1/3 of the onions until soft and brown for 350°F for 6 minutes.
4. Add garlic and cook for 1 minute.
5. Add meat and cook for 3 minutes stirring occasionally.
6. Add half the chipotle pepper, tomatoes, and jalapeno.
7. Add water just enough to submerge meat.
8. Select the bake function.
9. Bake at 300°F for 45- minutes to 1 hour.
10. In a baking tray, lay the remaining tomatoes evenly.
11. Broil for 3 minutes or until blackened.
12. Do not move tomatoes until they begin to caramelize.
13. Divide blackened tomatoes into two.
14. Dice half and use for garnish.
15. Puree half and use it as a sauce.

Serving Suggestion:

Serve on a toasted tortilla. Sprinkle 2 oz. of ground goat meat, a tablespoon of cheese, a tablespoon charred tomatoes, a teaspoon of onion, jalapenos avocado, sour cream, roasted peppers.

Tip:

Skim fat every 20 minutes while baking. Garnish with a lime wedge.

Ground Goat & Sweet Potatoes

A filling goat recipe with just the right amount of spice.
Prep Time and Cooking Time: 50 minutes | Serves: 4

Ingredients to Use:

- 1 tablespoon olive oil
- 1 clove garlic, minced
- 1/4 cup fresh cilantro, chopped
- 1 teaspoon coriander
- 2 lb. sweet potatoes, peeled and diced into 1/4-inch cubes
- 1 large onion, chopped
- 2 tablespoons lemon juice
- 1/4 teaspoon of garam masala
- 1 cup plain yogurt
- 1 lb. ground goat meat
- Salt to taste

Step-by-Step Directions

1. Add sweet potatoes to a pot and cover with water.
2. Choose bake function.
3. Bake for 400°F for 30 minutes until soft. Set aside.
4. Select the air fry function.
5. Air fry onion with some olive oil in a baking tray for 5 minutes until soft.
6. Add ground goat and cook until light brown.
7. Add the sweet potatoes, garam masala, cilantro, coriander, and salt.
8. Cook for 5 minutes at 350°F.
9. Combine yogurt, garlic, and lemon juice in a bowl to make the yogurt sauce.

Serve goat meat with a dollop of yogurt sauce on top.

Gently stir to avoid breaking or mashing the sweet potatoes.

Chevon Lahmacun

A Turkish classic with a brilliant twist. This recipe swaps lamb for sustainable and tasty goat meat.

Prep Time and Cooking Time: 1 hour 30 minutes | Serves: 8

Ingredients to Use:

- 2 teaspoons dry yeast
- 1-3/4 teaspoon sugar
- 3 cups strong white bread flour, plus more for dusting
- 2 teaspoons salt
- 1 cup lukewarm water
- 2 tablespoons tomato puree
- Pepper to taste
- 5 tablespoons olive oil
- 1 lb. minced goat
- 1 red pepper, seeded and chopped
- 3 garlic cloves, chopped
- 1 white onion, chopped
- 1 pinch red pepper or chili flakes
- 1 bunch parsley, chopped

Step-by-Step Directions

1. In a large bowl, mix flour and salt.
2. Dissolve yeast in lukewarm water.
3. Add 3 tablespoons olive oil and 1-3/4 teaspoon sugar to the yeast water. Mix.
4. Gently pour the liquid into the bowl with flour.
5. Using hands, mix until you get a rough dough.
6. Take out the dough and knead until soft and elastic.

7. Place the dough back in the bowl. Dust with flour and cover with a towel.
8. Let the dough rise in a warm area for an hour.
9. Combine goat along with all other ingredients in a food processor until a smooth paste consistency is achieved.
10. Divide dough into 4-8 balls, depending on your preference.
11. Roll each dough ball flat and top with a generous amount of goat mixture.
12. Place dough on a baking tray.
13. Choose the
14. cook for 6-10 minutes.

Serving Suggestion:

Add parsley and a drizzle of pomegranate molasses on top.

Tip:

If the dough is too wet, you can add a little flour. If it's too dry, add a little water. The lahmacun is ready if the goat is sizzling and the edges have become brown.

Easy Air Fryer Goat Curry

This is the most popular way to prepare goat meat and for good reason.

Prep Time and Cooking Time: 1 hour 10 minutes | Serves: 4

Ingredients to Use:

- 10 garlic cloves, finely grated
- 1 onion, sliced
- 2 tablespoons chili powder
- 2 teaspoons curry leaves
- 2 lb. goat shoulder, cubed
- 2 cinnamon quills
- 5 tablespoons vegetable oil
- 1 teaspoon castor sugar
- 1 lemon, juiced
- 8 fl. coconut cream
- 17 oz. water

- 2 tablespoons fennel seeds, ground
- 1 oz. ginger

1. In a small bowl, mix the garlic, fennel, and ginger into a paste.
2. Choose the bake option.
3. Coat pan with oil and put cinnamon quills, curry leaves, onions.
4. Cook for 5 minutes at 350°F.
5. Add the garlic, ginger, and fennel paste.
6. Add the goat and cook for 5 minutes until brown.
7. Add water and reduce temperature to 190°F.
8. Cook for 40 minutes.
9. Add the coconut milk, lemon juice, salt, and sugar.
10. Stir and continue cooking until liquids have evaporated.

Serving Suggestion:

Serve with a steamy bowl of rice.

Tip:

Garnish with fresh parsley.

Moorish Goat Skewers

Spicy and savory goat skewers ideal for any occasion.
Prep Time and Cooking Time: 6 hours 30 minutes | Serves: 4

Ingredients to Use:

- 1 teaspoon turmeric
- 2 oz. olive oil
- 2 garlic cloves, finely minced
- 1 teaspoon nutmeg, ground
- 1/2 teaspoon, plus 1/2 teaspoon cayenne pepper
- 1 bunch curly parsley, chopped
- 7 oz. fino, plus 2 oz. sherry
- 2 tablespoons cumin seeds, ground
- 1 tablespoon, plus 1 teaspoon sweet

Spanish paprika
- 1/2 lemon, squeezed
- 2 lb. goat meat, cut into 1-inch cubes
- Salt to taste

Step-by-Step Directions

1. In a large bowl, mix cumin, nutmeg, turmeric, garlic, parsley, ½ teaspoon cayenne powder, 1 tablespoon paprika, 7 oz. fino, and olive oil.
2. Add goat meat.
3. Cover and chill for 6 hours or overnight.
4. Thread goat cubes into metal skewers.
5. To create basting liquid, mix 2 oz. sherry, 1/2 teaspoon cayenne pepper, 1 teaspoon paprika, and lemon juice.
6. Choose the grill or use the rotisserie function in your air fryer oven.
7. Set the temperature to 200°F and cook for 15 minutes.
8. Brush basting liquid occasionally.

Serving Suggestion:

Allow meat to rest for a few minutes before serving.

Tip:

While marinating, turn or stir 2-3 times to coat goat meat evenly. Make a big batch and store it in the fridge to easily cook anytime in your air fryer.

Kid Goat Ragu with Pappardelle

This Greek-inspired goat dish is brilliantly well-balanced and undeniably delicious.
Prep Time and Cooking Time: 1 hour 45 minutes | Serves: 4

Ingredients to Use:

- 1 garlic clove, sliced
- 2 onions, chopped
- 1 cup of water
- 4 celery sticks, chopped

- 2 oz. extra virgin olive oil
- 1 carrot, cubed
- 18 oz. white wine
- 1 teaspoon thyme leaves
- 2 bird's eye chilis, thinly sliced
- 1/2 cup pecorino
- 2 lb. kid goat shoulders, cut into 3 pieces each
- 2 lb. pappardelle pasta, cooked al dente
- Salt and freshly ground pepper to taste

Step-by-Step Directions

1. Put olive oil in the pot.
2. Add garlic, celery, carrots, and onions.
3. Select the air fryer option.
4. Cook the vegetables for 3 minutes at 200°F.
5. Increase temperature to 350°F.
6. And add the meat. Cook for 8 minutes until golden brown.
7. Add water, thyme, white wine, and season with salt and pepper.
8. Cover and cook for 90 minutes.
9. Shred meat and remove from bone.
10. Toss pasta with sauce.

Serving Suggestion:

Sprinkle pecorino over the goat and pasta.

Tip:

Top with sliced chili as a garnish.

Kid Goat with Cranberries

A carefully seasoned goat dish cooked with honey and red wine.
Prep Time and Cooking Time: 2 hours| Serves: 4

Ingredients to Use:

- 2 bay leaves
- ½ cup red wine
- 2/3 cup olive oil
- 2/3 cup dried cranberries

- 2 garlic cloves, finely chopped
- 2 red onions, finely chopped
- 2 white onions, cut into wedges
- 2 tablespoons honey
- 1 tablespoon rosemary, chopped
- 1 tablespoon fresh thyme, chopped
- 2 large tomatoes, cut into wedges
- 3-1/2 lb. goat leg

Step-by-Step Directions

1. Score goat meat with a sharp knife.
2. Rub oil, salt, and pepper all over, making sure that meat is sufficiently coated.
3. Coat pot with some oil.
4. Choose the broil or roast function.
5. Cook red onions for 4 minutes at 400°F until soft.
6. Add garlic, thyme, cranberries, and rosemary. Cook for 2 minutes.
7. Next, add the wine and honey.
8. Season with salt and pepper. Set aside.
9. In a baking tray, cook the goat meat for 6 minutes until golden brown. Set aside.
10. Cook white onions and potatoes until soft. Season with salt and pepper.
11. Add meat to the pot with cranberries.
12. Add bay leaves and roast for 20 minutes.
13. Baste meat and turn temperature to 350 °F.
14. Add the onions and potatoes to the pot.
15. Cook for 30 minutes.

Serving Suggestion:

Cover meat with foil for 15 minutes before serving.

Tip:

Use fresh thyme sprig as garnish.

Jamaican Goat Curry

This goat recipe is a delightful introduction to Jamaican cuisine.
Prep Time and Cooking Time: 2 hours 45

minutes | Serves: 6

Ingredients to Use:

- 2 teaspoons minced garlic
- 1 medium onion, sliced
- 2 scallions, sliced
- 1 tablespoon tomato paste
- 1 tablespoon bouillon powder
- 3 lb. goat meat, cut into chunks
- 1 scotch bonnet pepper
- 3 medium potatoes
- 1/4 cup cooking oil
- 2 teaspoons minced ginger
- 4 tablespoons curry powder
- 2 teaspoons fresh thyme
- Salt and white pepper to taste

Step-by-Step Directions

1. Generously rub goat meat with salt and pepper. Set aside.
2. Choose the air fry option.
3. Lightly coat pot with oil.
4. Air fry goat meat until brown.
5. Add curry powder and cook for 2 minutes.
6. Stir in tomato paste, scallions, garlic, onion, ginger, scotch bonnet, thyme, and white pepper.
7. Add hot water enough to cover the goat.
8. Cook for 1-1/2 to 2 hours until meat is tender.
9. Add hot water or stock as needed.
10. Add potatoes and bouillon powder cook for 20 minutes.

Serving Suggestion:

Serve hot in a bowl with rice or mashed potatoes.

Tip:

Garnish with fresh herbs and lime wedges.

Easy Air Fried Goat

This recipe has savory and tangy flavors that go so well with goat meat.
Prep Time and Cooking Time: 45 minutes | Serves: 4

Ingredients to Use:

- 2 teaspoons garlic, minced
- 1 teaspoon paprika
- 4 tablespoons lemon juice
- 2 lb. kid goat meat, cubed
- 2 tablespoons cooking oil

Step-by-Step Directions

1. Season goat meat with salt, lemon juice, paprika, and garlic.
2. Cover and rest for 30 minutes at room temperature.
3. Choose the air fry function.
4. Lightly coat a baking tray with oil.
5. Air fry goat at 400°F until brown.

Serving Suggestion:

Serve with fresh salad. Drizzle some more lemon juice before serving.

Tip:

For a spicy version, sprinkle with chili powder or hot sauce.

Goat with Rosemary & Bay Leaf

A traditional Zimbabwe goat dish with a pleasant twist.
Prep Time and Cooking Time: 1 hour 30 minutes | Serves: 5

Ingredients to Use:

- 3 garlic cloves, minced
- 2 lb. goat meat, cubed
- 2 sprigs fresh rosemary
- 2 tablespoons cooking oil
- 1 bay leaf
- Salt to taste

Step-by-Step Directions

1. Coat pot with oil.
2. Choose the grill function.
3. Put goat in pot and season with salt.
4. Grill goat until golden brown at 400°F.
5. Add bay leaf, rosemary, and garlic to the pot.
6. Add hot water enough to cover the meat.
7. Cook until liquid evaporates.
8. Brown goat again for 5 minutes.

Serving Suggestion:

Serve with sadzaregorosi (wheatmeal pap)

Tip:

Goes well with sadzanemuriwo (sautéed meat and vegetables) and soup.

Punjabi-style Goat Curry

This traditional Indian curry is easy to make and is full of great flavors and aroma.
Prep Time and Cooking Time: 1 hour 40 minutes | Serves: 6

Ingredients to Use:

- 4 cloves, crushed
- 1 tablespoon turmeric powder
- 2 teaspoon garam masala powder
- 1 tablespoon chili powder
- 2 teaspoon paprika powder
- 1 tablespoon coriander powder
- 2 green cardamoms, crushed
- 3 tablespoons ginger, chopped
- 1 bay leaf
- 1 cup olive oil
- 1 large yellow onion (crushed in a food processor)
- 2 cups canned tomato sauce
- 2 tablespoon fresh Indian chili, chopped
- 1 bunch fresh coriander leaves
- 9 cups hot water
- 3 lb. goat meat, cut into chunks
- Salt to taste

Step-by-Step Directions

1. Coat pot with oil.
2. Choose the bake or roast function.
3. Add cloves, onion, bay leaf, cumin, and cardamom.
4. Cook until onion turns light brown.
5. Add chili paste, garlic, and ginger.
6. Add goat and cook for 15 minutes.
7. Add chili powder, paprika, coriander, turmeric, tomato sauce, and salt. Mix well.
8. Once the oil starts to form, add the hot water, and continue stirring.
9. Add water as needed.
10. Cover with foil and continue baking until meat is fork-tender.

Serving Suggestion:

Add the garam masala and coriander leaves a few minutes before serving.

Tip:

This goes well with steamed rice and Indian bread.

Spiced Masala Chops

If you're someone trying out goat meat for the first time, this spice-infused recipe is perfect for you.
Prep Time and Cooking Time: 40 minutes | Serves: 3

Ingredients to Use:

- 1 tablespoon white vinegar
- 1 tablespoon turmeric powder
- 1/2 tablespoon garam masala
- 1 tablespoon cumin powder
- 1-1/2 Kashmiri red chili powder
- 2 tablespoon ginger and garlic paste
- 1 lb. goat chops
- 2 tablespoon cooking oil

- Salt to taste

1. Coat pot with oil.
2. Choose the roast or bake function in your air fryer oven.
3. Set temperature at 350°F.
4. Add the garlic and ginger paste for a few seconds.
5. Put chops and cook until brown.
6. Put all remaining ingredients and add some water.
7. Add 1/2 cup of hot water and cook for 25 minutes until liquids evaporate.
8. Put chops in the air fryer basket.
9. Roast for 8-10 minutes at 356°F.

Serving Suggestion:

Serve with any yogurt dip and fresh salad.

Tip:

Goes well with steamed rice.

Air fryer Oven Grilled Goat

This easy goat recipe will make you want to cook goat meat more often.
Prep Time and Cooking Time: 1 hour 30 minutes | Serves: 2

Ingredients to Use:

- 4 garlic cloves, sliced
- 1 lb. goat meat, left for 30 minutes at room temperature
- 2 teaspoon soy sauce
- 1 tablespoon honey
- 2 teaspoons Worcestershire sauce
- 6 sprigs rosemary
- 2 tablespoons olive oil
- 1 beef cube stock. crumbled
- Salt and pepper to taste

Step-by-Step Directions

1. Lay out enough foil to coat goat meat.
2. Coat with 1 tablespoon olive oil, salt, and pepper.
3. Put goat meat and create small slices on the surface.
4. Insert garlic and rosemary in the incisions.
5. Sprinkle with beef stock and wrap.
6. In a small bowl, combine olive oil, Worcestershire sauce, soy sauce, and honey to make the sauce.
7. Choose the grill function and set the temperature to 338°F.
8. Cook goat for 30 minutes turning halfway.
9. Brush goat with the sauce after 15 minutes of cooking, and after 30 minutes.
10. Remove the foil and set the temperature to 374°F.
11. Cook for 15 minutes (medium-rare) to brown the surface.

Serving Suggestion:

Let the meat rest for 15 minutes before carving. Garnish with rosemary and parsley.

Tip:

After the foil is off, you can cook goat for 25 minutes for medium and 30 minutes for well-done.

Chapter 6: Chicken & Poultry Dishes

Szechuan Chicken

Enjoy oriental flavors in this simple but savory Szechuan chicken recipe.
Prep Time and Cooking Time: 30 minutes | Serves: 2

Ingredients to Use:

Chicken
- 1 lb. chicken breast, sliced into cubes
- 1/4 cup cornstarch
- Cooking spray

Sauce
- 1 tablespoon black bean sauce
- 1/4 cup mayonnaise
- 1 teaspoon hoisin
- 1 teaspoon ground Sichuan peppercorns
- 2 teaspoon honey
- 1/4 teaspoon garlic powder
- 1 tablespoon brown sugar
- 1 teaspoon rice wine vinegar

Step-by-Step Directions

1. Dredge chicken cubes with cornstarch.
2. Spray with oil.
3. Add to the air crisper tray.
4. Set your air fryer oven to air fry.
5. Cook at 350°F for 8 to 10 minutes, and flip once.
6. Mix the sauce ingredients in a bowl.
7. Toss the crispy chicken cubes in the sauce.
8. Put these back to the air fryer oven.
9. Set it to bake.
10. Bake at 350°F for 3 minutes.

Serving Suggestion:

Garnish with chopped green onions.

Tip:

You can also serve this with cooked white rice.

Barbecue Chicken Wings

Sticky barbecue sauce will make your chicken wings truly irresistible.
Prep Time and Cooking Time: 35 minutes | Serves: 6

Ingredients to Use:

Chicken
- 2 lb. chicken wings
- 2 teaspoon baking powder
- Salt and pepper to taste

Sauce
- 15 oz. tomato sauce
- 1/2 cup apple cider vinegar
- 1/3 cup honey
- 1/4 cup tomato paste
- 1/4 cup molasses
- 4 tablespoons Worcestershire sauce
- 2 teaspoons liquid smoke
- 1 teaspoon garlic powder
- 1 teaspoon paprika
- Salt and pepper to taste
- 1 teaspoon onion powder

Step-by-Step Directions

1. Season chicken with salt and pepper.
2. Coat with baking powder.
3. Place these in the air crisper tray.
4. Set it to air fry.
5. Cook at 350°F for 15 minutes, flipping once.
6. Increase temperature to 400°F.
7. Cook for another 5 minutes.
8. Toss the chicken in the sauce.
9. Place back to the air fryer oven.
10. Set it to bake.
11. Cook at 350°F for 15 minutes.

Garnish with chopped parsley.

Tip:

Dry chicken thoroughly before seasoning.

Air Fried Chicken with Roasted Tomatoes & Leafy Greens

Use your air fryer oven to air fry the chicken and roast the vegetables.

Prep Time and Cooking Time: 30 minutes | Serves: 4

Ingredients to Use:

Roasted veggies
- 1 cup cherry tomatoes
- 1 cup arugula
- 2 tablespoons olive oil

Air fried chicken
- 2 chicken breast fillets
- 2 teaspoons olive oil
- 2 tablespoons chicken rub
- Salt and pepper to taste

Step-by-Step Directions

1. Toss tomatoes and arugula in olive oil.
2. Transfer to the air fryer oven.
3. Select roast function.
4. Cook at 350°F for 3 minutes.
5. Transfer to a serving plate.
6. Drizzle chicken with olive oil.
7. Sprinkle with chicken rub, salt and pepper.
8. Place in the air fryer oven.
9. Set it to air fry.
10. Cook at 370°F for 4 to 5 minutes per side.
11. Serve the chicken on top of the roasted vegetables.

Serving Suggestion:

Sprinkle with pepper before serving.

Tip:

You can also use chicken thigh fillet for this recipe.

Korean Fried Chicken

It would seem like you've taken a trip to Korea when you prepare this amazing dish at home.

Prep Time and Cooking Time: 20 minutes | Serves: 4

Ingredients to Use:
- 1/4 cup flour
- 1/4 cup water
- Salt and pepper to taste
- 1 lb. chicken thigh fillet, sliced into cubes

Sauce
- 3 teaspoons Korean chilli garlic paste
- 1 tablespoon sugar
- 1 tablespoon apple cider vinegar

Step-by-Step Directions

1. Mix the flour, water, salt and pepper in a bowl.
2. Coat the chicken with the batter.
3. Transfer to the air crisper tray.
4. Choose the air fry setting in your air fryer oven.
5. Cook at 350°F for 5 minutes.
6. Turn and cook for another 5 minutes.
7. Toss the chicken in the sauce.
8. Place it back in the air fryer oven.
9. Select bake setting.
10. Bake at 350°F for 5 minutes.

Serving Suggestion:

Serve with radish and steamed carrots.

Chicken Teriyaki

You don't have to get stressed over dinner when you have a recipe like this one.

Prep Time and Cooking Time: 30 minutes | Serves: 4

Ingredients to Use:
- 1 lb. chicken breast fillets, sliced into

cubes
- Cooking spray

Sauce
- 1 clove garlic, minced
- 1 tablespoon sesame oil
- 3 tablespoons brown sugar
- 2 tablespoons mirin
- 3 tablespoons vinegar
- 1/4 cup soy sauce

Step-by-Step Directions

1. Combine the sauce ingredients in a bowl.
2. Soak the chicken cubes in the sauce.
3. Cover and marinate for 1 hour in the refrigerator.
4. Select roast setting in your air fryer oven.
5. Place the chicken inside the oven.
6. Cook at 375°F for 5 minutes per side.
7. Set it to broil.
8. Cook for another 2 minutes.

Serving Suggestion:

Serve with cooked white rice.

Tip:

Use rice wine vinegar if available.

Cajun Chicken Drumsticks

This chicken is oozing with so much enticing flavors.
Prep Time and Cooking Time: 40 minutes | Serves: 6

Ingredients to Use:

- 6 chicken drumsticks
- Olive oil

Cajun seasoning
- 1 teaspoon onion powder
- 1/2 teaspoon garlic powder
- 1 teaspoon paprika
- 1/2 teaspoon dried thyme
- 1/2 teaspoon dried basil
- 1/2 teaspoon dried oregano
- 1/2 teaspoon cayenne pepper

- Salt and pepper to taste

Step-by-Step Directions

1. Combine seasoning ingredients in a bowl.
2. Coat chicken with oil.
3. Sprinkle with seasoning.
4. Place in the air fryer oven.
5. Press roast or grill setting.
6. Cook at 400°F for 10 minutes per side.

Serving Suggestion:

Serve with hot pepper sauce.

Tip:

You can also use chicken wings for this recipe.

Paprika Chicken Wings

One of the simplest and easiest chicken recipes to prepare!
Prep Time and Cooking Time: 40 minutes | Serves: 6

Ingredients to Use:

- 2 lb. chicken wings
- 2 tablespoons olive oil
- 1 tablespoon smoked paprika
- 1 teaspoon garlic powder
- Salt and pepper to taste

Step-by-Step Directions

1. Toss the chicken wings in oil.
2. Mix the remaining ingredients in a bowl.
3. Cover the chicken with this mixture.
4. Add the chicken wings to the air fryer oven.
5. Choose air fry setting.
6. Cook at 400°F for 30 minutes, and flip once halfway through cooking.

Serving Suggestion:

Garnish with chopped green onions.

Baked Stuffed Chicken

Chicken stuffed with cream cheese and

seasoned with herbs—here's a wonderful treat for your taste buds.
Prep Time and Cooking Time: 30 minutes | Serves: 2

Ingredients to Use:

- 2 chicken breast fillets
- 1 cup cream cheese
- 1 teaspoon garlic powder
- 2 teaspoons dried Italian seasoning
- Salt and pepper to taste

Step-by-Step Directions

1. Create a pocket in your chicken breast.
2. Season both sides of chicken with salt and pepper.
3. Mix the remaining ingredients in a bowl.
4. Stuff the pocket with the mixture.
5. Place the stuffed chicken with the mixture.
6. Add to the air fryer oven.
7. Set it to bake.
8. Cook at 370°F for 15 minutes.
9. Flip and cook for another 15 minutes.

Serving Suggestion:

1. Let rest for 5 minutes before serving.

Tip:

You can also use cream cheese flavored with garlic and herbs.

Chipotle Lime Chicken

This lime chicken has the right balance of savory, sour and sweet flavors.
Prep Time and Cooking Time: 1 hour and 40 minutes | Serves: 6

Ingredients to Use:

- 2 lb. chicken wings

Sauce
- 2 tablespoons lime juice
- 1 teaspoon lime zest
- 1 tablespoon water
- 2 tablespoons chipotle in adobe sauce
- Salt and pepper to taste

Step-by-Step Directions

1. Add the sauce ingredients to a bowl.
2. Coat the chicken wings in the sauce.
3. Cover and marinate for 1 hour in the refrigerator.
4. Add the chicken to the air fryer oven.
5. Set it to roast.
6. Cook at 380°F for 15 minutes per side.
7. Set the oven to broil.
8. Broil the chicken for 5 minutes.

Serving Suggestion:

Serve with hot pepper sauce.

Tip:

You can also use drumsticks for this recipe.

Chinese Sesame Chicken

This will easily become your family's favorite dish.
Prep Time and Cooking Time: 40 minutes | Serves: 4

Ingredients to Use:

- 1 lb. chicken thigh fillet, sliced into cubes
- 1/2 cup potato starch
- Olive oil

Sauce
- 1/4 cup soy sauce
- 1/4 cup hoisin sauce
- 2 tablespoons brown sugar
- 2 tablespoons orange juice
- 1 teaspoon garlic powder
- 1 teaspoon ground ginger

Step-by-Step Directions

1. Coat the chicken cubes with potato starch.
2. Brush with oil.
3. Place in the air crisper tray inside the air fryer oven.

4. Select air fry setting.
5. Cook at 350°F for 7 to 10 minutes, flipping once.
6. Mix the sauce ingredients in a bowl.
7. Toss the chicken in the sauce.
8. Transfer back to the air fryer oven.
9. Choose broil setting.
10. Broil for 2 minutes.

Serving Suggestion:

Garnish with green onions and white sesame seeds.

Tip:

You can also use flour instead of potato starch.

Southern Fried Chicken

Enjoy Southern fried chicken without any fuss with the help of your air fryer oven.
Prep Time and Cooking Time: 45 minutes | Serves: 6

Ingredients to Use:
- 2 lb. chicken
- Cooking spray

Southern spice mixture
- 2 tablespoons olive oil
- 1 teaspoon onion powder
- 1 teaspoon dried oregano
- 1 teaspoon dried celery salt
- 1 teaspoon dried basil
- 1 teaspoon dried thyme
- 1 teaspoon dried paprika
- Salt and pepper to taste

Breading
- 1/4 cup cornstarch
- 1 cup flour
- 1-1/2 teaspoons baking powder
- Salt and pepper to taste

Buttermilk mixture
- eggs, beaten
- tablespoons hot sauce
- 2 tablespoons buttermilk
- 1/4 cup water

Step-by-Step Directions
1. Mix the southern spice mixture ingredients in a bowl.
2. In another bowl, combine the breading ingredients.
3. In a third bowl, mix the buttermilk mixture ingredients.
4. Coat the chicken evenly with the spice mixture.
5. Dredge with breading.
6. Dip in the buttermilk mixture.
7. Dredge with breading once more.
8. Spray chicken with oil.
9. Place chicken in the air crisper tray.
10. Set the air fryer oven to air fry function.
11. Cook at 350°F for 20 minutes.

Serving Suggestion:

Serve with mustard and ketchup.

Tip:

Omit hot sauce if you don't like your chicken spicy.

Turkey Pot Pie

This is an extremely convenient recipe that you can make whenever you have a busy schedule.
Prep Time and Cooking Time: 35 minutes | Serves: 1

Ingredients to Use:
- 1 frozen turkey pot pie

Step-by-Step Directions
1. Set your air fryer oven to bake.
2. Preheat it to 350°F for 10 minutes.
3. Add the frozen pie to the oven.
4. Bake it for 30 minutes.
5. Increase temperature to 400°F.
6. Bake it for 5 minutes.

Let cool before slicing and serving.

Tip:

You can also use frozen chicken pot pie for this recipe.

Honey Mustard Chicken Wings

This dish has just the right balance of sweet and sour flavors that you'd absolutely love.
Prep Time and Cooking Time: 40 minutes | Serves: 8

Ingredients to Use:

- 1 tablespoon lemon juice
- 1/4 cup honey
- 1/4 cup mustard
- 1/8 cup butter
- Salt and pepper to taste
- 2 lb. chicken wings

Step-by-Step Directions

1. Combine all the ingredients except chicken in a bowl.
2. Mix well.
3. Add the chicken wings to the air crisper tray.
4. Set it to air fry function.
5. Cook at 380°F for 12 minutes.
6. Flip and cook for another 12 minutes.
7. Toss the chicken wings in the sauce.
8. Place it back inside the oven.
9. Choose bake setting.
10. Bake at 350°F for 10 minutes.

Serving Suggestion:

Garnish with chopped green onion.

Tip:

Use spicy brown mustard if available.

Salt & Vinegar Chicken Wings

You're going to love the salty and sour flavors

of these chicken wings.
Prep Time and Cooking Time: 40 minutes | Serves: 8

Ingredients to Use:

- 2 lb. chicken wings

Marinade
- tablespoons apple cider vinegar
- 1/2 cup white vinegar
- 2-1/3 dry ranch mix
- 1 teaspoon garlic power
- 1 teaspoon sugar
- 2 tablespoons salt

Step-by-Step Directions

1. Add all the marinade ingredients to a bowl.
2. Mix well.
3. Add the chicken wings to the bowl.
4. Cover and marinate in the refrigerator for 30 minutes.
5. Arrange in a single layer in the air crisper tray.
6. Set your air fryer oven to air fry.
7. Cook at 380°F for 12 to 15 minutes per side.

Serving Suggestion:

Garnish with chopped scallions.

Tip:

Ranch dressing can also be used in place of dry ranch mix.

Roasted Whole Chicken

Yes, you can roast your own whole chicken at home when you have your air fryer oven!
Prep Time and Cooking Time: 1 hour and 10 minutes | Serves: 5

Ingredients to Use:

- 1 whole chicken, cleaned

Rub
- 3 tablespoons oil

- 1 teaspoon onion powder
- 1 teaspoons thyme
- 2 teaspoons paprika
- 1/2 teaspoon cayenne pepper
- 1/2 teaspoon garlic powder
- 1/4 cup fresh thyme, chopped
- 1/4 cup fresh rosemary, chopped
- Salt and pepper to taste

Step-by-Step Directions

1. Combine the rub ingredients in a bowl.
2. Rub the spice mixture all over the chicken.
3. Attach the chicken in the rotisserie spit inside the air fryer oven.
4. Set it to rotisserie.
5. Cook at 350°F for 2 hours.

Serving Suggestion:

Let cool for 5 minutes before serving.

Tip:

Internal temperature of chicken should be 180°F.

Garlic Parmesan Chicken

Here's a tasty chicken dish that would make you want to get another serving.
Prep Time and Cooking Time: 30 minutes | Serves: 2

Ingredients to Use:

- 1 cup breadcrumbs
- 1 tablespoon Italian seasoning
- 1/2 teaspoon poultry seasoning
- 1 lb. chicken breast fillet
- 1/2 cup mayonnaise
- 4 tablespoons butter
- 1 clove garlic, minced
- 2/3 cup Parmesan cheese, grated

Step-by-Step Directions

1. In a bowl, mix the breadcrumbs, Italian seasoning and poultry seasoning.

2. Dip the chicken breast fillets in mayo.
3. Coat with the breadcrumb mixture.
4. Add the chicken to the air crisper tray.
5. In a bowl, mix butter and garlic.
6. Set the air fryer oven to air fry.
7. Cook the chicken at 370°F for 5 minutes.
8. Flip and cook for another 5 minutes.
9. Add the Parmesan cheese and garlic butter on top of the chicken.
10. Select bake setting.
11. Cook the chicken for 3 minutes.

Serving Suggestion:

Garnish with chopped parsley.

Tip:

Flatten your chicken with meat mallet first before seasoning it.

Pesto Chicken

Make your chicken with pesto for a dinner meal that's truly unforgettable.
Prep Time and Cooking Time: 35 minutes | Serves: 8

Ingredients to Use:

- 2 lb. chicken thigh
- Salt and pepper to taste
- 1 cup pesto
- 2 tablespoons olive oil

Step-by-Step Directions

1. Season chicken with salt and pepper.
2. Spread the pesto on one side of the chicken.
3. Drizzle with olive oil.
4. Place these in the air fryer oven.
5. Set it to bake.
6. Cook at 350°F for 8 to 10 minutes per side or until chicken is fully cooked.

Serving Suggestion:

Garnish with fresh herbs.

Sweet & Sour Turkey

If you love sweet and sour chicken, for sure, you're going to enjoy this amazing dish that's very easy to do.
Prep Time and Cooking Time: 30 minutes | Serves: 4

Ingredients to Use:

- 1 lb. chicken breast fillet, trimmed and sliced
- 1/2 cup cornstarch
- Cooking spray

Sauce
- 4 tablespoons mayonnaise
- tablespoons sweet chili sauce
- 2 tablespoons vinegar
- 2 tablespoons chili garlic paste

Step-by-Step Directions

1. Coat the chicken slices with cornstarch.
2. Spray your chicken with oil.
3. Set your air fryer oven to air fry.
4. Cook at 400°F for 5 minutes.
5. Flip and cook for another 5 minutes.
6. Combine the ingredients for the sauce.
7. Toss the chicken in the sauce.
8. Put the chicken back to the air fryer oven.
9. Choose bake setting.
10. Bake at 400°F for 5 minutes.

Serving Suggestion:

Sprinkle with chopped scallions and roasted peanuts.

Tip:

Use rice vinegar.

French Onion Chicken with Cheese

Don't be intimidated by this dish. It's actually easier than it seems.
Prep Time and Cooking Time: 30 minutes | Serves: 2

Ingredients to Use:

- 1 onion, sliced thinly
- 2 tablespoons olive oil
- 1 teaspoon sugar
- Salt and pepper to taste
- 2 chicken breast fillets, sliced
- 2 teaspoons olive oil
- Salt and pepper to taste
- 3 oz. Fontina cheese

Step-by-Step Directions

1. Toss the onion slices in olive oil, salt, pepper and sugar.
2. Arrange in the air fryer basket.
3. Set the air fry oven to 350°F.
4. Cook for 5 minutes.
5. Transfer to a plate.
6. Coat the chicken with oil.
7. Season with salt and pepper.
8. Air fry at 350°F for 10 minutes.
9. Take the chicken out of the oven.
10. Top the chicken with the onions.
11. Top the onions with the cheese.
12. Set the air fryer oven to bake.
13. Bake at 350°F for 2 minutes.

Serving Suggestion:

Garnish with herb sprigs.

Tip:

You can also use other types of cheese for this recipe.

Chicken Shawarma

This recipe is a pleasure with every bite.

Prep Time and Cooking Time: 6 hours and 40 minutes | Serves: 4

Chicken
- 2 tablespoons olive oil
- 1 teaspoon lemon juice
- 2 cloves garlic, minced
- 1 teaspoon paprika
- 1 teaspoon ground cumin
- 1/2 teaspoon ground allspice
- 1/4 teaspoon ground cinnamon
- 1/4 teaspoon turmeric
- Salt and pepper to taste
- 1-1/2 lb. chicken breast fillet, sliced into cubes

For serving
- 4 pieces naan bread
- Tahini sauce
- 1 cup tomatoes, diced
- 1 cucumber, diced
- 1 red onion, minced

Step-by-Step Directions

1. Combine chicken ingredients in a bowl.
2. Cover and marinate in the refrigerator for 6 hours.
3. Transfer to the air fryer oven.
4. Choose air fryer option.
5. Cook at 380°F for 10 minutes per side.
6. Top the naan bread with chicken mixture.
7. Drizzle with sauce and top with tomatoes, cucumber and onion.
8. Roll up the naan bread and serve.

Serving Suggestion:

Drizzle with lemon juice and top with chopped parsley.

Tip:

You can also use pita bread for this recipe.

Turkey with Artichoke

The crispy texture and delicious flavors will make you go wow with this dish.
Prep Time and Cooking Time: 30 minutes | Serves: 2

Ingredients to Use:
- 1/2 teaspoon poultry seasoning
- 1 tablespoon Italian seasoning
- 1 cup breadcrumbs
- 1/4 cup cheddar cheese, shredded
- 2 tablespoon cream cheese
- 2 tablespoons onions, minced
- 1 lb. turkey breast fillet
- 1/2 cup mayonnaise
- Cooking spray
- 1/4 cup tomatoes, diced
- oz. baby artichokes, sliced

Step-by-Step Directions

1. Mix the herbs and breadcrumbs in a bowl.
2. In another bowl, mix the cheddar cheese, cream cheese and onions.
3. Spread both sides of turkey with mayo.
4. Dredge with breadcrumb mixture.
5. Add these to the air crisper tray.
6. Spray the turkey with oil.
7. Select air fry option in your air fryer oven.
8. Cook at 370°F for 7 minutes.
9. Flip and cook for 5 minutes.
10. Spread the topping on top of the turkey.
11. Place the tomatoes and artichokes on top.
12. Choose roast option.
13. Cook at 350°F for 10 minutes.

Serving Suggestion:

Sprinkle with pepper and serve.

Tip:

Flatten the turkey with meat mallet.

Onion Turkey

You'll find yourself speechless once you get a taste of this amazing turkey dish.

Prep Time and Cooking Time: 30 minutes | Serves: 4

Ingredients to Use:

- 1/2 cup flour
- Salt and pepper to taste
- 1 egg
- 2 tablespoons mayonnaise
- 1 lb. turkey breast fillet
- 1 cup fried onions, crushed
- Cooking spray

Step-by-Step Directions

1. Mix flour, salt and pepper in a bowl.
2. In another bowl, beat the egg.
3. Stir in the mayo.
4. In the third bowl, add the dried onions.
5. Coat the turkey with the flour mixture, egg mixture and then with the crushed dried onions.
6. Spray with oil.
7. Arrange in a single layer in the air crisper tray.
8. Select air fry function.
9. Cook the turkey at 370°F for 6 minutes per side.

Serving Suggestion:

Serve with fresh green salad.

Tip:

Spray both sides evenly with oil to get a crispy texture.

Red Pepper Jelly Chicken Wings

You'll love the spicy flavor of these chicken wings. These are delicious, crispy and easy to make.

Prep Time and Cooking Time: 40 minutes | Serves: 6

Ingredients to Use:

- Salt to taste
- 3 tablespoons baking powder
- 1 lb. chicken wings
- Cooking spray
- 1 cup red pepper jelly

Step-by-Step Directions

1. Combine salt and baking powder in a bowl.
2. Coat chicken wings with the mixture.
3. Spray with oil.
4. Add to the air fryer oven.
5. Choose the air fry option.
6. Cook at 380°F for 15 minutes.
7. Flip and cook for another 10 minutes.
8. Heat the jelly in a pan over medium heat.
9. Toss the chicken in the jelly before serving.

Serving Suggestion:

Garnish with red pepper flakes or chopped green onion before serving.

Tip:

You can also use turkey wings for this recipe.

Turkey & Veggie Stir Fry

Here's a light and filling meal that you'd surely enjoy.

Prep Time and Cooking Time: 20 minutes | Serves: 4

Ingredients to Use:

- 1 tablespoon sesame oil
- 1 lb. turkey breast fillet, sliced into cubes
- 16 oz. frozen vegetables
- 1 clove garlic, minced
- 1 teaspoon Italian seasoning

Step-by-Step Directions

1. Coat turkey and veggies with sesame oil.
2. Sprinkle with garlic and Italian seasoning.
3. Choose air fry setting in your air fryer

oven.

4. Cook the chicken at 370°F for 7 minutes.
5. Stir in the vegetables.
6. Cook for 5 minutes.

Serving Suggestion:

Garnish with chopped herbs.

Tip:

Thaw the vegetables first before air frying.

Chicken Piccata

A flavorful dish that will become a regular in your weekly menu.
Prep Time and Cooking Time: 30 minutes | Serves: 4

Ingredients to Use:

Chicken breasts
- 1 lb. chicken, sliced thinly
- Salt and pepper to taste
- 1 teaspoon garlic powder
- 1 tablespoon lemon juice
- 1 egg white, beaten
- 1/2 cup Italian bread crumbs
- Cooking spray

Piccata Sauce
- 1 tablespoon butter
- 3/4 cup chicken stock
- 2 tablespoons lemon juice
- Salt and pepper to taste

Step-by-Step Directions

1. Season chicken with salt and pepper.
2. In a bowl, combine the garlic powder, lemon juice and egg white.
3. In another bowl, add the breadcrumbs.
4. Dip the chicken in garlic powder mixture.
5. Dredge with breadcrumbs.
6. Spray both sides with oil.
7. Place chicken in the air crisper tray.
8. Cook at 350°F for 5 minutes.
9. In a pan over medium low heat, mix the butter, lemon juice and broth.

10. Season with salt and pepper.
11. Simmer for 5 minutes, stirring often.
12. Drizzle chicken with sauce and serve.

Serving Suggestion:

Garnish with capers.

Tip:

Be sure to trim the skin of chicken before cooking.

Balsamic Glazed Turkey

Be ready to fall head over heels in love with this savory balsamic glazed turkey.
Prep Time and Cooking Time: 30 minutes | Serves: 4

Ingredients to Use:

- 1 teaspoon garlic, minced
- 1/2 cup balsamic vinegar
- 4 tablespoons honey
- 1 teaspoon honey mustard
- Salt and pepper to taste
- 4 turkey thigh fillets

Step-by-Step Directions

1. Combine all the ingredients except turkey thigh fillets.
2. Add the turkey to an air fryer safe pan.
3. Place this inside the air fryer oven.
4. Pour the sauce over the turkey.
5. Select roast setting.
6. Cook at 350°F for 7 minutes per side.

Serving Suggestion:

Sprinkle with pepper before serving.

Tip:

If turkey is not fully cooked at 15 minutes, cook for 5 more minutes.

Lemon Garlic Turkey Kebab

These kebabs are always a big hit in parties!
Prep Time and Cooking Time: 8 hours and 30

minutes | Serves: 4

- 1 lb. turkey breast fillets, sliced into cubes
- 1 bell pepper, sliced
- 1 onion, sliced

Marinade

- 3 tablespoons lemon juice
- 1/4 cup olive oil
- 2 cloves garlic, minced
- Salt and pepper to taste

1. Combine the marinade ingredients in a bowl.
2. Divide into 2 bowl.
3. Marinate turkey cubes in the first bowl.
4. Marinate vegetables in the second bowl.
5. Cover and refrigerate for 8 hours.
6. Thread the turkey and vegetables onto skewers.
7. Add to the air crisper tray.
8. Choose grill setting.
9. Cook at 350°F for 5 minutes per side.

Garnish with lemon wedges.

You can also separate a small amount of sauce for basting.

Barbecue Turkey Fillets

Turkey fillets drenched in sweet savory barbecue sauce is truly delightful.
Prep Time and Cooking Time: 30 minutes | Serves: 4

- 1 lb. turkey fillets, sliced
- Cooking spray
- Salt and pepper
- 1/2 cup barbecue sauce, divided

1. Spray turkey with oil.
2. Sprinkle both sides of turkey with salt and pepper.
3. Brush with half of the barbecue sauce.
4. Add to the air fryer oven.
5. Select bake setting.
6. Cook at 350°F for 10 minutes per side.
7. Toss in the barbecue sauce.
8. Cook for another 5 minutes.

Garnish with chopped onions.

You can also make your own barbecue sauce by mixing ketchup, honey, soy sauce, lemon juice and pepper.

Garlic Herb Turkey

Turkey slices flavored with garlic and herbs—this is one dish that's definitely enticing.
Prep Time and Cooking Time: 1 hour | Serves: 6

- 4 tablespoons butter, melted
- 3 cloves garlic, minced
- 1 teaspoon rosemary, chopped
- 1 teaspoon thyme, chopped
- Salt and pepper to taste
- 2 lb. turkey breast, sliced

1. In a bowl, mix butter, garlic, herbs, salt and pepper.
2. Brush both sides of turkey with this mixture.
3. Add to the air crisper tray.
4. Select roast function.
5. Cook at 375°F for 40 minutes.

Let turkey rest for 5 minutes before serving.

Tip:

You can also use chicken for this recipe.

Chicken Tikka Masala

Enjoy Indian flavors at home with this simple but satisfying recipe.
Prep Time and Cooking Time: 40 minutes | Serves: 2

Ingredients to Use:

- 3 turkey breast fillets, diced
- 1 cup tikka masala sauce

Step-by-Step Directions

1. Marinate turkey in tikka masala sauce for 1 hour in the refrigerator.
2. Add the turkey to the air crisper tray.
3. Choose air fry option.
4. Cook at 350°F for 5 minutes per side.
5. Thread turkey slices onto skewers.
6. Baste with the marinade.
7. Place back to the air fryer oven.
8. Choose grill setting.
9. Cook at 350°F for 2 minutes.

Serving Suggestion:

Garnish with chopped green onions.

Tip:

You can also serve this dish with rice.

Chicken Skewers with Peanut Sauce

Chicken slices threaded onto skewers and basted with peanut sauce will absolutely delight everyone in your family.
Prep Time and Cooking Time: 30 minutes | Serves: 2

Ingredients to Use:

- 2 chicken breast fillets, diced
- Salt and pepper to taste
- 1 cup Thai peanut sauce

Step-by-Step Directions

1. Season chicken with salt and pepper.
2. Dip in peanut sauce.
3. Marinate for 15 minutes.
4. Thread onto skewers.
5. Place in the air fryer oven.
6. Select grill setting.
7. Cook at 350°F for 5 to 7 minutes per side.
8. Baste with the remaining sauce.
9. Cook for another 3 minutes.

Serving Suggestion:

Serve with hot white jasmine rice.

Tip:

If using wooden skewers, soak first in water before using.

Grilled Turkey Fillet

Succulent turkey fillets seasoned with herbs and spices to complete your day.
Prep Time and Cooking Time: 15 minutes | Serves: 2

Ingredients to Use:

- 2 turkey breast fillets
- Cooking spray
- 1 teaspoon dried rosemary
- 1 teaspoon dried thyme
- 2 tablespoons poultry seasoning

Step-by-Step Directions

1. Spray turkey fillets with oil.
2. Sprinkle with rosemary, thyme and poultry seasoning.
3. Arrange in a single layer in the air crisper tray.
4. Choose grill setting in your air fryer oven.
5. Cook at 350°F for 7 minutes per side.

Serving Suggestion:

Serve with roasted vegetables.

Tip:

Flatten the turkey fillet with meat mallet before seasoning.

Herb Crusted Turkey Breast

You can't say no to a dish like this—it's full of enticing flavors that you won't get enough of.
Prep Time and Cooking Time: 30 minutes | Serves: 2

Ingredients to Use:

- 1 lb. turkey breast fillets
- 1/2 cup mayonnaise
- 1 tablespoon Italian seasoning
- 1/2 teaspoon poultry seasoning
- 1 cup breadcrumbs
- Cooking spray

Step-by-Step Directions

1. Spread both sides of turkey with mayo.
2. In a bowl, mix the Italian seasoning, poultry seasoning and breadcrumbs.
3. Dredge turkey with breadcrumb mixture.
4. Spray both sides with oil.
5. Choose air fry setting in your air fryer oven.
6. Add turkey to the air crisper tray.
7. Cook at 370°F for 7 minutes per side.

Serving Suggestion:

Serve with tomato salad.

Tip:

Flatten the turkey fillet with meat mallet before seasoning.

Bacon-Wrapped Turkey Fillet

As they say, everything is better with bacon! This recipe gives your favorite turkey extra wow factor by wrapping it with bacon slices.
Prep Time and Cooking Time: 30 minutes | Serves: 2

Ingredients to Use:

- 2 turkey fillets
- 1/2 teaspoon sweet paprika
- 1 teaspoon garlic powder
- Salt and pepper to taste
- Bacon slices

Glaze

- 1 teaspoon Dijon mustard
- 2 tablespoons maple syrup
- Salt and pepper to taste

Step-by-Step Directions

1. Season turkey with paprika, garlic powder, salt and pepper.
2. Wrap the turkey with bacon slices.
3. Place these in the air crisper tray.
4. Choose air fry setting.
5. Cook at 380°F for 6 minutes per side.
6. In a bowl, mix the glaze ingredients.
7. Brush the turkey with the glaze.
8. Cook for another 3 minutes.

Serving Suggestion:

Garnish with chopped parsley.

Tip:

You can also use honey in place of maple syrup.

Barber Chicken

Have you tried barber chicken before? It's a dish of chicken breast fillet stuffed with cheesy broccoli. It's definitely a must-try!
Prep Time and Cooking Time: 20 minutes | Serves: 2

Ingredients to Use:

- 2 chicken breast fillets
- Salt and pepper to taste
- 1 cup broccoli florets, sliced
- 1 cup cheddar cheese, grated
- 1 egg, beaten
- 1 cup breadcrumbs

1. Flatten the chicken with a meat mallet.
2. Season both sides with salt and pepper.
3. Spread the broccoli and cheese on top.
4. Roll the chicken and secure with a toothpick.
5. Dip in egg and dredge with breadcrumbs.
6. Set the chicken inside the air fryer oven.
7. Select air fry function.
8. Cook at 390°F for 20 minutes, and flip once.

Serving Suggestion:

Serve with sautéed green beans and carrots.

Tip:

You can also chop the broccoli into smaller pieces.

Crispy Ranch Turkey with Roasted Carrots

Season your turkey with ranch dressing before air frying, and pair it with roasted carrots.

Prep Time and Cooking Time: 20 minutes | Serves: 4

Ingredients to Use:

- 4 turkey breast fillets
- 1/2 cup ranch dressing
- 1/2 cup breadcrumbs
- Cooking spray
- 2 carrots, diced
- 1 tablespoon olive oil
- 1 teaspoon Italian seasoning

Step-by-Step Directions

1. Soak turkey breast in ranch dressing.
2. Dredge with breadcrumbs.
3. Spray with oil.
4. Add the turkey breast in the air crisper tray.
5. Set your air fryer oven to air fry.

6. Cook at 370°F for 7 minutes per side.
7. Transfer to a plate.
8. Toss the carrots in the oil.
9. Season with Italian herbs.
10. Place in the air fryer.
11. Select roast setting.
12. Cook at 350°F for 5 minutes, and stir once.

Serving Suggestion:

Serve with cooked brown rice.

Tip:

Trim the turkey before seasoning.

Sweet Spicy Turkey Thighs

Enjoy these delicious turkey thighs drenched in sweet and spicy sauce.

Prep Time and Cooking Time: 35 minutes | Serves: 4

Ingredients to Use:

- 2 tablespoons hot pepper sauce
- 2 cloves garlic, minced
- 2 tablespoons honey
- 1/2 cup chicken broth
- 1 cup brown sugar
- 1/2 cup soy sauce
- Salt and pepper to taste
- 2 lb. turkey thighs

Step-by-Step Directions

1. Mix all the ingredients except turkey in a pan.
2. Place it over medium low heat.
3. Simmer for 5 minutes.
4. Toss turkey in the sauce.
5. Add to the air fryer oven.
6. Select grill setting.
7. Cook at 400°F for 10 minutes.
8. Flip and cook for another 10 minutes.

Serving Suggestion:

Garnish with herb sprigs.

Use low-sodium chicken broth and soy sauce.

Caribbean Chicken

Here's a recipe that's friendly in terms of both cost and time.
Prep Time and Cooking Time: 15 minutes | Serves: 4

Ingredients to Use:

- 4 chicken thighs
- Cooking spray

Seasoning
- 2 teaspoons cayenne pepper
- 1 teaspoon dried thyme
- 1 teaspoon dried basil
- 2 teaspoons paprika
- Salt and pepper to taste

Step-by-Step Directions

1. Combine all the seasoning ingredients.
2. Sprinkle both sides of chicken with this mixture.
3. Transfer chicken to the air fryer oven.
4. Select roast function.
5. Cook at 350°F for 10 minutes per side.
6. Spray with oil.
7. Put the chicken back to the air fryer.
8. Choose air fry setting.
9. Cook at 350°F for 5 minutes.

Serving Suggestion:

Garnish with lemon wedges.

Tip:

Remove skin of chicken before seasoning and cooking.

Orange Turkey

Here's a unique twist to orange chicken that you'll enjoy. This one uses turkey fillets instead of chicken.
Prep Time and Cooking Time: 30 minutes | Serves: 2

Ingredients to Use:

- 2 turkey breast fillets, diced
- Salt and pepper to taste
- 1/2 cup flour
- 1 teaspoon butter
- 3 tablespoons orange juice
- 2 teaspoons orange zest
- 1 teaspoon honey

Step-by-Step Directions

1. Season turkey breast slices with salt and pepper.
2. Cover with flour.
3. Add to the air fryer tray.
4. Set it to air fry.
5. Cook at 370°F for 10 minutes.
6. Flip and cook for another 7 minutes.
7. Add butter to a pan over medium heat.
8. Once melted, add the orange juice, orange zest and honey.
9. Simmer while stirring for 1 minute.
10. Toss the turkey slices in the mixture.
11. Put them back to the air fryer oven.
12. Select bake function.
13. Cook at 350°F for 2 minutes.

Serving Suggestion:

Garnish with orange slices.

Tip:

You can also add herbs to the breading if you like.

Grilled Herb Chicken

Simple but satisfying—there are so many wonderful words to describe this grilled herb chicken.
Prep Time and Cooking Time: 1 hour and 30 minutes | Serves: 2

- 2 chicken breast fillets

Marinade

- 1/4 cup olive oil
- 2 cloves garlic, minced
- 1 teaspoon orange zest
- 1 teaspoon lemon zest
- 1 teaspoon dried thyme
- 1 teaspoon dried oregano
- 1 teaspoon dried basil
- Salt and pepper to taste

Step-by-Step Directions

1. Mix marinade ingredients in a bowl.
2. Add the chicken to the bowl.
3. Cover and marinate for 1 hour.
4. Add chicken to the air fryer oven.
5. Select grill setting.
6. Cook at 350°F for 7 minutes per side.
7. Increase temperature to 400°F.
8. Cook for another 6 minutes.

Serving Suggestion:

Garnish with grilled onion slices and lemon wedges.

Tip:

You can also use fresh herbs if you like.

Spiced Turkey

This is another irresistible turkey recipe that you shouldn't take long to try.
Prep Time and Cooking Time: 20 minutes | Serves: 4

Ingredients to Use:

- 4 turkey breast fillets
- 4 tablespoons olive oil
- Salt and pepper to taste
- teaspoons harissa paste

Step-by-Step Directions

1. Brush turkey with olive oil.
2. Season both sides with salt, pepper and harissa paste.
3. Place the turkey inside the air fryer oven.
4. Select air fry option.
5. Cook at 370°F for 7 minutes per side.

Serving Suggestion:

Serve on top of vegetable salad.

Tip:

Dry the chicken thoroughly before seasoning.

Turkey with Creamy Lemon Sauce

With this recipe, you don't have to beat yourself up coming up with something fancy and special.
Prep Time and Cooking Time: 20 minutes | Serves: 4

Ingredients to Use:

- 4 turkey breast fillets
- Salt and pepper to taste
- 1 tablespoon olive oil, divided

Sauce

- 2 tablespoons butter
- 1 cup red onion, minced
- 3 tablespoons garlic, minced
- 1 cup chicken broth
- 1 tablespoon lemon juice
- 1/4 cup heavy cream
- 1 teaspoon fresh dill, minced

Step-by-Step Directions

1. Season the turkey with salt and pepper.
2. Drizzle with half of the oil.
3. Toss the onion slices in the remaining oil.
4. Place the turkey and onion slices in the air fryer oven.
5. Set the air fryer oven to air fry.
6. Cook at 370°F for 7 minutes per side.

7. Add the butter to a pan over medium heat.
8. Cook the onion and garlic for 2 minutes.
9. Combine the sauce ingredients in a pan over medium heat.
10. Simmer while stirring for 3 minutes.
11. Pour the sauce over the turkey and serve.

Serving Suggestion:

Serve with roasted zucchini slices.

Tip:

Use freshly squeezed lemon juice for this recipe.

Italian Chicken

Don't make the mistake of thinking that this chicken lacks in flavor. It's a lot tastier than it looks!
Prep Time and Cooking Time: 1 hour and 20 minutes | Serves: 4

Ingredients to Use:

- 4 chicken breast fillets
- 16 oz. Italian salad dressing
- 1 teaspoon dried rosemary

Step-by-Step Directions

1. Coat the chicken with dressing.
2. Sprinkle with rosemary.
3. Cover and refrigerate for 1 hour.
4. Transfer the chicken to the air fryer oven.
5. Select bake function.
6. Cook at 370°F for 7 minutes.
7. Flip and cook for another 7 minutes.

Serving Suggestion:

Garnish with rosemary sprigs.

Tip:

You can also use Italian herbs.

Orange Chili Chicken with Veggies

Combine savory, sour and spicy flavors in this tantalizing dish that won't leave you wanting.
Prep Time and Cooking Time: 20 minutes | Serves: 2

Ingredients to Use:

- 2 chicken breast fillets
- 1 clove garlic, minced
- 1 tablespoon ginger, minced
- 1 orange, sliced
- 1 cup bok choy, sliced
- 1/2 cup snap peas, trimmed
- 2 tablespoons tamari sauce
- 2 tablespoons chili garlic sauce

Step-by-Step Directions

1. Add the chicken breast fillets to a foil sheet.
2. Top the chicken with garlic, ginger, and orange slices.
3. Place the bok choy and peas beside the chicken.
4. Mix the tamari and chili garlic sauce.
5. Pour the sauce over the chicken.
6. Wrap the foil around the chicken and vegetables.
7. Place the foil packet inside the air fryer oven.
8. Cook at 370°F for 15 minutes.

Serving Suggestion:

Serve with Jasmine rice.

Tip:

Extend cooking time if chicken is not fully done.

Lemon Turkey with Oregano

This turkey recipe has just the right balance of lemon and herbs that you'd be delighted with.
Prep Time and Cooking Time: 10 minutes | Serves: 4

Ingredients to Use:

- 1 lb. turkey thigh fillet, diced
- 2 teaspoon olive oil
- 1 teaspoon ground oregano
- 1 tablespoon lemon juice

Step-by-Step Directions

1. Toss the turkey cubes in oil.
2. Season with oregano.
3. Drizzle with lemon juice.
4. Transfer to the air fryer oven.
5. Set the air fryer oven to bake.
6. Cook at 350°F for 5 minutes per side.

Serving Suggestion:

Serve with vegetables and rice.

Tip:

Slice chicken into 1-inch pieces.

Chicken with Zucchini & Tomatoes

Healthy and delicious—this can be your go-to recipe when you want to enjoy delicious flavors without any guilt.
Prep Time and Cooking Time: 30 minutes | Serves: 2

Ingredients to Use:

- 1 lb. chicken thigh fillets, diced
- 1 teaspoon dried oregano
- 1 teaspoon lemon juice
- 1/2 cup cherry tomatoes
- 1 zucchini, sliced
- 2 tablespoons olive oil
- Salt and pepper to taste

Step-by-Step Directions

1. Add the chicken to a bowl.
2. Stir in the oregano and lemon juice.
3. Place the chicken in the air fryer oven.
4. Set it to bake.
5. Cook at 370°F for 12 minutes per side.

6. Transfer chicken to a plate.
7. Drizzle the tomatoes and zucchini with oil.
8. Season with salt and pepper.
9. Add to the air fryer basket.
10. Set the oven to air fry.
11. Cook at 320°F for 5 minutes.

Serving Suggestion:

Sprinkle with Italian herbs before serving.

Tip:

You can also use chicken breast fillet for this recipe.

Chicken Fingers

Enjoy crispy chicken fingers without having to use loads of oil.
Prep Time and Cooking Time: 20 minutes | Serves: 6

Ingredients to Use:

- 1 lb. chicken strips
- 1 cup buttermilk
- 1-1/2 cups all-purpose flour
- Garlic salt to taste
- Cooking spray

Step-by-Step Directions

1. Dip chicken strips in buttermilk.
2. Mix the all-purpose flour and garlic salt.
3. Coat the chicken strips in flour mixture.
4. Spray with oil.
5. Add to the air fryer oven.
6. Select air fry function.
7. Cook at 370°F for 7 minutes per side.

Serving Suggestion:

Serve with green salad.

Tip:

You can choose to soak the chicken in buttermilk for 20 minutes before seasoning and cooking.

Mexican Chicken

Take your taste buds on a trip to Mexico with this amazing recipe.
Prep Time and Cooking Time: 20 minutes | Serves: 2

Ingredients to Use:

- 2 chicken breast fillets
- 1 teaspoon chili powder
- Salt and pepper to taste
- 1 cup salsa
- 1 cup black beans, rinsed and drained
- 1 cup corn kernels
- 1/2 cup Mexican cheese, shredded

Step-by-Step Directions

1. Add the chicken on top of a foil sheet.
2. Sprinkle with chili powder, salt and pepper.
3. Top with the salsa, black beans and corn.
4. Fold the foil to make a packet.
5. Place this inside the air fryer oven.
6. Select air fry setting.
7. Cook at 370°F for 7 minutes.
8. Flip and foil packet and cook for another 7 minutes.
9. Unwrap the foil.
10. Sprinkle with cheese.
11. Fold the foil and air fry for another 2 minutes.

Serving Suggestion:

Serve with rice.

Tip:

Add more chili powder if you want your Mexican chicken spicier.

Mediterranean Chicken

Spice things up at home with this fantastic Mediterranean chicken that only takes a few minutes to prepare.

Prep Time and Cooking Time: 20 minutes | Serves: 6

Ingredients to Use:

- 2 tablespoons ground cinnamon
- 2 tablespoons ground coriander
- 1 tablespoon ground nutmeg
- 1 tablespoon ground cumin
- Salt and pepper to taste
- chicken breast fillets
- Cooking spray

Step-by-Step Directions

1. Combine the spices, salt and pepper in a bowl.
2. Sprinkle both sides of chicken with this mixture.
3. Spray with oil.
4. Add to the air fryer oven.
5. Select air fry setting.
6. Cook at 370°F for 7 minutes per side.

Serving Suggestion:

Serve with marinara dip.

Tip:

Add chili powder if you like your chicken spicy.

Garlic & Ginger Chicken Wings

This well-marinated chicken dish can surely satisfy you and your family.
Prep Time and Cooking Time: 45 minutes | Serves: 6

Ingredients to Use:

- 2 tablespoons flour
- Salt and pepper to taste
- 1 tablespoon baking powder
- 1 lb. chicken wings

Sauce
- 1/2 cup soy sauce
- 2 tablespoons ginger, grated

- 1/2 cup brown sugar
- 3 cloves garlic, minced
- 2 tablespoons hot pepper sauce

Step-by-Step Directions

1. Mix flour, salt, pepper and baking powder in a bowl.
2. Coat wings with this mixture.
3. Place the wings in the air fryer oven.
4. Select air fry function.
5. Cook at 380°F for 25 minutes, and flip once or twice.
6. While waiting, mix the sauce ingredients in a bowl.
7. Toss the chicken wings in the sauce.
8. Put these back to the oven.
9. Select bake setting.
10. Cook at 350°F for 5 minutes.

Serving Suggestion:

Garnish with chopped scallions.

Tip:

You can also use honey in place of brown sugar.

Chapter 7: Fish & Seafood Dishes

Shrimp with Honey & Pecan

You'll be surprised at how much flavor this pecan crusted shrimp has!

Prep Time and Cooking Time: 25 minutes | Serves: 4

Ingredients to Use:

- 1/4 cup cornstarch
- Salt and pepper to taste
- 2 egg whites
- 2/3 cup pecans, chopped
- 1 lb. shrimp, peeled and deveined
- 2 tablespoons mayonnaise
- 1/4 cup honey

Step-by-Step Directions

1. In a bowl, mix cornstarch, salt and pepper.
2. Add egg whites to another bowl and the pecans to a third bowl.
3. Coat shrimp with cornstarch mixture.
4. Dip in egg whites.
5. Dredge with pecans.
6. Place in the air fryer oven.
7. Select air fry setting.
8. Cook at 330 degrees F for 5 minutes per side.
9. While waiting, mix honey and mayo.
10. Toss shrimp in the honey mixture and serve.

Serving Suggestion:

You can also serve the honey mayo sauce on the side.

Tip:

Do not overcook shrimp or it will have rubbery texture.

Baked Seafood with Dill & Garlic

This is a top-rated dish that would make it seem like you're dining in a restaurant.

Prep Time and Cooking Time: 50 minutes | Serves: 4

Ingredients to Use:

- 1 cup butter, melted
- 2 cloves garlic, minced
- 3 tablespoons dill, minced
- Salt and pepper to taste
- 4 cod fillets
- 1 cup shrimp, peeled and deveined
- 2 lemons, sliced

Step-by-Step Directions

1. In a bowl, mix butter, garlic, dill, salt and pepper.
2. Arrange the cod and shrimp on top of a foil sheet.
3. Pour the butter mixture all over.
4. Top with lemon slices.
5. Fold and pinch the sides to seal.
6. Place the foil packet inside the air fryer oven.
7. Choose bake function.
8. Bake at 350 degrees F for 30 to 40 minutes.

Serving Suggestion:

Serve with buttered rolls

Tip:

You can also add vegetables like potatoes and corn in the foil packet.

Broiled Scallops & Shrimp

Treat yourself to a delicious but healthy

dinner with this recipe made using your air fryer oven.

Prep Time and Cooking Time: 20 minutes | Serves: 6

Ingredients to Use:

- 1/4 cup butter, melted
- 1 tablespoon lemon juice
- 1 tablespoon Worcestershire sauce
- 1/3 cup dry white wine
- 3 cloves garlic, crushed
- Pinch red pepper flakes
- Salt and pepper to taste
- 1 lb. shrimp, peeled and deveined
- 1 lb. scallops
- 1 cup cherry tomatoes, sliced in half
- 5 oz. baby spinach

Step-by-Step Directions

1. Combine butter, lemon juice, Worcestershire sauce, wine, garlic, red pepper, salt and pepper in a bowl.
2. Toss shrimp and scallops in the bowl.
3. Transfer to the air fryer oven.
4. Choose broil setting.
5. Broil for 3 minutes.
6. Stir in tomatoes and spinach.
7. Broil for another 2 minutes.

Serving Suggestion:

Serve with slices of French bread.

Tip:

You can also use other leafy greens in place of spinach.

Garlic Roasted Seafood

This one-pan roasted seafood dish will result in something truly unforgettable.

Prep Time and Cooking Time: 40 minutes | Serves: 4

Ingredients to Use:

- 1/2 cup butter
- 3 cloves garlic, crushed
- 1 tablespoon lemon juice
- 2 teaspoons lemon zest
- 1 teaspoon smoked paprika
- 1 cup shrimp, peeled and deveined
- 2 squids, cleaned
- 12 mussels
- 2 cups baby potatoes
- 2 cobs corn, sliced

Step-by-Step Directions

1. Combine butter, garlic, lemon juice, lemon zest and paprika in a bowl.
2. Arrange the seafood in a baking pan.
3. Drizzle with the butter sauce.
4. Place inside the air fryer oven.
5. Select roast option.
6. Cook at 400 degrees F for 15 minutes, stirring once or twice.

Serving Suggestion:

Sprinkle with chopped parsley.

Tip:

Discard mussels that did not open during cooking.

Grilled Tilapia

Of the various ways to cook tilapia, grilling is the one that gives it the best flavor.

Prep Time and Cooking Time: 50 minutes | Serves: 2

Ingredients to Use:

- 1 tilapia

Marinade

- 2 tablespoons oil
- 5 cloves garlic
- 1 onion, sliced
- 1/2 teaspoon curry powder
- 2 seasoning cubes
- 2 sprigs fresh thyme
- 1 teaspoon nutmeg

- Salt and pepper to taste

1. Add marinade ingredients to a blender.
2. Process until smooth.
3. Make several slits on both sides of fish.
4. Coat with the marinade.
5. Cover and refrigerate for 30 minutes.
6. Place the fish inside the air fryer oven.
7. Select grill setting.
8. Cook at 350 degrees F for 15 minutes per side.

Serving Suggestion:

Serve on top of leafy greens and sliced tomatoes.

Tip:

You can also add chili powder to the marinade.

Bacon Wrapped Scallops

It's a party with these amazing bacon-wrapped scallops.
Prep Time and Cooking Time: 20 minutes | Serves: 4

Ingredients to Use:

- 16 scallops
- 8 slices bacon, sliced into 2
- 1/4 teaspoon paprika
- Pinch pepper

Step-by-Step Directions

1. Wrap the scallops with bacon slices.
2. Secure with toothpicks.
3. Season with pepper and paprika.
4. Preheat your air fryer oven to 350 degrees F.
5. Choose air fry setting.
6. Cook for 3 minutes.
7. Flip and cook for another 3 minutes.

Serving Suggestion:

Serve immediately.

Tip:

You can also pre-cook bacon by air frying at 400 degrees F for 3 minutes before wrapping it around the scallop.

Crab Cakes

Here's a quick and simple way to make crab cakes in your air fryer oven.
Prep Time and Cooking Time: 20 minutes | Serves: 4

Ingredients to Use:

- 1 lb. crab meat
- 1/4 cup onion, chopped
- 1/4 cup red bell peppers, chopped
- 1/4 cup parsley, chopped
- 1/4 cup breadcrumbs
- 2 eggs, beaten
- Salt to taste
- Cooking spray

Dip

- 3/4 cup mayonnaise
- 1/4 cup sour cream
- 1/4 cup sweet pickle relish
- 1 tablespoon mustard

Step-by-Step Directions

1. Combine crab meat, onion, bell pepper, parsley, breadcrumbs, egg and salt in a bowl.
2. Form patties from the mixture.
3. Spray both sides with oil.
4. Turn the knob of your air fryer oven to air fry.
5. Place the patties in the air crisper tray.
6. Cook at 380 degrees F for 5 minutes per side.
7. Mix the dip ingredients in a bowl.
8. Serve the crab cakes with the mixture.

Serving Suggestion:

Garnish with lemon wedges.

Check crab meat for any crab shell pieces.

Maple Salmon

Sweet and savory, this maple salmon dish is sure to please.

Prep Time and Cooking Time: 1 hour | Serves: 2

Ingredients to Use:

- 2 salmon fillets
- 1/4 cup maple syrup
- 1 teaspoon Worcestershire sauce
- 2 teaspoons Dijon mustard
- 1/2 cup walnuts, chopped
- Salt to taste

Step-by-Step Directions

1. Season salmon with salt.
2. Mix remaining ingredients except walnuts in a bowl.
3. Add salmon to a small baking pan.
4. Pour sauce over the salmon.
5. Refrigerate for 30 minutes.
6. Set your air fryer oven to roast.
7. Place the salmon inside the air fryer oven.
8. Top with the walnuts.
9. Roast the fish for 4 to 5 minutes per side.

Serving Suggestion:

Serve with roasted potatoes or steamed broccoli.

Tip:

You can also use brown mustard.

Halibut Fish Sticks

These fish sticks can be your go-to dish when you want something delicious but easy to cook.

Prep Time and Cooking Time: 50 minutes | Serves: 4

Ingredients to Use:

- 1/4 cup all-purpose flour
- 1/2 cup cornmeal
- 1/4 teaspoon ground cumin
- Salt and pepper to taste
- 1 lb. halibut, sliced into strips

Slaw

- 2 cups cabbage, shredded
- 1 tablespoon lime juice
- 1/4 cup Greek yogurt
- 1/4 cup mayonnaise
- 1/2 cup cilantro, chopped

Step-by-Step Directions

1. Preheat your air fryer oven to 350 degrees F.
2. Choose air fry setting.
3. Mix flour, cornmeal, cumin, salt and pepper in a bowl.
4. Coat the fish strips with this mixture.
5. Place in the air crisper tray.
6. Cook for 5 minutes per side.
7. While waiting, combine the slaw ingredients.
8. Serve fish sticks with slaw.

Serving Suggestion:

Garnish with lemon wedges.

Tip:

You can also use semolina or polenta instead of flour.

Baked Lemon Butter Fish

There's no way you could go wrong with this simple but satisfying dish.

Prep Time and Cooking Time: 20 minutes | Serves: 4

Ingredients to Use:

- 4 white fish fillets
- 1/4 cup butter, melted
- 3 cloves garlic, minced

- 2 tablespoons lemon juice
- 1 teaspoon lemon zest
- Salt and pepper to taste
- Lemon slices

1. Choose bake option in your air fryer oven.
2. Preheat it to 425 degrees F.
3. Arrange the fish fillets in a baking pan.
4. Combine the remaining ingredients except lemon slices in a bowl.
5. Pour the mixture over the fish.
6. Top with the lemon slices.
7. Bake in the air fryer oven for 6 minutes per side.

Serving Suggestion:

Garnish with chopped parsley.

Tip:

You can also use garlic powder instead of minced garlic.

Baked Swordfish Fillet with Cream Sauce

You won't run out wonderful things to say about this dish—swordfish baked with lemon slices and cream sauce.
Prep Time and Cooking Time: 20 minutes | Serves: 4

Ingredients to Use:

- 4 swordfish fillets
- Salt and pepper to taste
- 4 tablespoons butter
- 1/4 cup heavy cream
- 2 cloves garlic, minced
- 1 tablespoon mustard
- 1-1/2 tablespoons lemon juice

Step-by-Step Directions

1. Select bake setting in your air fryer oven.
2. Preheat it to 400 degrees F.

3. Place the fish fillets in a baking dish.
4. Season with salt and pepper.
5. In a pan over medium heat, melt the butter.
6. Stir in the rest of the ingredients.
7. Simmer for 3 minutes.
8. Pour the sauce over the fish.
9. Place inside the air fryer oven.
10. Bake for 10 minutes.

Serving Suggestion:

Sprinkle chopped parsley on top.

Tip:

If fish is frozen, thaw completely and dry with paper towels before preparing.

Baked Miso Tuna

This dish will fill you up and at the same time, satisfy your cravings.
Prep Time and Cooking Time: 1 hour and 15 minutes | Serves: 4

Ingredients to Use:

- 2 tuna steaks
- 1/2 tablespoon miso paste
- 2 tablespoons mirin
- 1 tablespoon garlic, minced
- 1 teaspoon rice wine
- 1/2 teaspoon vinegar

Step-by-Step Directions

1. Add tuna steaks to a baking pan.
2. Combine remaining ingredients in a bowl.
3. Pour the marinade over the tuna.
4. Cover and refrigerate for 1 hour.
5. Transfer to the air fryer oven.
6. Choose bake setting.
7. Cook at 360 degrees F for 5 to 7 minutes per side.

Serving Suggestion:

Garnish with chopped green onion.

Tuna steaks should be at least ½ inch thick.

Tuna Casserole

Here's a good source of protein and healthy fats that you can enjoy.
Prep Time and Cooking Time: 10 minutes | Serves: 2

Ingredients to Use:

Casserole
- 10 oz. canned tuna flakes, drained
- 1/4 cup Mexican cheese blend, shredded
- 1/4 cup onion, chopped
- 1/4 teaspoon onion powder
- 1/4 cup celery, chopped
- 2 tablespoons mayonnaise
- 1/4 cup breadcrumbs
- 1 tablespoon Parmesan cheese
- Salt and pepper to taste

Topping
- 1/4 cup cheddar cheese, grated

Step-by-Step Directions

1. Combine all the casserole ingredients in a baking pan.
2. Top with the grated cheese.
3. Set your air fryer oven to bake.
4. Preheat your air fryer oven to 380 degrees F for 5 minutes.
5. Place the baking pan inside the air fryer oven.
6. Bake for 6 to 10 minutes or until cheese has melted.

Serving Suggestion:

Sprinkle with chopped green onion.

Tip:

You can also add a little cayenne pepper to the casserole if you like.

Pesto Fish Fillets with Walnuts

Flavorful and tender, these pesto fish fillets are bound to make everyone in the dinner table go wow.
Prep Time and Cooking Time: 15 minutes | Serves: 2

Ingredients to Use:
- 2 salmon fillets
- Salt and pepper to taste
- 2 tablespoons pesto sauce
- 1 tablespoon mayonnaise
- 1/4 cup walnuts, chopped

Step-by-Step Directions

1. Season fish with salt and pepper.
2. Mix pesto and mayo.
3. Spread pesto sauce on top of fish.
4. Top with walnuts.
5. Place in the air crisper tray.
6. Choose air fry setting.
7. Place the fish in the air fryer oven.
8. Cook at 380 degrees F for 10 minutes.

Serving Suggestion:

Sprinkle with Parmesan cheese before serving.

Tip:

Dry the fish thoroughly with paper towel before seasoning.

Thai Fish

With minimal preparation, this dish comes out beautifully from your air fryer oven.
Prep Time and Cooking Time: 15 minutes | Serves: 2

Ingredients to Use:
- 1 teaspoon soy sauce
- 2 teaspoons fish sauce
- 1 tablespoon oyster sauce
- 1 clove garlic, minced
- 1/2 tablespoon lime juice

- 1 tablespoon brown sugar
- 2 flounder fillets

Step-by-Step Directions

1. Combine soy sauce, fish sauce, oyster sauce, garlic, lime juice and brown sugar in a bowl.
2. Brush both sides of fish with this mixture.
3. Add the fish fillets to the air fryer oven.
4. Set the air fryer oven to roast.
5. Cook at 370 degrees F for 5 minutes per side.

Serving Suggestion:

Sprinkle with thinly sliced fresh basil leaves.

Tip:

Use low-sodium fish sauce and soy sauce.

Tuna & Avocado Croquettes

Here's a croquette recipe that won't load you up with carbs.
Prep Time and Cooking Time: 15 minutes | Serves: 4

Ingredients to Use:

- 2 cups canned tuna flakes
- 1/4 teaspoon onion powder
- 1/2 avocado, pitted
- 2 tablespoons lemon juice
- 1/4 cup roasted almonds, chopped
- 1/2 cup breadcrumbs
- Salt and pepper to taste

Step-by-Step Directions

1. Combine all the ingredients in a bowl.
2. Form balls from the mixture.
3. Set your air fryer oven to air fry.
4. Place the tuna balls in the air crisper tray.
5. Cook at 380 degrees F for 8 minutes or until golden.

Serving Suggestion:

Serve with marinara dip.

Tip:

You can also add chopped onion in the mixture.

Cod Fillet with Curry Butter

This delicious cod recipe is ready in under 30 minutes.
Prep Time and Cooking Time: 20 minutes | Serves: 2

Ingredients to Use:

- 1 tablespoon butter, melted
- 1/4 teaspoon curry powder
- 1/8 teaspoon paprika
- Pinch garlic powder
- Salt to taste
- 2 cod fillets

Step-by-Step Directions

1. Combine butter, curry powder, paprika, garlic powder and salt in a bowl.
2. Coat cod fillets with this mixture.
3. Add cod fillets to the air fryer oven.
4. Set it to roast.
5. Cook at 360 degrees F for 4 to 5 minutes per side.
6. Drizzle with cooking liquid and serve.

Serving Suggestion:

Sprinkle with thinly sliced basil.

Tip:

Add more curry powder if you like your fish spicier.

Cod with Soy Ginger Sauce

This Asian style cod recipe will give you outstanding flavors you can't get enough of.
Prep Time and Cooking Time: 15 minutes | Serves: 2

- 1 tablespoon butter, melted
- 1-1/2 tablespoons rice wine
- 2 teaspoons honey
- 1 tablespoon soy sauce
- 2 cod fillets
- 1 tablespoon ginger, sliced thinly

Step-by-Step Directions

1. Combine butter, rice wine, honey and soy sauce in a bowl.
2. Place the cod fillets on top of a foil sheet.
3. Sprinkle the ginger slices on top.
4. Pour the butter sauce over the fish.
5. Fold the foil to wrap the fish.
6. Pinch sides to seal.
7. Place in the air fryer oven.
8. Select air fry setting.
9. Cook at 360 degrees F for 10 minutes.

Serving Suggestion:

Garnish with cilantro.

Tip:

You can also add sliced onions inside the packet.

Lemon Caper Fish Fillet

Your whole family will be delighted with this light yet delicious fish dish.
Prep Time and Cooking Time: 10 minutes | Serves: 2

Ingredients to Use:

- 2 cod fillets
- Salt and pepper to taste
- 1-1/2 tablespoons butter
- 1/2 teaspoon lemon zest
- 3 tablespoons lemon juice
- 1 tablespoon capers

Step-by-Step Directions

1. Spray fish with oil.

2. Season with salt and pepper.
3. Place the fish inside the air fryer oven.
4. Choose air fry setting.
5. Cook at 360 degrees F for 3 minutes per side.
6. In a pan over medium heat, add the butter.
7. Once melted, stir in lemon zest, lemon juice and capers.
8. Simmer for 1 minute.
9. Transfer fish to a serving plate.
10. Pour sauce over the fish and serve.

Serving Suggestion:

Sprinkle with pepper.

Tip:

Extend cooking time until fish is flaky.

Sweet & Sour Salmon

When you want a change in your weekly menu, here's a dish that will do the trick.
Prep Time and Cooking Time: 20 minutes | Serves: 4

Ingredients to Use:

- 4 salmon fillets, sliced into strips
- Salt and pepper to taste
- 2 tablespoons tapioca starch

Sauce
- 1 teaspoon olive oil
- 2 tablespoons garlic, minced
- 2 tablespoons ginger, grated
- 2 tablespoons sugar
- 2 tablespoons oyster sauce
- 4 tablespoons black vinegar

Step-by-Step Directions

1. Season salmon with salt and pepper.
2. Coat salmon with tapioca starch.
3. Place salmon inside air fryer oven.
4. Choose air fry option.
5. Cook at 400 degrees F for 3 to 4 minutes per side.

6. In a pan over medium heat, add the olive oil.
7. Once hot, cook the garlic and ginger for 1 minute.
8. Stir in sugar, oyster sauce and vinegar.
9. Toss salmon in the sauce and serve.

Sprinkle with crispy garlic flakes.

You can also use all purpose flour in place of tapioca starch.

Chinese-Style Roasted Salmon

Roasted salmon drenched in sweet savory sauce—this will make you feel like you're inside a fancy Chinese restaurant.
Prep Time and Cooking Time: 20 minutes | Serves: 4

Ingredients to Use:

- 4 salmon fillets
- Salt and pepper to taste
- 1 tablespoon vegetable oil
- 2 stalks green onion, chopped
- 3 slices ginger
- 1/4 cup carrot, sliced into strips
- 2 tablespoons soy sauce paste
- 2 tablespoons soy sauce
- 4 tablespoons mirin
- 2 tablespoons rice wine
- 1/4 cup water

Step-by-Step Directions

1. Season both sides of salmon with salt and pepper.
2. Add salmon to the air fryer oven.
3. Select roast setting.
4. Cook at 380 degrees F for 15 minutes, flipping once.
5. Pour oil into a pan over medium heat.
6. Cook ginger, green onion and carrot for 1 minute, stirring often.

7. Stir in the rest of the ingredients.
8. Simmer for 4 minutes.
9. Pour sauce over the salmon and serve.

Serving Suggestion:

Garnish with chopped scallions.

Tip:

Dry salmon with paper towel before seasoning with salt and pepper.

Japanese Mackerel

In Japan, this dish is known as Saba shioyaki. It's very simple but gives you stellar results.
Prep Time and Cooking Time: 50 minutes | Serves: 2

Ingredients to Use:

- 2 mackerel fillets
- 1 tablespoon rice wine
- Salt to taste
- 1 lemon, sliced into wedges

Step-by-Step Directions

1. Brush the fish fillets with wine.
2. Let sit for 10 minutes.
3. Season with salt.
4. Let sit for 30 minutes.
5. Add fish fillet to the air fryer oven.
6. Place in the air crisper tray.
7. Select air fry setting.
8. Cook at 400 degrees F for 4 minutes per side.

Serving Suggestion:

Drizzle with lemon juice and serve.

Tip:

You can add 2 more minutes cooking time to thicker fillets.

Garlic Salt and Pepper Shrimp

Here's a dish that you can prepare without any hassle—shrimp, flavored with garlic, salt and pepper

Prep Time and Cooking Time: 15 minutes | Serves: 8

- 16 shrimp
- 2 teaspoons olive oil
- 1 teaspoon rice wine
- Salt and pepper to taste
- 2 cloves garlic, minced

Step-by-Step Directions

1. Combine all the ingredients in a bowl.
2. Set the air fryer oven to air fry.
3. Add the shrimp mixture to the air crisper tray.
4. Cook at 400 degrees F for 3 minutes per side.
5. Mix all ingredients together and let sit for 5 minutes.

Serving Suggestion:

Garnish with crispy garlic bits.

Tip:

You can also use frozen shrimp for this recipe.

Kimchi Tuna Patties

This is not your regular tuna patty. This one is made with kimchi!
Prep Time and Cooking Time: 15 minutes | Serves: 4

Ingredients to Use:

- 2 cups canned tuna flakes, drained
- 1/2 cup kimchi
- 2-1/2 tablespoons mayo
- 1/4 cup saltine crackers, crushed
- 1 egg, beaten
- 2 cups breadcrumbs

Step-by-Step Directions

1. Cover your air fryer basket with foil.
2. Combine tuna flakes, kimchi, mayo, crackers and egg in a bowl.

3. Shape mixture into 4 patties.
4. Dredge the patties with breadcrumbs.
5. Place inside the air fryer oven.
6. Choose air fry option.
7. Cook at 360 degrees F for 5 minutes per side.

Serving Suggestion:

Serve with green salad or slaw.

Tip:

Squeeze the liquid out of the kimchi.

Almond Crusted Tuna

You won't have a hard time getting this amazing dish done.
Prep Time and Cooking Time: 10 minutes | Serves: 2

Ingredients to Use:

- 2 tuna steaks, sliced into cubes
- 1 egg, beaten
- 1/2 cup roasted almonds, crushed

Step-by-Step Directions

1. Dip tuna cubes in egg.
2. Dredge with almonds.
3. Cover and refrigerate for 15 minutes.
4. Transfer tuna cubes to the air crisper tray.
5. Set your air fryer oven to air fry.
6. Preheat it to 400 degrees F for 5 minutes.
7. Cook the tuna cubes for 3 minutes per side.

Serving Suggestion:

Serve with wasabi mayo dip.

Tip:

Cook longer if you want your tuna fully cooked

Sweet & Spicy Salmon

Create this golden crust on your sweet and

spicy flavored salmon.

Prep Time and Cooking Time: 20 minutes | Serves: 4

- 4 salmon fillets
- 1 tablespoon butter, melted
- 1/2 tablespoon chili powder
- 1/4 teaspoon paprika
- 2 tablespoons brown sugar
- 1 teaspoon cumin
- Pinch cayenne pepper
- Salt and pepper to taste

Step-by-Step Directions

1. Brush both sides of salmon with butter.
2. Mix the remaining ingredients in a bowl.
3. Sprinkle salmon with the spice mixture.
4. Add salmon to the air fryer oven.
5. Choose roast setting.
6. Preheat your air fryer oven to 380 degrees F for 5 minutes.
7. Cook the salmon for 6 minutes per side.

Serving Suggestion:

Let rest for 5 minutes before serving.

Tip:

You can also brush with melted butter in between cooking.

Parmesan Fish Fillet

This is another easy and delicious way to prepare fish fillet in the air fryer oven.

Prep Time and Cooking Time: 20 minutes | Serves: 2

Ingredients to Use:

- 1/4 teaspoon paprika
- 1/2 teaspoon Italian seasoning
- Salt and pepper to taste
- 2 fish fillets
- 1/4 cup Parmesan cheese, grated

Step-by-Step Directions

1. Mix paprika, Italian herbs, salt and pepper in a bowl.
2. Season fish with the mixture.
3. Cover with Parmesan cheese.
4. Set the air fryer oven to bake.
5. Preheat it to 370 degrees F for 5 minutes.
6. Place the fish inside the air fryer oven.
7. Cook for 5 minutes per side.

Serving Suggestion:

Garnish with chopped green onion.

Tip:

You can also add breadcrumbs to the breading.

Salmon Shioyaki

This is another Japanese style fish dish that you can prepare without stress using the air fryer oven.

Prep Time and Cooking Time: 6 hours and 10 minutes | Serves: 4

Ingredients to Use:

- 4 salmon fillets
- 2 tablespoons rice wine
- 4 teaspoons salt

Step-by-Step Directions

1. Coat salmon with rice wine.
2. Let sit for 10 minutes.
3. Sprinkle with salt.
4. Place inside a sealable plastic bag.
5. Refrigerate for 6 hours.
6. Transfer salmon to the air crisper tray.
7. Choose air fry setting.
8. Cook the salmon at 400 degrees F for 4 to 5 minutes per side.

Serving Suggestion:

Garnish with lime wedges.

Dry salmon with paper towel before seasoning.

Sweet Chili Shrimp

This shrimp dish has the perfect balance of spicy and sweet flavors.

Prep Time and Cooking Time: 20 minutes | Serves: 4

Ingredients to Use:

Shrimp
- 12 shrimp, peeled and deveined
- 1 egg, beaten
- 1/4 cup tapioca flour
- Cooking spray

Sauce
- 1 tablespoon olive oil
- 1 tablespoon garlic, minced
- 2 tablespoon lime juice
- 2 teaspoons brown sugar
- 3 tablespoons Thai sweet chili sauce

Step-by-Step Directions

1. Dip shrimp in eggs.
2. Coat with tapioca flour.
3. Spray shrimp with oil.
4. Transfer to the air crisper tray.
5. Cook at 380 degrees F for 3 minutes per side.
6. In a pan over medium heat, cook the garlic in oil for 1 minute.
7. Stir in the rest of the sauce ingredients.
8. Toss shrimp in sauce and serve.

Serving Suggestion:

Garnish with chopped cilantro.

Tip:

If using frozen shrimp, add 2 more minutes to cooking time.

Fish in Lime Butter Sauce

Things don't get easier than this recipe—fish in lime butter sauce.

Prep Time and Cooking Time: 20 minutes | Serves: 4

Ingredients to Use:

- 1 tablespoon butter, melted
- 1 teaspoon paprika
- 1/2 teaspoon garlic powder
- 1/2 teaspoon chili powder
- 1/4 teaspoon cumin
- Salt and pepper to taste
- 4 cod fillets

Sauce
- 1-1/2 tablespoons butter, melted
- 1 tablespoon lime juice
- 1 teaspoon dried parsley flakes

Step-by-Step Directions

1. Combine all the fish ingredients except cod in a bowl.
2. Brush cod with the mixture.
3. Place cod in the air fryer oven.
4. Select grill setting.
5. Cook at 380 degrees F for 3 to 4 minutes per side.
6. Mix the sauce ingredients in a bowl.
7. Microwave on high for 30 seconds.
8. Pour the butter parsley sauce over the fish and serve.

Serving Suggestion:

Garnish with lemon wedges.

Tip:

You can also use other types of white fish fillet for this recipe.

Baked Chinese Fish Fillet

This baked fish fillet will not leave you wanting!

Prep Time and Cooking Time: 20 minutes | Serves: 2

- 2 swordfish fillets
- 1 tablespoon rice wine
- 2 tablespoon olive oil
- 2 tablespoons ginger, grated
- 1/4 cup dark soy sauce
- 2 tablespoon Shaoxing wine
- 1 tablespoon sugar
- Salt to taste
- 1 tablespoon corn starch mixed with 1/4 cup water

Step-by-Step Directions

1. Brush both sides of fish with rice wine.
2. Add to the air crisper tray.
3. Select bake setting.
4. Cook at 380 degrees F for 5 minutes.
5. Flip and cook for another 5 minutes.
6. Transfer to a serving plate.
7. In a pan over medium heat, sauté ginger and green onion in oil.
8. Stir in the rest of the ingredients.
9. Simmer for 3 minutes.
10. Pour sauce over the fish and serve.

Serving Suggestion:

Garnish with slices green onions.

Tip:

You can also use regular cooking wine if Shaoxing wine is not available.

Fish Nachos

Here's a different way to enjoy fish sticks—serve it nacho style.
Prep Time and Cooking Time: 15 minutes | Serves: 2

Ingredients to Use:

- 8 frozen fish sticks
- 1/4 cup Mexican cheese blend

- 1/4 cup tomato, chopped
- 1/4 cup sour cream
- 1/2 cup avocado, diced
- 2 tablespoons jalapeno, chopped
- 2 tablespoons green onion, chopped
- 2 tablespoons cilantro, chopped

Step-by-Step Directions

1. Add the fish sticks to the air crisper tray.
2. Select air fry setting.
3. Cook at the fish sticks at 380 degrees F for 4 minutes per side or until crispy and golden.
4. Transfer fish to a cutting board.
5. Chop and place on a serving platter.
6. Sprinkle cheese on top.
7. Select bake setting.
8. Bake in the air fryer oven for 1 minute.
9. Spread the sour cream on top.
10. Top with the remaining ingredients and serve.

Serving Suggestion:

Drizzle with hot sauce.

Tip:

You can also use cheddar cheese for this recipe.

Tuna with Ponzu Sauce

This will surely become a regular dish in your weekly menu.
Prep Time and Cooking Time: 20 minutes | Serves: 2

Ingredients to Use:

- 1/2 cup Japanese Ponzu sauce
- 1 tablespoon olive oil
- 1-1/2 tablespoons ginger, grated
- 2 tuna steaks

Step-by-Step Directions

1. Mix Japanese Ponzu sauce, olive oil and ginger in a bowl.

2. Marinate fish in the mixture for 1 hour.
3. Preheat your air fryer to 400 degrees F for 2 minutes.
4. Select air fry setting.
5. Cook fish for 3 minutes per side.

Serving Suggestion:

Sprinkle with chopped green onion and sesame seeds.

Tip:

If Ponzu sauce is not available, you can replace this with a mixture of ¼ cup soy sauce, 3 tablespoons lemon juice and 3 tablespoons mirin.

Cheesy Kimchi Fish

East meets West in this simple but enticing dish that you'd love each time.
Prep Time and Cooking Time: 15 minutes | Serves: 4

Ingredients to Use:

- 4 cod fillets
- Salt and pepper to taste
- 1/2 cup kimchi, chopped
- 1/2 cup mozzarella cheese, shredded

Step-by-Step Directions

1. Arrange the fish in a baking pan.
2. Season with salt and pepper.
3. Top with kimchi.
4. Sprinkle cheese on top.
5. Place the baking pan inside the air fryer oven.
6. Select bake function.
7. Bake at 380 degrees F for 5 minutes.

Serving Suggestion:

Garnish with chopped green onions.

Tip:

Internal temperature of fish should be at least 145 degrees F.

Korean Barbecue Tuna Patties

Tender and flavorful, these Asian tuna patties will surely be a star in the dinner table.
Prep Time and Cooking Time: 20 minutes | Serves: 4

Ingredients to Use:

- 6 oz. canned tuna flakes, drained
- 1 tablespoons Korean barbecue sauce
- 1 egg, beaten
- 1/4 cup green onion, chopped
- Pepper to taste
- 1/2 cup breadcrumbs
- 2 tablespoons mayonnaise
- 1/4 teaspoon garlic powder

Step-by-Step Directions

1. Add all the ingredients to a large bowl.
2. Form patties from the mixture.
3. Select air fry setting.
4. Set temperature to 380 degrees F.
5. Add the tuna patties to the air crisper tray.
6. Cook for 10 minutes, flipping once.

Serving Suggestion:

Serve with spicy mayo dip.

Tip:

You can also add hot sauce to the patty mixture.

Baked Fish with Garlic & Basil

This only takes minimal effort to prepare.
Prep Time and Cooking Time: 30 minutes | Serves: 6

Ingredients to Use:

- 2 lb. white fish fillets
- 1 teaspoon sweet paprika
- 1 teaspoon ground coriander
- 1-1/2 teaspoon dried oregano
- Salt and pepper to taste

- 10 cloves garlic, minced
- 15 basil, chopped
- 1 tablespoon lemon juice
- 6 tablespoons olive oil
- 2 green onions, chopped
- 1 red bell pepper, sliced
- 1 green bell pepper, sliced

Step-by-Step Directions

1. Mix paprika, coriander, oregano, salt and pepper in a bowl.
2. Sprinkle both sides of fish with this mixture.
3. Marinate in the refrigerator for 1 hour.
4. In a bowl, mix garlic, basil, lemon juice and olive oil.
5. Preheat your air fryer oven to 425 degrees F.
6. Select bake function.
7. Arrange the green onions and bell peppers in the baking pan.
8. Top with the fish.
9. Bake in the oven for 15 minutes.
10. Pour garlic basil sauce over the fish and serve.

Serving Suggestion:

Serve with salad or pasta.

Tip:

You can also use fresh basil leaves to garnish the dish.

Korean Yellow Croaker Fish

For sure, you and your family will enjoy these Korean style yellow croaker fish that's ready in a few minutes.
Prep Time and Cooking Time: 20 minutes | Serves: 3

Ingredients to Use:

- 6 yellow croaker fish
- 1-1/2 teaspoons Korean chilli garlic paste

- 1 tablespoon rice wine
- 1/2 teaspoon soy sauce
- 2 tablespoons honey

Step-by-Step Directions

1. Brush fish with rice wine.
2. Let sit for 5 minutes.
3. In a bowl, mix the remaining ingredients.
4. Spread the sauce on both sides of the fish.
5. Place the fish inside the air fryer oven.
6. Select air fry option.
7. Set temperature to 400 degrees F.
8. Cook for 5 minutes per side.

Serving Suggestion:

Serve with lemon and soy sauce mixture for dipping.

Tip:

Make shallow slices on the fish before spreading with the sauce.

Cheesy Tuna & Egg Bake

This dish is so good you probably would want another round!
Prep Time and Cooking Time: 15 minutes | Serves: 2

Ingredients to Use:

- 10 oz. canned tuna flakes
- 1 egg, beaten
- 1/4 cup breadcrumbs
- 1 teaspoon hot sauce
- 3 tablespoons mayonnaise
- 1/4 cup celery, chopped
- 1/4 cup mozzarella cheese

Step-by-Step Directions

1. Combine all the ingredients except the egg in a bowl.
2. Transfer mixture to a baking pan.
3. Crack the egg on top of the mixture.
4. Place inside the air fryer oven.

5. Set the air fryer oven to bake.
6. Cook at 380 degrees F for 10 minutes.

Garnish with chopped scallions.

Make sure egg is fully cooked before serving. Extend cooking time if necessary.

Tuna & Black Bean Bake

This dish is as delicious as it is colorful!
Prep Time and Cooking Time: 30 minutes | Serves: 4

Ingredients to Use:

- 10 oz. canned tuna flakes, drained
- 1/2 cup canned black beans, rinsed and drained
- 1/2 cup sour cream
- 1/2 cup tomatoes, chopped
- Salt and pepper to taste
- 1/2 cup Mexican blend cheese, shredded

Step-by-Step Directions

1. Combine all the ingredients in a baking pan.
2. Place inside the air fryer oven.
3. Select bake function.
4. Set the temperature to 360 degrees F.
5. Cook for 15 minutes.

Serving Suggestion:

Serve with tortilla chips.

Tip:

You can also use salmon flakes for this recipe.

Tuna & Corn Croquettes

If there's a party at your home, you can prepare these tuna and corn croquettes.
Prep Time and Cooking Time: 15 minutes | Serves: 4

Ingredients to Use:

- 10 oz. canned tuna flakes
- 1/4 cup breadcrumbs
- 1/4 cup corn kernels
- 1 egg, beaten
- 1/4 teaspoon dried basil
- 1/4 teaspoon garlic powder
- 2 tablespoons mayonnaise

Step-by-Step Directions

1. Mix all the ingredients in a bowl.
2. Form balls from the mixture.
3. Place the balls in the air crisper tray.
4. Set the air fryer oven to air fry.
5. Cook at 360 degrees F for 10 minutes, turning once.

Serving Suggestion:

Serve with sriracha mayo dip.

Tip:

You can also add red pepper flakes to the mixture.

Egg & Tuna Salad

This is a low-carb version of your favorite egg and tuna salad.
Prep Time and Cooking Time: 10 minutes | Serves: 2

Ingredients to Use:

- 2 cans tuna flakes, drained
- 2 tablespoons pickled jalapenos, chopped
- 1/4 cup tomato, chopped
- 1 hard-boiled egg, chopped
- 1 tablespoon mayonnaise
- Salt and pepper to taste
- 1/4 cup cheddar, grated
- 1/4 cup mozzarella cheese

Step-by-Step Directions

1. Add all the ingredients to a bowl.
2. Mix well.

3. Choose air fry setting.
4. Preheat your air fryer to 400 degrees F for 2 minutes.
5. Transfer mixture to a ramekin.
6. Place inside the air fryer oven.
7. Cook for 4 minutes.

Serving Suggestion:

Garnish with chopped parsley.

Tip:

You can also sprinkle with Parmesan cheese.

Cheesy Fish Salsa

This fish recipe combines two things that you love cheese and salsa!
Prep Time and Cooking Time: 15 minutes | Serves: 2

Ingredients to Use:

- 2 cod fillets
- 1 cup salsa
- 1/4 cup Mexican cheese blend

Step-by-Step Directions

1. Arrange the cod fillets in a baking pan.
2. Top with the salsa.
3. Sprinkle cheese on top of salsa.
4. Select air fry setting in your air fryer oven.
5. Cook at 360 degrees F for 10 minutes.

Serving Suggestion:

Garnish with fresh basil leaves.

Tip:

You can also use haddock fillet for this recipe.

Fish with Cordia Dichotoma

This is a Taiwanese fish dish that you'd enjoy with every spoonful.
Prep Time and Cooking Time: 15 minutes | Serves: 2

Ingredients to Use:

- 2 cod fillets
- 2 teaspoon rice wine
- 2 tablespoons Taiwanese pickled Cordia Dichotoma
- 2 tablespoon pickled seed juice
- 2 teaspoon ginger, thinly sliced

Step-by-Step Directions

1. Add the cod fillets on top of a foil sheet.
2. Pour rice wine, Cordia Dichotoma and pickled seed juice on top of the fish.
3. Sprinkle the ginger slices on top.
4. Wrap the foil and pinch the sides to seal.
5. Place the foil packet inside the air fryer oven.
6. Select bake setting.
7. Set it to 360 degrees F.
8. Cook for 8 to 10 minutes.

Serving Suggestion:

Sprinkle sliced green onion on top.

Tip:

Let cool for 10 minutes before unwrapping.

Chili Garlic Sardines

This dish is a good source of omega 3 fatty acids and protein.
Prep Time and Cooking Time: 15 minutes | Serves: 2

Ingredients to Use:

- 2 cans sardines in oil
- 1 tablespoon sesame oil
- 2 cloves garlic, minced
- ¼ cup green onion, chopped
- 1 tablespoon Gochujang Korean chili paste
- 1 teaspoon soy sauce
- 2 tablespoons honey
- 3 tablespoons water

1. Add the sardines in a greased pizza pan.
2. Place inside the air fryer oven.
3. Select air fry setting.
4. Cook at 400 degrees F for 4 to 5 minutes per side.
5. Pour the oil into a pan over medium heat.
6. Cook the garlic and green onion for 1 minute, stirring often.
7. Stir in the rest of the ingredients.
8. Turn off heat.
9. Pour the sauce over the fish and serve.

Serving Suggestion:

Garnish with sliced green onions.

Tip:

Arrange the sardines in a single layer to cook evenly.

Fish with Butter & Cayenne Pepper Sauce

This is a spectacular dish that only takes a few minutes to prepare.
Prep Time and Cooking Time: 15 minutes | Serves: 2

Ingredients to Use:

- 2 Swai fish fillets
- Salt and pepper to taste
- 2 tablespoons butter, melted
- 2 tablespoon rice wine
- 2 tablespoon lemon juice
- 1/4 teaspoon cayenne pepper

Step-by-Step Directions

1. Place the fish fillets in a baking pan.
2. Season with salt and pepper.
3. Combine the butter, rice wine, lemon juice and cayenne pepper in a bowl.
4. Pour the sauce over the fish.
5. Place inside the air fryer oven.
6. Choose bake setting.

7. Bake at 380 degrees F for 6 to 8 minutes.

Serving Suggestion:

Sprinkle with chopped parsley.

Tip:

Use white wine if rice wine is not available.

Garlic Shrimp Scampi

This garlic shrimp scampi is an incredible seafood dish that's bursting with so much flavor.
Prep Time and Cooking Time: 15 minutes | Serves: 4

Ingredients to Use:

- 4 tablespoons butter, melted
- 1 teaspoon red pepper flakes
- 3 tablespoons garlic, minced
- 1/2 lb. shrimp, peeled and deveined
- 1/4 cup chicken broth
- 3 tablespoons capers
- 3 tablespoons lemon juice

Step-by-Step Directions

1. Mix the butter, red pepper flakes and garlic in a cake pan.
2. Place inside the air fryer oven.
3. Select air fry setting.
4. Cook at 400 degrees F for 2 minutes.
5. Stir in the shrimp and remaining ingredients.
6. Choose bake function.
7. Bake at 370 degrees F for 6 to 8 minutes.

Serving Suggestion:

Garnish with fresh basil.

Tip:

Use low-sodium chicken broth.

Garlic Miso Tuna

Combine miso and garlic for the ultimate tuna dish that you'll never get bored with.

Prep Time and Cooking Time: 15 minutes | Serves: 3

Ingredients to Use:

- 1 clove garlic, minced
- 1/2 teaspoon miso
- 1-1/2 tablespoons mayo
- Pepper to taste
- 3 tuna steaks

Step-by-Step Directions

1. Mix the garlic, miso, mayo and pepper in a bowl.
2. Spread mixture on top of tuna steak.
3. Place on top of the air crisper tray.
4. Turn to air fry setting.
5. Cook at 380 degrees F for 6 to 8 minutes.

Serving Suggestion:

Sprinkle fried garlic flakes and chopped green onions on top.

Tip:

You can also use salmon fillets for this recipe.

Korean Fried Shrimp

Now you can enjoy Korean fried shrimp without any guilt!
Prep Time and Cooking Time: 20 minutes | Serves: 4

Ingredients to Use:

- 16 shrimp, peeled and deveined
- 1 egg, beaten
- 1/4 cup tapioca starch

Sauce
- 1 tablespoon sesame oil
- 1/4 cup onion, chopped
- 3 cloves garlic, minced
- 2 teaspoons Gochujang Korean hot pepper paste
- 2 tablespoons honey
- 2 tablespoons oyster sauce
- 2 tablespoons soy sauce

- 1 tablespoons lemon juice
- 2 tablespoons water

Step-by-Step Directions

1. Dip shrimp in egg.
2. Coat with tapioca starch.
3. Add to the air crisper tray.
4. Select air fry setting.
5. Cook at 400 degrees F for 4 to 5 minutes per side.
6. To make the sauce, add oil to a pan over medium heat.
7. Cook onion and garlic for 1 minute, stirring often.
8. Stir in the rest of the ingredients.
9. Simmer for 3 minutes.
10. Toss the shrimp in the sauce and serve.

Serving Suggestion:

Garnish with green onion and sesame seeds.

Tip:

Extend cooking time if using frozen shrimp.

Crispy Cod Fillets

Crunch with every bite—this is what you'll get from this amazing but easy to prepare dish.
Prep Time and Cooking Time: 15 minutes | Serves: 2

Ingredients to Use:

- 2 cod fillets
- 1 teaspoon Sriracha hot sauce
- 1 tablespoon mayo
- 1/2 teaspoon garlic powder
- Salt to taste
- 1/4 cup breadcrumbs

Step-by-Step Directions

1. Combine the hot sauce, mayo, garlic powder and salt in a bowl.
2. Sprinkle cod fillets with this mixture.
3. Dredge with breadcrumbs

4. Add breaded cod fillets in the air fryer oven.
5. Choose air fry setting.
6. Cook at 380 degrees F for 10 minutes.

Serving Suggestion:

Serve with spicy mayo dip.

Tip:

You can also make this ahead of time by freezing bread fish and air frying when ready to serve.

Cracker Crusted Fish Fillet

It's not often that you get this incredible idea to use crackers for breading for your fish!
Prep Time and Cooking Time: X minutes | Serves: X

Ingredients to Use:

- 4 cod fillets
- 2 tablespoons rice wine
- Salt and pepper to taste
- 3 tablespoons garlic, minced
- 1/4 cup saltine crackers, crushed
- 3 tablespoons butter, melted

Step-by-Step Directions

1. Drizzle cod with rice wine.
2. Season with salt and pepper.
3. In a bowl, mix the garlic, crackers and butter.
4. Press mixture on top of side of fish.
5. Choose air fry setting in your air fryer oven.
6. Add fish to the air crisper tray.
7. Cook at 280 degrees f for 15 minutes.

Serving Suggestion:

Garnish with parsley flakes.

Tip:

You can also use other white fish fillets for this recipe.

Chapter 8: Meatless Dishes

Sriracha Cauliflower Stir-Fry

This is a traditional lamb dish that you will surely fall in love with over and over again.
Prep Time and Cooking Time: 30 minutes | Serves: 4

Ingredients to Use:

- 1 head cauliflower, cut into florets
- 1 tablespoon Sriracha
- 1-1/2 tablespoons tamari or gluten free tamari
- 3/4 cup onion white, thinly sliced
- 5 cloves garlic, minced
- 1 tablespoon rice vinegar
- 2 tablespoons olive oil
- 1/2 teaspoon coconut sugar

Step-by-Step Directions

1. Combine all the ingredients in a bowl.
2. Place the mixture in the air fryer.
3. Set the oven in air fry mode.
4. Cook at 350°F for 30 minutes, shaking the pot every 10 minutes.

Serving Suggestion:

Garnish with scallions.

Tip:

You can use other hot sauces instead of sriracha.

Baked Buddha Bowl with Tofu

This vegan-friendly recipe is packed with protein and flavors.
Prep Time and Cooking Time: 50 minutes | Serves: 6

Ingredients to Use:

- 2 cups quinoa, cooked
- 14 oz. extra firm tofu, pressed dry
- 3 medium carrots, peeled and thinly sliced
- 1 lb. fresh broccoli florets
- 1 red bell pepper, thinly sliced
- 3 tablespoons molasses
- 2 tablespoons sesame oil
- 2 tablespoons lime juice
- 1/4 cup soy sauce
- 1 tablespoon sriracha
- 8 oz. spinach, sautéed with olive oil and garlic

Step-by-Step Directions

1. Whisk sesame oil, lime juice, soy sauce, and sriracha in a large bowl.
2. Using the mixture, marinate the tofu and the vegetables in two separate bowls for 10 minutes.
3. Select the bake setting on your air fryer oven at 370°F.
4. Cook the tofu and the vegetable mix separately for 10 minutes each.
5. Layer quinoa, veggies, spinach, and tofu in a bowl.
6. Pour over remaining marinade.

Serving Suggestion:

Garnish with sesame seeds.

Tip:

You can also use brown rice instead of quinoa.

General Tso's Cauliflower

This homemade version of a favorite Chinese takeout is just as tasty if not better.
Prep Time and Cooking Time: 30 minutes | Serves: 3

General Tso's Sauce

- 1/4 cup soy sauce
- 1 tablespoon sesame oil
- 2 cloves garlic, minced
- 1/4 cup rice vinegar
- 1 tablespoon ginger, grated
- 1/4 cup brown sugar
- 2 tablespoons tomato paste
- 1/2 cup vegetable broth
- 2 tablespoons cornstarch, dissolved in cold water

Cauliflower

- 1/2 cup flour
- 2 large eggs, beaten
- 1 cup panko breadcrumbs
- Salt and pepper to taste

Step-by-Step Directions

1. Cook the sauce ingredients over medium heat for 2 minutes, or until simmering.
2. Set the flour, egg, and breadcrumbs in three separate bowls.
3. Dredge the florets in flour, egg, and breadcrumbs.
4. Cook on bake mode at 400°F for 15 to 20 minutes.
5. Drizzle sauce over the cauliflower florets.

Serving Suggestion:

Serve warm as rice toppings.

Tip:

You can also use quinoa instead of rice.

Roasted Potatoes& Asparagus

This simple recipe is packed with nutrients but low in calories.
Prep Time and Cooking Time: 20 minutes | Serves: 4

Ingredients to Use:

- 4 new potatoes, cut and cooked
- 1 lb. asparagus, chopped
- 1 teaspoon dried dill
- 2 stalks scallions, chopped
- Salt and pepper to taste

Step-by-Step Directions

1. Combine the asparagus, scallions, and olive oil in a small bowl.
2. Select the roast function and cook the mixture at 350°F for 5 minutes.
3. Combine the mixture with the potatoes in a large bowl.
4. Season with dill, salt, pepper, and olive oil.

Serving Suggestion:

Garnish with fresh parsley.

Tip:

Drain the potatoes well.

Sweet Potato Casserole with Marshmallows

This sweet recipe is so filling that it can be an all-in-one dish and dessert.
Prep Time and Cooking Time: 32 minutes | Serves: 4

Ingredients to Use:

- Mini marshmallows
- 3 cups sweet potatoes, cooked and mashed
- 1/2 cup pecans, diced
- 1/2 cup brown sugar
- 1 teaspoon vanilla extract
- 1/3 cup melted butter
- 1 teaspoon ground cinnamon
- Salt and pepper to taste

Step-by-Step Directions

1. Combine all the ingredients, except for

the mini marshmallows.

2. Set the mixture on a greased casserole dish.
3. Arrange the mini marshmallows on top.
4. Select the bake function on your air fryer oven.
5. Bake at 320°F for 10 to 12 minutes.

Serving Suggestion:

Serve immediately.

Tip:

Use gluten-free marshmallows.

Grilled Vegetable Platter

Enjoy authentic chargrill taste and aroma with this summery platter recipe.
Prep Time and Cooking Time: 30 minutes | Serves: 6

Ingredients to Use:

- 2 ears corn, quartered crosswise
- 8 oz. cremini mushrooms, halved
- 1 lb. asparagus, trimmed
- 1 lb. cherry tomatoes, stemmed
- 2 zucchinis, quartered lengthwise
- 3 tablespoons olive oil
- Salt and pepper to taste

Step-by-Step Directions

1. Grease the vegetables by brushing with olive oil.
2. Season with salt and pepper.
3. Set the oven in grill mode at medium heat.
4. Cook the vegetables, turning occasionally: mushrooms, asparagus, and mushrooms for about 3 or 4 minutes; corn and zucchini for 5 to 8 minutes.
5. Serve in a platter immediately.

Serving Suggestion:

Garnish with fresh basil leaves.

Tip:

Use Kosher salt and freshly ground black pepper, if available.

Baked Cheesy Eggplant

This recipe is a good alternative for meatballs.
Prep Time and Cooking Time: 30 minutes | Serves: 2

Ingredients to Use:

- 2 tablespoons vegan Parmesan cheese, grated
- 1/2 cup Panko breadcrumbs
- Salt and pepper to taste
- Onion and garlic powder to taste
- 1/2 cup flour
- 1/2 cup almond milk
- 1 large eggplant, sliced
- 1/2 cup vegan mozzarella, shredded
- 1 cup marinara sauce

Step-by-Step Directions

1. Mix the Parmesan, Panko, salt, pepper, onion powder, and garlic powder in a bowl.
2. Coat the eggplant slices in flour, then dredge in almond milk.
3. Coat with the Panko mixture.
4. Cook on bake mode at 400°F for 15 minutes.
5. Top with marinara sauce and mozzarella cheese, and then cook until the cheese starts to melt.

Serving Suggestion:

Garnish with Parmesan and parsley and serve with cooked spaghetti noodles.

Tip:

You can also serve with rice or quinoa.

Nori Crab Cakes

The seaweed flavor makes this recipe taste like the real thing.

Prep Time and Cooking Time: 35 minutes | Serves: 4

Ingredients to Use:

- 4 sheets nori
- 2 tablespoons red curry paste
- 1-1/2 inch fresh ginger
- 1 lime, juice and zest
- 1 tablespoon soy sauce
- 100 grams artichoke hearts, drained and shredded
- 200 grams palm hearts, drained and chopped
- 4 cups potatoes, mashed

Step-by-Step Directions

1. Using a food processor, blend the nori, red curry paste, ginger, lime juice, and lime zest into a paste.
2. Mix the artichoke hearts, palm hearts, and mashed potatoes.
3. Evenly combine the mixture with the paste.
4. Shape into patties and put in the air fryer basket.
5. Cook at 400°F for 4 to 5 minutes on each side.

Serving Suggestion:

Serve with a side of green salad.

Tip:

Use tamari instead of soy sauce, if available.

Vegan Mini Lasagna

This recipe offers a heartily healthier version to an all-time comfort food.

Prep Time and Cooking Time: 30 minutes | Serves: 1

Ingredients to Use:

- 2 lasagna noodles, halved and cooked
- 1/2 cup pasta sauce
- 1 cup baby spinach leaves, chopped
- 3 tablespoons zucchini
- 1 cup fresh basil leaves, chopped
- 1/4 cup tofu ricotta

Step-by-Step Directions

1. Spread pasta sauce on a mini loaf pan.
2. Alternately layer the noodles with a mix of pasta sauce, spinach, zucchini, basil, and tofu ricotta.
3. Cover the loaf pan with aluminium foil.
4. Set the oven at 400°F on bake mode for 3 to 5 minutes.

Serving Suggestion:

Garnish with chopped parsley.

Tip:

Use egg-free lasagna noodles.

Baked Zesty Tofu

This recipe has all the flavors of the deep-fried version but with none of the oil.

Prep Time and Cooking Time: 40 minutes | Serves: 4

Ingredients to Use:

Sauce
- 2 tablespoons organic sugar
- 1/3 cup lemon juice
- 2 teaspoons arrowroot powder
- 1/2 cup water
- 1 teaspoon lemon zest

Tofu
- 1 tablespoon tamari
- 1 lb. extra-firm tofu, drained and pressed
- 1 tablespoon arrowroot powder

Step-by-Step Directions

1. Combine all the sauce ingredients in a small bowl.

2. Coat the tofu with tamari, and then with arrowroot powder.
3. Set oven in bake function at 390°F.
4. Bake for 10 minutes, shaking halfway through.
5. Heat the tofu and sauce in a skillet over medium to high setting until the sauce thickens.

Serving Suggestion:

Serve with steamed rice and vegetables.

Tip:

Use Meyer lemons to use less sugar.

Potato & Kale Nuggets

This recipe will be a hit to kids and those who are still kids at heart.
Prep Time and Cooking Time: 20 minutes | Serves: 4

Ingredients to Use:

- 1 teaspoon extra virgin olive oil
- 4 cups kale, chopped
- 1 clove garlic, minced
- 1/8 cup almond milk
- 2 cups potatoes, cooked
- Salt and pepper to taste

Step-by-Step Directions

1. Sauté the garlic and kale in oil for 2 or 3 minutes.
2. Mash the potato, adding milk, salt and pepper.
3. Combine the two mixtures, and then roll into 1-inch nuggets.
4. Cook on bake mode at 390°F for 12 to 15 minutes.

Serving Suggestion:

Serve with steamed rice or quinoa.

Tip:

You may omit the olive oil, if desired.

Crunchy Sushi Rolls

These veggie rolls are fun to make and filling to eat.
Prep Time and Cooking Time: 1 hour, 10 minutes | Serves: 3

Ingredients to Use:

Kale Salad

- 3/4 teaspoon toasted sesame seeds
- 1/4 teaspoon ground ginger
- 1/2 teaspoon rice vinegar
- 1/8 teaspoon garlic powder
- 3/4 teaspoon soy sauce
- 1-1/2 cups kale, ribbed and chopped

Sushi Rolls

- 3 sheets sushi nori
- Sushi rice, cooked
- 1/2 Haas avocado, sliced
- 1/4 cup mayo
- 1/2 cup Panko breadcrumbs

Step-by-Step Directions

1. Massage the kale with the kale salad ingredients until wilted.
2. Spread a layer of thin rice on the nori sheet, leaving a half-inch of naked seaweed along one edge.
3. Layer the kale salad, and then top with avocado slices.
4. Roll up the sushi.
5. Coat with mayo, and then with Panko.
6. Cook on air fryer, setting at 390°F for 10 minutes.
7. Let it cool before slicing.

Serving Suggestion:

Serve with soy sauce dipping.

Tip:

Add sriracha sauce to the mayo to taste.

Crispy BBQ Soy Curls

This dish is so versatile that you can pair it with almost anything.
Prep Time and Cooking Time: 21 minutes|
Serves: 2

Ingredients to Use:

- 1 cup soy curls
- 1 cup warm water
- 1 teaspoon vegetable broth
- 1/4 cup vegan barbecue sauce

Step-by-Step Directions

1. Soak soy curls in warm water with vegetable broth for 10 minutes.
2. Drain and shred into a mixing bowl.
3. Cook on air fry setting at 400°F for 3 minutes.
4. Put back in mixing bowl and coat with barbecue sauce.
5. Air fry for another 5 minutes.

Serving Suggestion:

Serve with potato salad and collard greens.

Tip:

You can use plain water instead of broth.

Vegan Omelettes

This recipe makes it easy to give up egg and cheese.
Prep Time and Cooking Time: 31 minutes |
Serves: 3

Ingredients to Use:

- 1/2 block of organic tofu
- 1/2 cup spinach, finely chopped
- 3 tablespoons nutritional yeast
- 1/2 teaspoon cumin
- 1/4 cup chickpea flour
- 1/2 teaspoon turmeric
- 1/4 teaspoon onion powder
- 1/4 teaspoon basil
- 1/4 teaspoon garlic powder
- 1 tablespoon apple cider vinegar
- 1/2 cup vegan cheese, grated
- 1 tablespoon water
- Salt and pepper to taste

Step-by-Step Directions

1. Blend all the ingredients in a processor, except for the spinach and cheese.
2. Combine the batter with spinach and cheese.
3. Make six omelettes into desired shape.
4. Cook on bake mode set at 370°F for 4 minutes on each side.

Serving Suggestion:

Serve in a sandwich.

Tip:

Use a cookie cutter to shape your omelettes.

Lentil Meatballs with BBQ Sauce

This tastes just like the savory meatballs you grew up eating.
Prep Time and Cooking Time: 45 minutes |
Serves: 5

Ingredients to Use:

- 1 cup white onion, diced and sautéed
- 1 clove garlic, minced and sautéed
- 1 tablespoon tomato paste
- 1/2 cup dried mushrooms, chopped and boiled
- 1 cup dry brown lentils, boiled
- 2 cups vegetable broth
- 1/2 cup vital wheat gluten
- 2 tablespoons avocado oil
- 3 tablespoons vegan BBQ sauce
- 1 tablespoon vegan low-sodium soy sauce
- 1 teaspoon dried parsley
- 1 teaspoon onion powder
- 1/2 teaspoon smoked paprika

- Salt and pepper to taste

Step-by-Step Directions

1. Blend all the ingredients in a food processor until chunky.
2. Make meat balls, each using 2 tablespoons of the mixture.
3. Select grill function on your air fryer oven.
4. Cook at 350°F for 12 minutes.

Serving Suggestion:

Slather with vegan barbecue sauce.

Tip:

You can use vegan Worcestershire sauce, if available.

Cajun Fishless Filets with Pecan Crust

This quick and easy recipe is a mix of tasty, flaky, and crispy texture.
Prep Time and Cooking Time: 20 minutes | Serves: 3

Ingredients to Use:

- 3/4 cup water
- 1 teaspoon Cajun seasoning blend
- 3/4 cup pecans, minced
- 3 tablespoons flax seed, ground
- 1/4 cup plus 2 tablespoons cornmeal, finely ground
- 10.1 oz. Gardein Golden Fishless Filets

Step-by-Step Directions

1. Make batter by combining all the ingredients except for the filets.
2. Coat the filets with the batter.
3. Cook on roast mode at 390°F for 10 minutes.
4. Flip and roast for another 3 to 5 minutes.

Serving Suggestion:

Serve with rice and hot sauce.

Tip:

You can check if the center is piping hot—meaning it's cooked—by poking with a fork.

BBQ Tofu Wings

This sticky recipe is perfect for a munchies style dinner.
Prep Time and Cooking Time: 35 minutes | Serves: 4

Ingredients to Use:

- 1 block extra firm tofu, cut in triangle wings
- 3/4 cup barbecue sauce
- 1/2 cup white wheat flour
- 1/4 cup cornstarch

Step-by-Step Directions

1. Lightly brush the tofu with barbecue sauce.
2. Coat with cornstarch and flour.
3. Arrange on a lined baking sheet.
4. Cook using the bake setting at 350°F for 10 minutes.
5. Remove from air fryer and coat with sauce again.
6. Bake for another 10 minutes.

Serving Suggestion:

Top on a salad with a side of tahini dressing.

Tip:

Use a rubber spatula when removing from air fryer to keep the tofu and coating intact.

Brussels Sprouts & Sweet Potatoes

This recipe is great for a weekly make-ahead meal.
Prep Time and Cooking Time: 35 minutes | Serves: 4

Ingredients to Use:

- 4 cups Brussels sprouts, sliced lengthwise
- 6 cups sweet potato, diced
- 2 tablespoons low-sodium soy sauce
- 2 teaspoons garlic powder

Step-by-Step Directions

1. Season the veggies with garlic powder.
2. Set the air fryer oven to roast mode at 400°F.
3. Roast the Brussels sprouts for 5 minutes.
4. Roast the sweet potatoes for 15 minutes.
5. Season the veggies with soy sauce, and then cook for another 5 minutes.

Serving Suggestion:

Serve with quinoa and peanut butter sauce.

Tip:

Also try with tahini sauce.

Bacon Tofu

This might just be the recipe that will make you say goodbye to pork.
Prep Time and Cooking Time: 30 minutes | Serves: 4

Ingredients to Use:

- 1 block tofu, pressed and sliced
- 1 tablespoon olive oil
- 1/4 cup soy sauce
- 1 tablespoon liquid smoke
- 3 tablespoons balsamic vinegar
- 1 teaspoon garlic powder

Step-by-Step Directions

1. Combine all the ingredients in a small bowl, except for the tofu.
2. Marinate the tofu with the mixture for 30 minutes.
3. Use the air fry setting of your oven.

4. Air fry at 400°F for 18 to 22 minutes.

Serving Suggestion:

Serve with grains or in a sandwich.

Tip:

You can dice the tofu for salads and soups.

Broccoli with Bang Bang Sauce

This recipe is easy but tasty—sweet, spicy and crispy!
Prep Time and Cooking Time: 35 minutes | Serves: 4

Ingredients to Use:

- 3/4 cup unsweetened almond milk
- 3/4 cup all-purpose flour
- 1/2 cup cornstarch
- 1/2 teaspoon onion powder
- 1 tablespoon sambal oelek
- 1 teaspoon garlic powder
- Salt and pepper to taste
- 1 lb. broccoli florets
- 1 cup Panko breadcrumbs

Bang Bang Sauce
- 1/4 cup sriracha
- 1/2 cup vegan mayonnaise
- 2 tablespoons maple syrup

Step-by-Step Directions

1. Combine the sauce ingredients in a bowl, and then set aside.
2. Make a batter by mixing the rest of the ingredients, except for the broccoli and breadcrumbs.
3. Coat the broccoli with the batter, the panko, and then with sauce.
4. Bake at 400°F for 8 minutes.

Serving Suggestion:

Garnish with sesame seeds.

Tip:

You can use other chili paste for the sauce.

Sticky Orange Tofu

This is the low-calorie version of the classic Chinese orange chicken.
Prep Time and Cooking Time: 40 minutes | Serves: 4

Ingredients to Use:

- 1 tablespoon tamari
- 1 tablespoon cornstarch
- 1 oz. extra-firm tofu, cubed

Sauce
- 1/3 cup orange juice
- 1 tablespoon pure maple syrup
- 2 teaspoons cornstarch
- 1/2 cup water
- 2 teaspoons cornstarch
- 1 teaspoon orange zest
- 1 teaspoon fresh ginger, minced
- 1 teaspoon fresh garlic, minced
- 1/4 teaspoon crushed red pepper flakes

Step-by-Step Directions

1. Make the sauce by combining all the ingredients.
2. Coat the tofu with tamari, and then with cornstarch.
3. Use the air fry setting of your oven at 390°F.
4. Cook for 10 minutes, shaking halfway through.

Serving Suggestion:

Serve with steamed rice and vegetables.

Tip:

You can also pair this with vegan noodles and fried rice.

Salted Broccoli with Lemon

This simple recipe is packed with healthy calories.
Prep Time and Cooking Time: 15 minutes |

Serves: 4

Ingredients to Use:

- Salt and pepper to taste
- 1.1 teaspoon garlic powder
- 2 tablespoons olive oil
- Fresh lemon wedges
- 1 lb. broccoli

Step-by-Step Directions

1. Drizzle broccoli with olive oil.
2. Toss in salt, pepper, and garlic powder.
3. Set the oven on air fry mode at 380°F.
4. Air fry for 12 to 15 minutes.

Serving Suggestion:

Serve with lemon wedges.

Tip:

Flip and shake for at least three times while cooking.

Cheesy Brussels Sprouts with Garlic

This recipe will compliment a romantic home dinner or movie night with wine.
Prep Time and Cooking Time: 60 minutes | Serves: 4

Ingredients to Use:

- 3/4 cup Parmesan cheese, grated
- 1-1/2 lb. Brussels sprouts, halved
- 4 cloves garlic, minced
- 1 tablespoon balsamic vinegar
- 2 tablespoons olive oil
- Salt and pepper to taste

Step-by-Step Directions

1. Toss all the ingredients together, except for the Parmesan cheese.
2. Select the roast function on your air fryer oven.
3. Roast Brussels sprouts for 20 minutes.
4. Sprinkle cheese, and then roast for

another 3 minutes.

Serving Suggestion:

Serve warm.

Tip:

You may vegan cheese instead of Parmesan cheese.

Tofu Piccata with Citrusy Sauce

Don't let the ingredients list fool you; this is recipe is so easy to make.
Prep Time and Cooking Time: 50 minutes | Serves: 4

Ingredients to Use:

Marinade
- 1 clove garlic
- 2 tablespoons parsley
- 1 cup fresh lemon juice
- Salt and pepper to taste

Sauce
- 1 cup vegetable broth
- 2 teaspoons cornstarch
- 1/4 cup lemon juice
- 2 tablespoons parsley
- 1 clove garlic
- 2 tablespoons capers
- Salt and pepper to taste

Tofu
- 1/2 cup vegan mayo
- 1 cup Panko breadcrumbs
- 1 block extra firm tofu, cut into rectangles

Step-by-Step Directions

1. Puree the marinade ingredients, then marinate the tofu for 15 to 30 minutes. Set aside.
2. Puree the sauce ingredients, except for the capers.
3. Simmer the sauce in a pan, and then add the capers. Boil for 5 to 7 minutes, and then set aside.
4. Dip the tofu in mayo, and then coat with breadcrumbs.
5. Cook on bake mode at 370°F for 20 minutes.
6. Plate and put sauce over tofu.

Serving Suggestion:

Garnish with parsley sprig and serve with round lemon slices.

Tip:

You can use potato starch instead of cornstarch, if available.

Quinoa Pilaf with Garlic Tofu

This quick and easy recipe is perfect for brunch.
Prep Time and Cooking Time: 25 minutes | Serves: 4

Ingredients to Use:

- 1 cup quinoa, cooked in vegetable broth
- 1 cup green peas, cooked
- 1 block extra firm tofu, pressed and sliced
- 2 cloves garlic, minced
- 2 lemons, zested and juiced
- Salt and pepper to taste

Step-by-Step Directions

1. Make a marinade with garlic, lemon zest, lemon juice, salt, and pepper.
2. Marinate the tofu for 15 minutes.
3. Cook tofu on air fry setting at 370°F for 15 minutes.
4. Mix the quinoa pilaf, boiled green peas, and tofu.

Serving Suggestion:

You can serve warm or cold.

Tip:

You can also try this with rice instead of quinoa.

Fried Tofu with Peanut Sauce

This vegan-friendly version is just as seasoned as the classic Southeast Asian dish.
Prep Time and Cooking Time: 40 minutes | Serves: 4

- 1 tablespoon lime juice
- 1 tablespoon maple syrup
- 1 teaspoon sriracha sauce
- 2 tablespoons soy sauce
- 2 cloves garlic
- 2 teaspoons ginger, chopped
- 1 block extra firm tofu, cut into strips
- 6 tablespoons peanut butter sauce

Step-by-Step Directions

1. Puree all ingredients, except tofu and sauce, to make marinade.
2. Marinade the tofu for 15 to 30 minutes.
3. Skewer the tofu strips, and then put in the air fryer.
4. Select the roast function, and set temperature to 370°F.
5. Roast for 15 minutes.

Serving Suggestion:

Serve with peanut butter sauce.

Tip:

The marinade can also be used as salad dressing.

Tofu & Veggies Rancheros

This is an all-day breakfast recipe for a quick high-protein meal.
Prep Time and Cooking Time: 40 minutes | Serves: 4

Ingredients to Use:

- 4 large gluten-free tortillas
- 1/3 cup yellow squash, grated

- 1/3 cup carrot, grated
- 1 cup vegan cheese
- 1/3 cup zucchini, grated
- 20 oz. extra firm tofu, cubed
- 1/2 teaspoon smoked paprika
- 1 teaspoon ground cumin powder
- 1 teaspoon ground chili powder
- Salt to taste

Salsa Beans

- 1/4 cup cilantro salsa
- 1/8 teaspoon cayenne powder
- 1/4 teaspoon liquid smoke
- 1/8 teaspoon cumin powder
- 15.5 oz. organic black beans, drained
- Salt to taste

Step-by-Step Directions

1. Make the salsa beans by mixing all the salsa bean ingredients in a bowl.
2. Season the tofu cubes with paprika, cumin, chili powder, and salt.
3. Cook on air fry mode at 400°F for 15 minutes.
4. Place tortilla on baking sheet, top with vegan cheese and salsa beans.
5. Air fry at 350°F for 15 minutes.
6. Add the tofu and veggies.

Serving Suggestion:

Top with a spoonful of salsa.

Tip:

You can use chipotle powder instead of cayenne.

Buffalo Cauliflower

This is a delicious and low-carb alternative to chicken wings.
Prep Time and Cooking Time: 25 minutes | Serves: 4

Ingredients to Use:

- 3 tablespoons parsley
- 1/2 cup almond flour

- 1/2 tablespoon garlic powder
- Salt to taste
- 5 cups cauliflower florets
- 1/2 cup hot sauce
- 2 tablespoons butter, melted
- 1 tablespoon olive oil

Step-by-Step Directions

1. Combine parsley, flour, garlic powder and salt in a bowl.
2. In a separate bowl, mix the hot sauce, melted butter, and olive oil.
3. Dredge the florets in the hot sauce mix, and then coat with the flour mix.
4. Cook on air fry setting at 350°F for 15 minutes.

Serving Suggestion:

Serve with blue cheese dip and celery sticks.

Tip:

Put florets in the broiler for 2 minutes for an added crunchiness.

Potato & Tofu Scramble

This recipe is all about timing to achieve crispy, soft, and eggy textures in one.
Prep Time and Cooking Time: 35 minutes | Serves: 3

Ingredients to Use:

- 2 tablespoons olive oil
- 2-1/2 cups red potato, cubed
- 2 tablespoons soy sauce
- 1 block tofu, cubed
- 1/2 teaspoon garlic powder
- 1/2 cup onion, chopped
- 1/2 teaspoon onion powder
- 1 teaspoon turmeric
- 4 cups broccoli florets

Step-by-Step Directions

1. Toss the potato in olive oil.
2. Make a marinade out of the remaining ingredients.
3. Marinate the tofu and the broccoli in two separate bowls.
4. Air fry the potatoes at 400°F for 15 minutes.
5. Add the tofu and air fry for another 15 minutes at 370°F.
6. Add the broccoli with 5 minutes remaining cooking time.

Serving Suggestion:

Serve with ketchup.

Tip:

Shake the air fryer basket to get evenly cooked results.

Vegan Tempura

You can't go wrong with this amazingly simple vegan tempura recipe.
Prep Time and Cooking Time: 35 minutes | Serves: 4

Ingredients to Use:

- 1/2 cup all-purpose flour
- 2 eggs, beaten with 2 tablespoons water
- 1 cup breadcrumbs, mixed with 2 teaspoons vegetable oil
- 1/2 cup whole green beans
- 1/2 cup sweet pepper rings
- 1/2 cup avocado wedges
- 1/2 cup whole asparagus spears
- 1/2 cup zucchini slices
- 1/2 cup red onion rings

Step-by-Step Directions

1. Dip the vegetables in flour, egg mixture, and then breadcrumbs.
2. Sprinkle salt and pepper taste.
3. Cook on air fry mode at 400°F for 10 minutes.

Serving Suggestion:

Serve with Asian dressing or ranch dip.

You may try using your favorite vegetables instead of the ones mentioned in the recipe.

Curried Cauliflower

Enjoy the classic Indian flavor with this one pan recipe.

Prep Time and Cooking Time: 20 minutes | Serves: 3

Ingredients to Use:

- 12 oz. cauliflower florets
- 1 cup vegetable stock
- 1 cup sweet corn kernels
- 3/4 cup light coconut milk
- 1 teaspoon garlic purée
- 3 scallions, sliced
- 1-1/2 teaspoon garam masala
- 1 teaspoon turmeric
- 1 teaspoon mild curry powder
- Salt to taste

Step-by-Step Directions

1. Combine all the ingredients a large bowl until vegetables are fully coated.
2. Put in a deep dish.
3. Select the air fry function, and set the temperature to 375°F.
4. Cook the vegetables for 12 to 15 minutes.

Serving Suggestion:

Top with dried cranberries and lime wedges.

Tip:

Stir every 3 or so minutes while cooking.

Baked Mushroom Pulled Pork

This recipe gives a similar texture and taste of the real stuff.

Prep Time and Cooking Time: 25 minutes | Serves: 3

Ingredients to Use:

- 2 cloves garlic, minced

- 1/4 teaspoon cayenne pepper
- 2 tablespoons extra virgin olive oil
- 1 teaspoon smoked paprika
- Salt to taste
- 4 king oyster mushrooms, shredded
- 1/4 cup barbecue sauce

Step-by-Step Directions

1. Mix all the ingredients, except barbecue sauce, until mushrooms are coated evenly.
2. Set on a lined baking sheet.
3. Cook on bake mode at 400°F for 10 minutes.
4. Transfer in large pan and sauté with barbecue sauce for 3 to 5 minutes.

Serving Suggestion:

Pair with corn or potatoes and serve with barbecue sauce.

Tip:

You can also serve in a sandwich or with salad.

Vegan Burrito Bowl

Preparing a full meal in a bowl has never been this easy.

Prep Time and Cooking Time: 25 minutes | Serves: 4

Ingredients to Use:

- 8 oz. mushroom, sliced
- 1 cup sweet corn
- 2 cups black beans
- 1 teaspoon onion powder
- 1 cup white onion, chopped
- 1/2 cup red onion, chopped
- 1/2 cup green onion, chopped
- 1 cup tomatoes, diced
- 1/2 teaspoon paprika
- 1 teaspoon chili powder
- 2 teaspoons cumin, ground
- 1 teaspoon garlic, minced

- Salt and pepper to taste

1. Combine all the ingredients in a large bowl.
2. Place mixture in air fryer basket.
3. Spritz with avocado oil.
4. Set to air fry function at 370°F.
5. Cook for 15 minutes.

Serving Suggestion:

Serve with quinoa and top with guacamole.

Tip:

Shake the basket halfway through cooking.

Asparagus & Mushroom Stir-Fry

Dinner will be ready in less than 15 minutes with this recipe.
Prep Time and Cooking Time: 12 minutes | Serves: 2

Ingredients to Use:

- 4 stalks asparagus, cut in half
- 50 grams extra firm tofu, cut into strips
- 3 brown mushrooms, sliced
- 4 brussels sprouts, halved
- 2 cloves garlic, minced
- 1/2 teaspoon sesame oil
- 1 teaspoon Italian seasoning
- 1/4 teaspoon soy sauce
- Salt and pepper to taste

Step-by-Step Directions

1. Toss all the ingredients in a bowl to combine.
2. Place in the air fryer basket.
3. Select the air fry option on your oven, and set to 350°F.
4. Cook for 7 or 8 minutes.

Serving Suggestion:

Garnish with toasted sesame seeds.

Tip:

You may extend cooking time depending on your doneness preference.

Tofu & Broccoli Stir-Fry

This is a low-calorie and keto-friendly recipe.
Prep Time and Cooking Time: 30 minutes | Serves: 4

Ingredients to Use:

- 2 heads broccoli
- 1 cup red bell pepper, thinly sliced
- 2 cloves garlic, minced
- 1 onion, diced
- 1 tablespoon rice vinegar
- 2 tablespoon soy sauce
- 1/2 teaspoon ginger, ground
- 1 tablespoon sesame oil
- 12 oz. extra firm tofu

Step-by-Step Directions

1. Toss and coat the vegetables with spices, vinegar, soy sauce.
2. Spritz sesame oil on the air fryer basket.
3. Air fry the tofu at 400°F for 5 minutes each side.
4. Add the vegetables, and then cook at 370°F for 15 to 30 minutes.

Serving Suggestion:

Garnish with roasted sesame seeds.

Tip:

You may extend the cooking time until the vegetables are cooked to desired texture.

Crispy Southern Tofu with BBQ Sauce

This light recipe is reminiscent of a certain Louisville flavor.
Prep Time and Cooking Time: 2 hour, 20 minutes | Serves: 2

Ingredients to Use:

- 1 block extra firm tofu, drained

- 1 tablespoon gluten free tamari
- 1 cup vegetable broth
- 1-1/4 cups corn flakes
- 1 teaspoon onion powder
- 1/4 teaspoon smoked paprika
- 1 tablespoon nutritional yeast
- 1/2 teaspoon celery salt
- 1/4 teaspoon kala namak

Step-by-Step Directions

1. Marinate the tofu in tamari and broth mix for two hours.
2. Blend corn flakes using food processor to make fine powdery crumbs.
3. Combine crumbs with the rest of the ingredients, except for the tofu.
4. Coat tofu by pressing onto the crumb mix.
5. Arrange on a lined baking sheet, and then set oven to bake function.
6. Cook at 350°F for 7 minutes on each side.

Serving Suggestion:

Coat with barbecue sauce.

Tip:

Marinate the tofu overnight.

Mashed Eggplant

This easy recipe is originated in India and is called baingan bharta.
Prep Time and Cooking Time: 45 minutes | Serves: 4

Ingredients to Use:

- 4 medium eggplants, sliced
- 1 tablespoon olive oil
- 1/2 cup peas
- 1/2 cup onion, chopped
- 2 teaspoon lemon juice
- 1 teaspoon serrano peppers
- 1/2 tablespoon coriander powder

- 6 cloves garlic
- 1 teaspoon powder
- Salt to taste

Step-by-Step Directions

1. Cook the eggplants on roast mode at 390°F for 20 to 25 minutes.
2. Mash the eggplant pulps, and then heat on a skillet with oil.
3. Add the rest of the ingredients, and then cook for 2 or 3 minutes.

Serving Suggestion:

Garnish with cilantro leaves and serve hot with naan, roti, or poori.

Tip:

This will last up to 3 days in the refrigerator, and one month in the freezer.

Low-Fat Chinese Noodles

A serving of this filling recipe has 166 calories and only 4 grams of fat.
Prep Time and Cooking Time: 25 minutes | Serves: 6

Ingredients to Use:

- 13 oz. Chinese noodles, precooked
- 5 oz. button mushrooms, washed
- 1 onion, finely chopped
- 5 oz. soya beans, washed and soaked overnight
- 8 oz. carrots, peeled and cut into strips
- 4 tablespoons soy sauce
- 1 tablespoon vegetable stock powder
- 4 tablespoons water

Step-by-Step Directions

1. Dilute the stock powder in water.
2. Place the noodles on the line baking pan.
3. Add the rest of the ingredients.
4. Air fry at 350°F for 15 minutes.

Serving Suggestion:

Drizzle with sriracha.

Soak the beans overnight.

Dry Curry with Eggplant

This flavorful recipe is based on a cooking style in South India.

Prep Time and Cooking Time: 17 minutes | Serves: 4

Ingredients to Use:

- 2 cups eggplants, cubed
- 1 large onion, chopped
- 1-1/2 teaspoon cayenne powder
- 1/2 teaspoon cumin seeds
- 2 tablespoons curry powder
- 1/2 teaspoon mustard seeds
- 1/2 teaspoon turmeric powder
- 6 cloves garlic, minced
- 2 tablespoons olive oil
- Salt to taste

Step-by-Step Directions

1. Place the eggplants and onion in a greased air fryer basket.
2. Season with the rest of the ingredients, except for the curry powder and cayenne powder.
3. Cook on air fryer, setting at 390°F for 10 minutes.
4. Mix in the curry powder and cayenne powder.
5. Cook for another 3 minutes.

Serving Suggestion:

Garnish with chopped coriander.

Tip:

Refrigerate for up to 5 days.

Beet Noodles with Balsamic Vinegar

This vibrant recipe enhances the distinct flavor of beets.

Prep Time and Cooking Time: 35 minutes | Serves: 4

Ingredients to Use:

- 2 large beets, peeled and spiralized
- 2 tablespoons balsamic vinegar
- 2 tablespoons olive oil
- Salt and pepper to taste

Step-by-Step Directions

1. Season the beet noodles with vinegar, oil, salt, and pepper.
2. Place the beet on a baking sheet.
3. Cook on roast mode at 350°F for 20 minutes.

Serving Suggestion:

Sprinkle with orange zest and parsley.

Tip:

Use a 5-mm spiralizer blade to make the noodles.

Spaghetti Squash with Kale & Chickpeas

The versatility of this recipe will give you a lot of serving ideas.

Prep Time and Cooking Time: 40 minutes | Serves: 4

Ingredients to Use:

- 1 spaghetti squash, halved lengthwise

Step-by-Step Directions

1. Scoop out and discard of the seeds.
2. Put into the air fryer basket.
3. Cook on bake mode at 360°F for 20 minutes.
4. Scrape with fork to make noodles.

Serving Suggestion:

Top with fresh kale and cooked chickpeas.

Tip:

Cooking times may vary depending on the

squash size.

Zoodles with Marinara Sauce

You will love the slight crispiness, and pasta-like tenderness of this recipe.
Prep Time and Cooking Time: 35 minutes | Serves: 2

Ingredients to Use:

- 2 large zucchinis, spiralized
- 1 tablespoon olive oil
- Salt to taste

Step-by-Step Directions

1. Salt the zoodles in a colander, and then let sit for 10 minutes.
2. Squeeze out excess water using a tea towel.
3. Toss zoodles in a bowl with salt and oil.
4. Press the air fry button and set temperature to 400°F.
5. Cook for 20 minutes, or until tender.

Serving Suggestion:

Top with marinara sauce and cheese.

Tip:

Draining affects the tenderness of the zoodles.

Air Fried Instant Ramen

These crispy and crunchy noodles will compliment any juicy vegetable dish.
Prep Time and Cooking Time: 45 minutes | Serves: 4

Ingredients to Use:

- 4 cups water, boiling
- 4 packs ramen noodles
- 1 tablespoon olive oil

Step-by-Step Directions

1. Put the noodles in boiling water for 5 minutes.

2. Drain, and then toss in oil.
3. Place noodles on aluminium foil, and then put in the air fryer basket.
4. Select air fry function and set temperature to 350°F.
5. Cook for 15 to 20 minutes.

Serving Suggestion:

Serve with meatless chop suey.

Tip:

Cook in batches.

Chickpea Patties

This is a vegan take on the classic burger that can pair easily with any dish.
Prep Time and Cooking Time: 25 minutes | Serves: 3

Ingredients to Use:

- 1 medium sweet potato, boiled and mashed
- 1 cup chickpeas, boiled and mashed
- 1 onion, chopped
- 1 green chili, chopped
- 3 twigs coriander leaves, chopped
- 2 tablespoons chickpea flour
- 1 teaspoon cumin
- Salt to taste

Step-by-Step Directions

1. Combine all the ingredients to make the batter.
2. Make small balls and flatten by pressing in between your palms.
3. Place the patties on a greased air fryer basket.
4. Air fry at 390°F for 8 or 9 minutes.
5. Flip and cook for another 5 or 6 minutes.

Serving Suggestion:

Serve with rice and your favorite sauce for dipping.

Tip:

Soak the chickpeas overnight.

Grilled Veggie Skewers

This recipe spells summertime all year round.
Prep Time and Cooking Time: 35 minutes | Serves: 4

Ingredients to Use:

- 1 medium red onion, cut into 2-inch chunks
- 1 medium yellow squash, cut into 1-inch slices
- 1 medium zucchini, cut into 1-inch slices
- 3 red, yellow, or orange bell peppers, cut into 1-inch slices
- 1/4 cup extra-virgin olive oil
- 2 garlic cloves, pressed
- Salt and pepper to taste

Step-by-Step Directions

1. Season the vegetables and onion with garlic, salt, pepper, and oil.
2. Alternate the onions and vegetables on the skewers.
3. Grill on medium to high heat for 15 minutes, or until slightly charred.

Serving Suggestion:

Serve hot with rice and a dipping sauce.

Tip:

Soak wooden skewers in water for 10 minutes to prevent them from burning.

Grilled Lime Cabbage

This grilled recipe is sure to be a hit, even mong meat lovers.
Prep Time and Cooking Time: 20 minutes | Serves: 4

Ingredients to Use:

- 4 tablespoons olive oil

- 2 tablespoons fresh lime juice
- 1 large Napa cabbage
- 1 tablespoon nam pla fish sauce
- 1 teaspoon fresh ginger, minced or grated
- 2 tablespoons fresh cilantro, stems removed
- teaspoon lemongrass, minced
- Salt to taste

Step-by-Step Directions

1. Make the dressing by whisking together oil, lime juice, fish sauce, ginger, lemongrass, and cilantro.
2. Season the cabbage with oil and salt.
3. Select the grill function at medium to high setting.
4. Grill for 3 to 5 minutes on both sides.
5. Drizzle the dressing or serve on the side.

Serving Suggestion:

Garnish with parsley sprigs.

Tip:

For a vegan option, use soy sauce or liquid aminos instead of fish sauce.

Grilled Purple Caponata

This recipe is a Sicilian specialty that will surely add color and flavor to your table spread.
Prep Time and Cooking Time: 45 minutes | Serves: 8

Ingredients to Use:

- 8 oz. purple cauliflower florets
- 1 tablespoon sugar
- Salt to taste
- 1/2 cup shallots, thinly sliced
- Cooking spray
- 1 lb. Japanese eggplant, cut into 1-inch cubes
- 1/2 cup purple basil leaves
- 1 cup Cherokee purple tomatoes, seeded

- and chopped
- 1/4 cup red wine vinegar
- 1 oz. kalamata olives, pitted and chopped
- 3 tablespoons capers, drained
- 1/4 cup extra-virgin olive oil

Step Directions

1. In a large bowl, combine the cauliflower, sugar, salt, and shallots. Let stand for 30 minutes.
2. Coat the eggplant cubes with cooking spray, and then spread on oiled grill grates.
3. Set the oven to grill function and the temperature at 350°F.
4. Grill the for 5 to 6 minutes, or until tender.
5. Add the eggplant and the rest of the ingredients to the cauliflower mix.

Serving Suggestion:

Let stand for about 15 minutes before serving.

Tip:

Store in an airtight container and refrigerate for up to a week.

Tofu Steaks with Chimichurri Sauce

These churrasco-style tofu steaks are amazingly meaty, zesty, and herbaceous.
Prep Time and Cooking Time: 45 minutes | Serves: 6

Ingredients to Use:

- 2 tablespoons hemp seeds
- 1 cup fresh parsley leaves
- 1/4 teaspoon red pepper, crushed
- 1 cup fresh cilantro leaves
- 1 garlic clove
- 1 tablespoon red wine vinegar
- 1 tablespoon fresh lime juice

- 1 teaspoon kosher salt, divided
- 2 teaspoons garlic powder
- 1 teaspoon smoked paprika
- 1 teaspoon onion powder
- 1 teaspoon ground cumin
- Salt and pepper to taste
- 1 block extra firm tofu, drained and cut into triangles
- 5 tablespoons extra virgin olive oil, divided
- Cooking spray
- 1/4 teaspoon red pepper, crushed

Step-by-Step Directions

1. Season the tofu triangles with salt, pepper, garlic powder, smoked paprika, onion powder, and cumin.
2. Coat the tofu with cooking spray and arrange on an oiled grill pan.
3. Set the oven on grill mode at medium to high temperature
4. Grill the tofu steaks for 3 to 5 minutes, or until chargrill marks appear.
5. Transfer steaks to a baking sheet.
6. Cook on bake mode at 400°F for 5 minutes.
7. Blend the hemp seeds, parsley, red pepper, cilantro, garlic, vinegar, lime juice, oil, and salt using a food processor.
8. Pour the sauce over the tofu steaks.

Serving Suggestion:

Serve with roasted vegetables and whole grain bread.

Tip:

Drain the tofu by pressing with paper towel.

Roasted Root Traybake

You can't go wrong with these offerings in one tray--crispy, crunchy, soft, zesty and herbaceous.
Prep Time and Cooking Time: 1 hour, 15

minutes | Serves: 4

- 1kg mixed roots (carrots, parsnips and swede), cut into batons and halved
- 4 thyme sprigs
- 4 rosemary sprigs
- 3 garlic cloves, with skin
- 220g new potatoes, halved
- 2 tablespoon olive oil
- 50g mixed nuts
- 45g feta cheese

Dressing

- 1 lemon, juiced
- 1 cup parsley, finely chopped
- 2 tbsp olive oil

Step-by-Step Directions

1. Combine the roots, herbs, garlic, and potatoes on a grill pan.
2. Drizzle with oil, and then cook on roast mode at 400°F for 10 minutes or until tender.
3. Skin the toasted garlic and whisk together with the rest of the dressing ingredients.
4. Toss the roots in the dressing.

Serving Suggestion:

Top with nuts and feta cheese.

Tip:

You may use vegan cheese instead of feta.

Cheddar Quinoa & Grilled Corn

This creamy recipe is bursting with flavor even with just a few ingredients.

Prep Time and Cooking Time: 30 minutes | Serves: 4

Ingredients to Use:

- 4 ears of sweet corn
- 2 tablespoons olive oil
- 1 cup quinoa, boiled in chicken stock
- 4 oz. cheddar cheese, grated
- 2 tablespoons butter
- 1/4 cup fresh cilantro, chopped
- Salt and pepper to taste

Step-by-Step Directions

1. Brush corn with olive oil and season with salt and pepper.
2. Cover one side of the corn in aluminium oil.
3. Set oven on grill mode at the highest temperature.
4. Grill the corn ears for 10 minutes.
5. Let stand and then remove the kernels from the cob.
6. Heat cooked quinoa in a saucepan with cheese, butter, salt, and pepper.
7. Add in the corn kernels and stir to mix the ingredients.

Serving Suggestion:

Garnish with fresh cilantro.

Tip:

Rotate the corn ears while grilling to cook evenly.

Chapter 9: Snacks

Baked Potato Wedges

This easy and delicious recipe is perfect for game or movie nights.
Prep Time and Cooking Time: 25 minutes | Serves: 4

Ingredients to Use:

- 1 lb. fingerling potatoes, washed and sliced
- 1/2 teaspoon garlic powder
- Salt and pepper to taste
- 1 teaspoon olive oil

Step-by-Step Directions

1. Preheat your air fryer oven at 400°F for 3 minutes.
2. Combine garlic powder, salt, pepper, and olive oil in a bowl.
3. Coat the potatoes with the mixture.
4. Cook using the bake function in your air fryer oven at 400°F for 16 minutes.

Serving Suggestion:

Drizzle with cheese sauce.

Tip:

You can opt for a no-oil version by omitting the olive oil.

Grilled Cheese Sandwich

This is a classic go-to snack for the kids and those who are still kids at heart.
Prep Time and Cooking Time: 12 minutes | Serves: 1

Ingredients to Use:

- 1 tablespoon mayonnaise
- 2 slices toast bread
- 1 slice cheese
- Cooking spray

Step-by-Step Directions

1. Spread the mayonnaise and put cheese on the bread.
2. Lightly spray both sides of the sandwich with oil.
3. Secure the sandwich with a toothpick.
4. Select the grill option on your air fryer oven.
5. Grill at 350°F for 8 minutes.

Serving Suggestion:

Serve with potato fries. You may cook the fries with your grilled cheese at the same time. Just place the fries in your air fryer basket and cook for 12 minutes at 350°F.

Tip:

Use a good melting cheese for a super delicious treat.

Crispy Roasted Chickpeas

This is a simple recipe for healthy snacking at any time of the day.
Prep Time and Cooking Time: 15 minutes | Serves: 3

Ingredients to Use:

- 425 grams chickpeas, drained and patted dry
- 1 tablespoon olive oil
- Salt to taste

Step-by-Step Directions

1. Lightly grease the chickpeas with olive oil.
2. Add salt to taste.
3. Spread the chickpeas in one layer on a sheeted baking pan.

4. Select the roast function in your air fryer oven.
5. Cook for 10 minutes at 390°F.

Serving Suggestion:

Put in a take-away container and snack away throughout the day. Also try them as toppings on your salad or soup.

Tip:

Store in a paper bag or loosely covered container at room temperature for up to a week.

Crunchy Pasta Chips

This gives a nice twist for an alternative to regular chips or biscuits.
Prep Time and Cooking Time: 40 minutes | Serves: 2

Ingredients to Use:

- 1 tablespoon nutritional yeast
- 1-1/2 teaspoon Italian seasoning
- Salt to taste
- 1 tablespoon olive oil
- 2 cups dry whole wheat bowtie pasta, cooked and drained

Step-by-Step Directions

1. Combine the nutritional yeast, Italian seasoning, salt, and olive oil in a bowl.
2. Toss the pasta with the mixture.
3. Cook at 390°F for 10 minutes.
4. Shake the air fryer to cook evenly.

Serving Suggestion:

Enjoy as is or with your favorite dip.

Tip:

Let the chips cool down completely to enjoy their maximum crunchiness.

Breaded Avocado Fries

These crispy and rich avocado fries need no oil at all.
Prep Time and Cooking Time: 20 minutes | Serves: 4

Ingredients to Use:

- 1 cup aquafaba
- 1/2 cup panko breadcrumbs
- Salt to taste
- 1 Haas avocado, peeled and sliced

Step-by-Step Directions

1. Put aquafaba into a shallow bowl.
2. In a separate bowl, mix the panko breadcrumbs and salt.
3. Dip the avocado slices in aquafaba, and then dredge them with the panko and salt mixture.
4. Arrange the slices in a single layer on a greased baking sheet.
5. Select the bake function on your air fryer oven.
6. Bake for 10 minutes at 390°F.

Serving Suggestion:

Serve immediately with a creamy sauce such as spicy mayo or ranch dressing.

Tip:

For best results, use a slightly under-ripe avocado—neither too firm nor too soft.

Tomato & Cheese Pizza

This is a quick and easy recipe that will revolutionize your pizza nights.
Prep Time and Cooking Time: 12 minutes | Serves: 2

Ingredients to Use:

- 12 inches pizza dough
- 1 teaspoon olive oil
- 1 tablespoon tomato sauce
- Buffalo mozzarella

1. Roll out the dough to the size of two personal pan pizzas.
2. Lightly brush the dough with olive oil.
3. Spread a layer of tomato sauce.
4. Top with chunks of buffalo mozzarella.
5. Place the dough on a greased baking pan.
6. Select the bake function on your air fryer oven.
7. Bake at 375°F for 7 minutes.

Serving Suggestion:

Top with grated Parmesan cheese, basil, and pepper flakes.

Tip:

The pizza will be piping hot so allow ample time for it to cool down before taking a bite.

Mozzarella Sticks

Say hello to your new favorite crunchy and cheesy snack.
Prep Time and Cooking Time: 2 hours & 25 minutes | Serves: 2

Ingredients to Use:

- 6 mozzarella sticks
- 3 tablespoons all-purpose flour
- 2 eggs, beaten
- 1 cup panko breadcrumbs

Step-by-Step Directions

1. Freeze mozzarella sticks for at least 2 hours.
2. Set the flour, eggs, and panko in separate bowls.
3. Coat the mozzarella sticks in flour, and then dip them in egg, and then panko.
4. Dip the sticks in egg, and then panko again.
5. Arrange the sticks in a single layer on a baking sheet.

6. Select the bake function on your air fryer oven.
7. Bake at 400°F for 6 minutes.

Serving Suggestion:

Serve with warm marinara sauce.

Tip:

Keep an eye while cooking, and do not let the cheese ooze out.

Guilt-Free Fries

This no-oil recipe will have you snacking on fries every day.
Prep Time and Cooking Time: 40 minutes | Serves: 2

Ingredients to Use:

- 1/4 teaspoon basil
- 1 teaspoon garlic powder
- 1 teaspoon onion powder
- 1/4 teaspoon paprika
- 1/4 teaspoon chili powder
- Salt to taste
- 3 medium potatoes

Step-by-Step Directions

1. Combine the basil, garlic powder, onion powder, paprika, chili powder, and salt in a bowl.
2. Peel and rinse the potatoes, and then slice them into fries.
3. Pat them dry, and then toss the fries with the mixture in a bowl.
4. Air fry at 400°F for 25 to 30 minutes.
5. Shake the basket every 5 to 10 minutes.

Serving Suggestion:

Serve with ketchup, nacho cheese or gravy.

Tip:

You may also soak the fries in a bowl of cold water for an hour to remove some starch and yield more crispy results.

High-Protein Onion Rings

This healthy and crave-worthy recipe definitely has a nice ring to it.
Prep Time and Cooking Time: 40 minutes | Serves: 3

Ingredients to Use:

- 2 yellow onions
- 1/2 cup flour
- 1/2 teaspoon turmeric
- 1 teaspoon paprika
- Salt to taste
- 2/3 cup unsweetened milk
- 1 cup chickpea breadcrumbs
- 3 yellow onions

Step-by-Step Directions

1. Peel the outer skin of the onions, and then cut them into ½-inch circular portions.
2. Combine the flour and milk with ¼ teaspoon of turmeric and ½ teaspoon of paprika. Add salt to taste.
3. In a separate bowl, combine the panko with the remaining dry ingredients.
4. Coat the onion rings.
5. Choose the bake function on your air fryer oven.
6. Bake at 400°F for 10 minutes.

Serving Suggestion:

Serve warm with ketchup or ranch dip.

Tip:

Bread very lightly as chickpea breadcrumbs tend to stay drier than regular ones.

Sausage & Apple Slaw

This is a well-balanced recipe for a quick but filling snack.
Prep Time and Cooking Time: 20 minutes | Serves: 4

Ingredients to Use:

- 2 large Granny Smith apples
- 1/2 small red onion
- 1 teaspoon spicy brown mustard
- 1 tablespoon mayonnaise
- 1 tablespoon cider vinegar
- Celery salt to taste
- 4 wedge bratwurst links
- 4 hoagie rolls

Step-by-Step Directions

1. Select the grill function on your air fryer oven.
2. Preheat on medium to high setting.
3. Grate the apples and onion into a bowl.
4. Toss the mixture with spicy brown mustard, mayonnaise, cider vinegar, and celery salt.
5. Grill bratwurst links for 10 to 12 minutes.
6. Set the grilled sausage in between the hoagie rolls.
7. Top the sausage with the apple coleslaw.

Serving Suggestion:

Serve with stone ground mustard dipping sauce.

Tip:

Turn sausage once or twice during cooking for evenly cooked results.

Low-Calorie Calzones

This delicious calzone recipe is stuffed with 348 calories only.
Prep Time and Cooking Time: 27 minutes | Serves: 2

Ingredients to Use:

- 2 oz. rotisserie chicken breast, shredded
- 1/3 cup low-sodium marinara sauce
- 1/4 cup red onion, finely chopped
- 1 teaspoon olive oil

- 3 oz. baby spinach leaves
- 6 oz. whole wheat pizza dough
- 1-1/2 oz. mozzarella cheese, shredded
- Cooking spray

Step-by-Step Directions

1. Heat the olive oil in a non-stick skillet over medium to high setting.
2. Sauté the onion and spinach for 2 minutes.
3. Stir evenly with the chicken and marinara sauce.
4. Fill four 6-inch dough circles with the mix and cheese.
5. Evenly coat the calzones with cooking spray.
6. Select the bake function on your air fryer oven.
7. Bake at 325°F for 12 minutes.

Serving Suggestion:

Serve with marinara sauce.

Tip:

Do not overfill your calzones to prevent the dough from bursting.

Healthy Roasted Nuts

This crunchy protein and fiber-filled recipe is the perfect all-day snack.
Prep Time and Cooking Time: 12 minutes | Serves: 4

Ingredients to Use:

- 1/4 cup cashew
- 1/4 cup almond
- 1/4 cup hazelnut
- 1/4 cup peanut

Step-by-Step Directions

1. Set your air fryer oven to roast function.
2. Arrange the nuts in a single layer, side by side per kind. Do not mix.
3. Roast at 325°F for 6 to 10 minutes.
4. Toss halfway through to cook evenly.

5. Mix them all in a bowl.

Serving Suggestion:

Eat with your favorite cheese or yogurt.

Tip:

Cool them completely before storing them in a glass container away from direct sunlight.

Cooking times:

cashew and almond – 6 minutes; hazelnut – 8 minutes; peanut – 10 minutes.

Cheesy Zucchini Chips

This is an easy and healthy recipe to help you ditch store-bought chips.
Prep Time and Cooking Time: 24 minutes | Serves: 4

Ingredients to Use:

- 1 medium zucchini, thinly sliced
- 1 large egg, beaten
- 1 cup panko breadcrumbs
- 3/4 Parmesan cheese, grated
- Cooking spray

Step-by-Step Directions

1. Combine the panko and cheese.
2. Dip the zucchini slices into the beaten egg, and then coat with the mixture.
3. Lightly grease with cooking spray.
4. Cook using the bake function on your air fryer oven at 350°F for 12 minutes.

Serving Suggestion:

Serve with marinara sauce or ranch dressing for dipping.

Tip:

Flip with tongs to cook evenly.

Sweet Potato Fries

This dish tastes sweeter than traditional potato fries.

Prep Time and Cooking Time: 20 minutes | Serves: 4

Ingredients to Use:

- 1/4 teaspoon paprika
- 1/2 teaspoon garlic powder
- 1/2 teaspoon fine sea salt
- 2 medium sweet potatoes, cut into strips
- 1 tablespoon olive oil

Step-by-Step Directions

1. Mix all the ingredients except for the sweet potatoes and oil.
2. Coat the fries with oil and the mixture.
3. Set the air fryer oven to bake function at 380°F.
4. Cook for 18 minutes.

Serving Suggestion:

Garnish with parsley and serve with ketchup for dipping.

Tip:

Keep an eye will cooking as the fries will brown at different rates depending on the size.

Three-Ingredient Ravioli Bites

This quick and easy snack will become a household regular in no time.
Prep Time and Cooking Time: 11 minutes | Serves: 2

Ingredients to Use:

- 12 frozen ravioli
- 1/2 cup buttermilk
- 1/2 cup Italian breadcrumbs

Step-by-Step Directions

1. Dip ravioli into the buttermilk.
2. Coat with breadcrumbs.
3. Cook using bake function at 400°F for 6 minutes or until golden brown.

Serving Suggestion:

Serve immediately with marinara sauce.

Tip:

You may also freeze them for up to 3 months.

Grilled Veggie Sandwich

This is a vegetarian recipe that even meat-eaters will surely love.
Prep Time and Cooking Time: 50 minutes | Serves: 4

Ingredients to Use:

- 1 tablespoon lemon juice
- 3 cloves garlic, minced
- 1/4 cup mayonnaise
- 1 small yellow squash, sliced
- red onion, sliced
- bell pepper, sliced
- 1 small zucchini, sliced
- 12 focaccia bread, sliced
- 1/2 cup crumbled feta cheese

Step-by-Step Directions

1. Mix the lemon juice, garlic and mayonnaise; and then set aside in refrigerator.
2. Brush all the vegetables with olive oil.
3. Cook using grill function at high setting for 6 minutes, and then set aside.
4. Spread mayonnaise mix and cheese on the bread.
5. Grill for 2 to 3 minutes.
6. Transfer to plate and layer with the grilled veggies.

Serving Suggestion:

Top with alfalfa sprouts.

Tip:

You may also enjoy it as an open sandwich.

Curled Zucchini Fries

The crispiness of these healthy fries will keep you curling back for more.
Prep Time and Cooking Time: 35 minutes |

Serves: 4

- 1 cup panko breadcrumbs
- 1/2 cup Parmesan cheese, grated
- 1 teaspoon Italian seasoning
- 1 large zucchini, sliced using spiralizer
- 1 large egg, beaten

Step-by-Step Directions

1. Mix the panko, cheese and Italian seasoning in a large resealable plastic bag.
2. Dip the zucchini in the beaten egg, and then put inside the bag with the mix to coat.
3. Use the bake function at 400°F for 10 minutes.

Serving Suggestion:

Serve with a zesty ranch dipping sauce.

Tip:

Cook in batches for evenly crisped results.

Chilled Veggie Pizza

This recipe gives a raw twist to your vegetarian pizza.
Prep Time and Cooking Time: 2 hours, 25 minutes | Serves: 16

Ingredients to Use:

- 1 oz. ranch dressing mix
- 8 oz. cream cheese, softened
- 1 cup sour cream
- 1 teaspoon dried dill
- 1/4 teaspoon garlic salt
- 8 oz. crescent rolls, refrigerated
- 1-1/2 cup fresh broccoli, chopped
- 1 small carrot, grated
- 1/2 cup radish, thinly sliced
- 1 small onion, finely chopped
- 1 stalk celery, thinly sliced
- 1 red bell pepper, chopped

Step-by-Step Directions

1. Combine the ranch, cream cheese, sour cream, dill, and garlic salt in a bowl.
2. Put the crescent roll dough on a greased jellyroll pan. Leave for 5 minutes.
3. Cook using the bake function at 350°F for 10 minutes.
4. Once cooled, spread with ranch mixture and top with the vegetables.
5. Cover and chill.

Serving Suggestion:

Cut into squares and serve chilled.

Tip:

Use low-fat or non-fat sour cream for an even healthier version.

Cinnamon Apple Chips

This recipe will let you have an apple a day to keep the doctor away.
Prep Time and Cooking Time: 23 minutes | Serves: 2

Ingredients to Use:

- 2 medium apples, thinly sliced

Step-by-Step Directions

1. Sprinkle the apple slices with cinnamon.
2. Put them in the air fryer basket. Weigh them down with a metal rack to prevent from flying around the basket.
3. Cook on air fryer mode at 300°F for 16 minutes.
4. Allow to cool and crisp for at least 5 minutes before serving.

Serving Suggestion:

Consume immediately once crisp.

Tip:

Store in an airtight container for later. The chips will soften when exposed in the air for too long.

Zucchini Pizza Boats

This keto-friendly recipe is a great low-carb snack at any time of the day.
Prep Time and Cooking Time: 12 minutes | Serves: 6

Ingredients to Use:

- 3 medium zucchinis, halved
- 1/2 cup pizza sauce
- 4 cup mozzarella cheese, shredded

Step-by-Step Directions

1. Scoop out the center of the zucchinis to make boats.
2. Fill in the center with pizza sauce and cheese.
3. Cook in the air fryer at 350°F for 7 minutes.
4. Plate and enjoy.

Serving Suggestion:

Top with more cheese and serve warm.

Tip:

You can tweak this recipe to load your boat with other fillings of your choice.

Roasted Shishito Peppers

This recipe will bring summer to your snack time in any time of the year.
Prep Time and Cooking Time: 15 minutes | Serves: 4

Ingredients to Use:

- 2 tablespoons olive oil
- Salt and pepper to taste
- 8 oz Shishito peppers

Step-by-Step Directions

1. Rub the Shishito peppers with olive oil, salt and pepper.
2. Cook on roast setting at 380°F for 5 to 7 minutes.

Serving Suggestion:

Enjoy by itself, or with cornbread.

Tip:

You may also dice them to garnish your salad or soup.

Garlic Carrot Fingers

This recipe balances the sweet and sour flavors of carrots with garlic.
Prep Time and Cooking Time: 22 minutes | Serves: 4

Ingredients to Use:

- 1 lb. carrot, peeled and cut
- 2 teaspoons garlic powder
- Salt and pepper to taste
- 1 tablespoon olive oil

Step-by-Step Directions

1. Coat the carrots by mixing all the ingredients.
2. Set the air fryer oven to roast mode at 390°F.
3. Roast for 10 to 12 minutes.

Serving Suggestion:

Garnish with parsley and cream cheese.

Tip:

If you want a spicy version, just add ground cinnamon and chili powder into the mix.

Roasted Cauliflower

Here's a simple and straightforward recipe that gives you outstanding results.
Prep Time and Cooking Time: 18 minutes | Serves: 4

Ingredients to Use:

- 1 tablespoon sesame oil
- Salt and pepper to taste
- 1 head cauliflower florets
- 3 teaspoons garlic powder

1. Season the florets with sesame oil, salt, pepper, and garlic powder.
2. Roast in your air fryer oven at 400°F for 15 minutes.
3. Flip the florets halfway through.

Serving Suggestion:

Garnish with grated parmesan cheese.

Tip:

You may also coat with panko breadcrumbs.

Black Bean Burger

This vegan and oil-free recipe is also a great make-ahead snack.
Prep Time and Cooking Time: 35 minutes | Serves: 6

Ingredients to Use:

- 16 oz. black beans, drained
- 1/2 cup corn kernels
- 1-1/3 cups rolled oats
- ¾ cup salsa
- 1/2 teaspoon garlic powder
- 1-1/4 teaspoons mild chili powder
- 1/2 teaspoon chipotle chili powder
- 1 tablespoon soy sauce

Step-by-Step Directions

1. Except for the corn, blend all ingredients in a food processor.
2. Add the corn and refrigerate for 15 minutes.
3. Shape the mixture into patties.
4. Set the air fryer oven to bake mode at 375°F.
5. Bake for 15 minutes or until crispy.

Serving Suggestion:

Make a sandwich and serve with guilt-free air fryer fries.

Tip:

Wrap the patties tightly and freeze for up to 3

months.

Spicy Veggie Wontons

This is a better and healthier version of a deep-fried takeout favorite.
Prep Time and Cooking Time: 25 minutes | Serves: 6

Ingredients to Use:

- 30 wonton wrappers
- 1/2 cup carrot, grated and cooked
- 3/4 cup cabbage, grated and cooked
- 1/2 cup mushrooms, finely chopped and cooked
- 1/2 cup white onion, grated and cooked
- 3/4 cup red pepper, finely chopped and cooked
- 1 tablespoon chili sauce
- 1 teaspoon garlic powder
- Salt and pepper to taste
- Cooking spray

Step-by-Step Directions

1. Mix the cooked vegetables with chili sauce, garlic powder, salt and pepper.
2. Stuff the wonton wrappers using the mixture.
3. Spray with olive oil and cook using the air fryer function at 320°F.
4. Cook for 6 minutes or until golden brown.

Serving Suggestion:

Serve with sesame soy or duck sauce for dipping.

Tip:

You may or not preheat your air fryer for at least 3 minutes before putting the wontons in the air fryer basket.

Crispy Falafel

Bring a well-loved street food into your

kitchen with this easy recipe.
Prep Time and Cooking Time: 25 minutes |
Serves: 6

Ingredients to Use:

- 2 cups dried chickpeas, soaked
- 1 tablespoon chickpea flour
- 3/4 cup parsley, chopped
- 1 medium onion, diced
- 1/4 cup cilantro, chopped
- 2 cloves garlic, minced
- 2 teaspoons ground coriander
- 2 teaspoons cumin powder
- 1/2 teaspoon cayenne pepper
- Salt and pepper to taste

Step-by-Step Directions

1. Pulse all the ingredients in a food processor to make a coarse mixture.
2. Shape the mixture into 1.5-inch balls.
3. Set in a single layer on a lined baking pan.
4. Cook on bake mode at 370°F for 15 minutes or until crispy and golden brown.

Serving Suggestion:

Serve with tzatziki sauce.

Tip:

You may soak the chickpeas overnight for best results.

Roasted Brussels Sprouts

Enjoy the crispy on the outside and tender on the inside with this recipe.
Prep Time and Cooking Time: 17 minutes |
Serves: 2

Ingredients to Use:

- 1 tablespoon olive oil
- 10 Brussels sprouts, halved
- Salt and pepper to taste

Step-by-Step Directions

1. Season the Brussels sprouts with olive oil, salt, and pepper.
2. Select the roast function on your air fryer oven.
3. Cook at 360°F for 12 minutes or until lightly browned.

Serving Suggestion:

Drizzle with lime juice and serve with garlic mayo.

Tip:

You may add garlic powder for additional flavor.

Garlic Parmesan Asparagus

This easy recipe packs flavors in an otherwise simple healthy snack.
Prep Time and Cooking Time: 20 minutes |
Serves: 4

Ingredients to Use:

- 1 lb. asparagus, trimmed
- 2 teaspoons garlic, minced
- 1/4 cup Parmesan cheese, grated
- 2 tablespoons olive oil
- Salt and pepper to taste

Step-by-Step Directions

1. Coat the asparagus with the rest of the ingredients.
2. Place on the air fryer oven in a single layer.
3. Use the roast function at 400°F for 7 minutes or until cooked as desired.

Serving Suggestion:

Garnish with grated Parmesan cheese.

Tip:

Roast for another minute if you prefer melted cheese.

Roasted Green Beans with Garlic

This tasty low-carb recipe is a perfect keto diet snack.
Prep Time and Cooking Time: 13 minutes | Serves: 4

- 1 lb. green beans, cut
- 1 teaspoon garlic powder
- 2 tablespoons olive oil
- Salt to taste

Step-by-Step Directions

1. Mix all the ingredients.
2. Spread the green beans on the air fryer tray.
3. Cook on roast mode at 370°F for 4 minutes.
4. Flip and roast for another 4 minutes.

Serving Suggestion:

Grate butter on top and add a squeeze of lemon.

Tip:

Cut the ends and remove the string of the beans.

Zesty Roasted Artichokes

This is an easy recipe that can uplift your mood.
Prep Time and Cooking Time: 22 minutes | Serves: 2

Ingredients to Use:

- 2 tablespoons lemon juice
- 2 tablespoons olive oil
- Salt and pepper to taste
- 2 fresh artichokes, halved

Step-by-Step Directions

1. Combine the lemon juice, olive oil, salt, and pepper in a bowl.
2. Brush the mixture on the artichokes.

3. Set the air fryer oven at 340°F on roast mode.
4. Cook for 9 to 12 minutes.

Serving Suggestion:

Serve with spinach dip.

Tip:

Use freshly squeezed lemon juice.

Baked Corn Nuts

This recipe makes enough for storing a ready-to-eat snack at any time.
Prep Time and Cooking Time: 50 minutes | Serves: 6

Ingredients to Use:

- 1 lb. hominy, dried
- 2 tablespoons olive oil
- 3 tablespoons ranch seasoning
- Salt to taste

Step-by-Step Directions

1. Drizzle olive oil over the kernels.
2. Toss with ranch seasoning and salt.
3. Cook using the bake function of your air fryer oven at 400°F.
4. Bake for 45 minutes or until golden brown.

Serving Suggestion:

Top with Parmesan cheese.

Tip:

Soak the kernels overnight.

Jalapeño Poppers

This recipe makes a satisfyingly filling snack that you will surely love.
Prep Time and Cooking Time: 20 minutes | Serves: 6

Ingredients to Use:

- 4 oz. cream cheese
- 1 cup Monterey Jack cheese

- 1 teaspoon cumin
- 5 jalapeños, cleaned and halved lengthwise
- 5 slices bacon, halved lengthwise
- Olive oil spray

Step-by-Step Directions

1. Combine the cream cheese, cheese, and cumin in a bowl.
2. Fill the jalapeños with the mixture.
3. Wrap a bacon strip around each stuffed jalapeño and secure with a toothpick.
4. Use the air fryer function and set at 370° F.
5. Cook for 6 to 8 minutes, or until the top turns golden brown.

Serving Suggestion:

Serve with ranch dressing.

Tip:

Cook in batches to avoid overcrowding.

Sweet Potato Chips

This simple recipe will cover your next snack attack in a healthier way.
Prep Time and Cooking Time: 20 minutes | Serves: 2

Ingredients to Use:

- 1 large sweet potato, thinly sliced
- 1 teaspoon dried thyme
- 1 tablespoon olive oil
- Salt and pepper to taste

Step-by-Step Directions

1. Toss the sweet potato slices with the rest of the ingredients in a medium bowl.
2. Select the air fryer function on your oven.
3. Cook at 350°F for 14 minutes, or until golden brown.

Serving Suggestion:

Serve hot with ranch sauce for dipping.

Tip:

Use a mandolin slicer to make thinly sliced chips.

Crispy Tacos

Bring Mexican flavors to your home with this simple but amazing recipe.
Prep Time and Cooking Time: 19 minutes | Serves: 6

Ingredients to Use:

- 1 lb. ground turkey, cooked
- 1 pack taco seasoning
- 2 cups lettuce, shredded
- 1/2 cup black beans
- 2 cups Mexican cheese
- 1/2 cup onion, sliced
- 1/2 cup tomatoes, sliced
- 12 hard taco shells

Step-by-Step Directions

1. Mix the taco seasoning with cooked meat.
2. Stuff the taco shells with meat and the rest of the ingredients.
3. Arrange the tacos in the air fryer basket.
4. Cook at 360°F for 4 minutes, or until crispy.

Serving Suggestion:

Serve with salsa.

Tip:

Use a greased foil line to avoid sticking.

Frozen Chicken Fries

You are never too busy to cook this straight from your freezer.
Prep Time and Cooking Time: 8 minutes | Serves: 2

Ingredients to Use:

- 1 pack frozen chicken fries
- 2 tablespoons ketchup

1. Place frozen chicken fries in the air fryer basket.
2. Set the oven to air fryer mode at 340°F.
3. Cook for 8 minutes.

Serving Suggestion:

Serve with ketchup or other dipping sauce.

Tip:

Make sure not to overcrowd the air fryer basket.

Zucchini Foil Packets

Here is another take on an all-time favorite grilled vegetable.
Prep Time and Cooking Time: 40 minutes | Serves: 4

Ingredients to Use:

- 2 medium zucchinis, sliced
- 1/4 cup Parmesan cheese, grated
- 1 teaspoon Italian seasoning
- 1 teaspoon dried parsley
- 1 teaspoon dried basil
- 1 teaspoon lemon zest
- 1 teaspoon lemon juice
- 1 tablespoon butter, melted
- 1 tablespoon olive oil

Step-by-Step Directions

1. Combine all ingredients in a bowl.
2. Divide and put the mixture into aluminium foil packets.
3. Set them in the air fryer.
4. Cook on air fryer mode at 350°F for 25 to 30 minutes.

Serving Suggestion:

Top with bits of fresh parsley.

Tip:

You may also use other seasonings of your choice.

Fried Pickles with Ranch Dip

This oil-free recipe will get pickle fans excited.
Prep Time and Cooking Time: 55 minutes | Serves: 3

Ingredients to Use:

- 1/2 cup breadcrumbs
- 1/4 cup Parmesan cheese, grated
- 1 teaspoon garlic powder
- 1 teaspoon dried oregano
- 1 egg, whisked with 1 tablespoon water
- 2 cups dill pickle slices, dried
- 2 tablespoons ranch, for dipping

Step-by-Step Directions

1. Combine the breadcrumbs, cheese, garlic powder, and oregano in a bowl.
2. Dip each pickle chip in egg and then coat with the mixture.
3. Cook on air fryer setting at 400°F for 10 minutes.

Serving Suggestion:

Serve immediately with ranch dip.

Tip:

Do not overlap when placing in the air fryer.

Cheesy Tortellini Bites

This snack only takes a few minutes using your air fryer oven!
Prep Time and Cooking Time: 25 minutes | Serves: 6

Ingredients to Use:

- 2 large eggs, beaten
- 1 cup all-purpose flour
- 1 cup Panko breadcrumbs
- 1/3 cup Parmesan cheese, grated
- 1/2 teaspoon crushed red pepper flakes
- 1 teaspoon dried oregano
- 1/2 teaspoon garlic powder

- Salt and pepper to taste
- 9 oz. cheese tortellini, cooked
- 2 tablespoons marinara, for dipping

Step-by-Step Directions

1. Create a mixture of breadcrumbs, cheese, pepper flakes, oregano, garlic powder, salt and pepper.
2. Coat the tortellini in flour, dip in eggs, and then coat with the Panko mixture.
3. Air fry at 370°F for 10 minutes.

Serving Suggestion:

Serve warm with marinara sauce.

Tip:

Pair with a red wine mule, if available.

Taquitos

No need to wait for a party; you can snack on these any day.
Prep Time and Cooking Time: 15 minutes | Serves: 4

Ingredients to Use:

- 12 small corn tortillas, microwaved
- 8 oz. block cream cheese, softened
- 1-1/2 cups cheddar cheese, shredded
- 1-1/2 cups Pepper Jack, shredded
- 3 cups shredded chicken, cooked
- 1-1/2 cups cheddar cheese, shredded
- 1-1/2 cups Pepper Jack, shredded
- 1 teaspoon cumin
- 1 chipotle in adobo sauce, chopped
- 1 tbsp. sauce
- 1 teaspoon chili powder
- Salt and pepper to taste

Step-by-Step Directions

1. Except for the tortillas, mix the rest of the ingredients.
2. Fill the tortillas with the mixture and roll them tightly.
3. Air fry at 400°F for 7 minutes.

Serving Suggestion:

Serve with Pico de Gallo and avocado cream sauce.

Tip:

Place in the air fryer with the seam side down.

Cauliflower Tots with Cheese

Cheese lovers are going to love munching on these one-bite snack.
Prep Time and Cooking Time: 30 minutes | Serves: 6

Ingredients to Use:

- 4 cups cauliflower florets, steamed and riced
- 2/3 Panko breadcrumbs
- 1 cup Parmesan cheese, grated
- 1 cup cheddar cheese, shredded
- 1 large egg, lightly beaten
- 2 tablespoons chives, chopped
- Salt and pepper to taste

Step-by-Step Directions

1. Mix all the ingredients.
2. Shape the mixture into tater tots.
3. Arrange them in a single layer in the air fryer.
4. Cook on air fryer mode at 375°F for 10 minutes, or until golden brown.

Serving Suggestion:

Serve warm with hot sauce.

Tip:

Use Kosher salt and freshly ground black pepper, if available.

Ham & Cheese Egg Rolls

This homemade recipe will warm both your heart and your tummy.
Prep Time and Cooking Time: 30 minutes |

Serves: 2

- 6 egg roll wrappers
- 1 cup shredded mozzarella
- 6 slices provolone
- 12 slices pepperoni
- 6 slices deli ham

Step-by-Step Directions

1. Place the egg roll wrapper in a diamond shape.
2. Equally divide the rest of the ingredients to fill each egg roll wrapper.
3. Fold the sides, roll tightly, and seal the fold with water.
4. Air fry at 390°F for 12 minutes, or until golden brown.

Serving Suggestion:

Serve immediately with Italian dressing for dipping.

Tip:

Garnish with Parmesan cheese and fresh parsley, if available.

Salted Potato Chips

This classic recipe will never go out of style.
Prep Time and Cooking Time: 1 hour, 35 minutes | Serves: 4

Ingredients to Use:

- 1 medium unpeeled russet potato, thinly sliced and soaked
- Salt and pepper to taste
- 1 tablespoon canola oil
- 1 teaspoon fresh rosemary, chopped

Step-by-Step Directions

1. Season the potato chips with salt, pepper, and canola oil.
2. Air fry at 375°F for 25 to 30 minutes.
3. Cook in two batches to avoid overcrowding the basket.

4. Sprinkle with chopped fresh rosemary.

Serving Suggestion:

Serve immediately with your favorite dip.

Tip:

Use freshly ground black pepper, if available.

Air Fried Turkey Fingers

This recipe will take the guilt away from your deep-fried chicken cravings.
Prep Time and Cooking Time: 35 minutes | Serves: 4

Ingredients to Use:

- 1/2 cup buttermilk
- 1 pack taco seasoning
- 3 cups corn chips, crushed
- 1 cup all-purpose flour
- 3/4 lb. turkey breasts, cut into strips
- Pepper to taste

Step-by-Step Directions

1. Set aside flour in a bowl.
2. In a separate bowl, whisk the buttermilk with pepper in a bowl.
3. Mix corn chips and taco seasoning in another bowl.
4. Coat turkey with flour, dip in buttermilk, and then coat with the corn chip mixture.
5. Air fry at 400°F for 8 minutes on each side.

Serving Suggestion:

Serve with sour cream, ranch or salsa for dipping.

Tip:

Cook in batches for evenly browned and crisped results.

Pumpkin Fries

These fries are a little sweet just the way you

like it.

Prep Time and Cooking Time: 35 minutes | Serves: 4

Ingredients to Use:

- 1 medium pumpkin, peeled and cut into strips
- 1/4 chili powder
- 1/4 teaspoon garlic powder
- 1/4 teaspoon cumin
- Salt and pepper to taste

Step-by-Step Directions

1. Combine all the ingredients in a bowl.
2. Set the oven to air fryer mode.
3. Cook at 400°F for 9 to 13 minutes.

Serving Suggestion:

Serve with maple-chipotle sauce.

Tip:

You can also use butternut squash instead of pumpkin.

Baked Turnovers with Pear

This recipe combines the worlds of a healthy salad crusty pizza.

Prep Time and Cooking Time: 30 minutes | Serves: 4

Ingredients to Use:

- 1 medium pear, thinly sliced
- 1/4 lb. black forest deli ham, thinly sliced
- 1/4 cup toasted walnuts, chopped
- 2 tablespoons crumbled blue cheese
- 13.8 oz. refrigerated pizza crust, cut into 3x3-inch squares

Step-by-Step Directions

1. Layer all the ingredients on the pizza crust squares.
2. Fold into triangles, and seal with a fork.
3. Arrange in a single layer on a greased baking sheet.
4. Cook using the bake function at 400°F

for 4 to 6 minutes on each side.

Serving Suggestion:

Serve with fresh pear slices.

Tip:

You may also use apples instead of pears.

Creamy Beef Pockets

The cheese and flavorful seasonings make this a comforting recipe.

Prep Time and Cooking Time: 30 minutes | Serves: 4

Ingredients to Use:

- 1 large egg, beaten
- 2 tablespoons water
- 1 lb. ground beef, cooked
- 1-1/2 cups mushrooms, sliced and cooked
- 1/2 cup onion, chopped and cooked
- 1-1/2 teaspoons garlic, minced
- 4 teaspoons Worcestershire sauce
- 3/4 teaspoon dried rosemary, crushed
- 3/4 teaspoon paprika
- 1 sheet frozen puff pastry, thawed
- 1 cup Swiss cheese, shredded
- Salt and pepper to taste

Step-by-Step Directions

1. Beat egg and water, and then set aside.
2. Place all ingredients in a skillet, except for the egg mix and the puff pastry, and cook for 1 minute.
3. Stuff 4 puff pastry rectangles with the cooked filling and pinch the seams to seal.
4. Brush over with the egg mix, and place on a baking sheet.
5. Cook on bake mode at 375°F for 10 to 12 minutes, or until golden brown.

Serving Suggestion:

Serve with fresh pear slices.

You may also use apples instead of pears.

Fruity Wontons

This recipe will surely put a warm summer party in your belly.

Prep Time and Cooking Time: 40 minutes | Serves: 4

- 1 oz. cream cheese, beaten
- 1 tablespoon sweetened shredded coconut
- 1 tablespoon ripe banana, mashed
- 1/2 tablespoon walnuts, chopped
- 1/2 tablespoon canned pineapple, crushed
- 1/4 cup marshmallow creme
- 6 wonton wrappers

Step-by-Step Directions

1. Make the filling by combining all the ingredients in a bowl, except for the wonton wrappers.
2. Stuff the wonton wrappers with the filling, and fold and press to seal.
3. Spritz with cooking oil, and then arrange in a single layer on the air fryer basket.
4. Cook at 350°F for 10 to 12 minutes.

Serving Suggestion:

Garnish with cinnamon powder and strawberry sauce.

Tip:

You may use confectioners' sugar instead of cinnamon powder.

Turkey Croquettes

This recipe will make you feel thankful for Thanksgiving leftovers.

Prep Time and Cooking Time: 30 minutes | Serves: 6

Ingredients to Use:

- 3 cups leftover turkey, chopped
- 1/2 cup Swiss cheese, shredded
- 1/2 cup Parmesan cheese, grated
- 1 shallot, finely chopped
- 2 cups mashed potatoes
- 1 teaspoon fresh sage leaves, minced
- 2 teaspoons fresh rosemary, minced
- 1 large egg, beaten
- 2 tablespoons water
- 1-1/4 cups Panko breadcrumbs
- Salt and pepper to taste

Step-by-Step Directions

1. Whisk egg and water in a shallow bowl.
2. In a separate bowl, mix the rest of the ingredients except for the breadcrumbs.
3. Make 12 1-inch patties with the mixture.
4. Dip the patties in the egg mixture, and then coat with panko.
5. Layer on a greased tray in a single layer.
6. Air fry at 350°F for 4 to 5 minutes.

Serving Suggestion:

Serve with sour cream for dipping.

Tip:

You may also use dried rosemary and sage leaves instead of fresh ones.

Vegan Pakoras

Travel to the origin of this fried snack with this air fryer recipe.

Prep Time and Cooking Time: 30 minutes | Serves: 4

Ingredients to Use:

- 1 cup cauliflower, chopped
- 1/2 cup yellow potatoes, chopped
- 1/2 clove garlic, minced
- 1/4 red onion, chopped
- 1/2 teaspoon curry powder
- 1/4 teaspoon cumin

- 2/3 tablespoons chickpea flour
- 1/3 tablespoons water
- 1/2 teaspoon coriander
- Salt and cayenne pepper to taste
- Cooking spray

Step-by-Step Directions

1. Mix all the ingredients in a large bowl. Let it sit for 10 minutes.
2. Scoop 2 tablespoons of the mixture on the air fryer basket, and then flatten. Repeat without overcrowding the basket.
3. Spritz with cooking spray.
4. Air fry at 350°F for 16 minutes, flipping halfway through.

Serving Suggestion:

Serve with vegan yogurt for dipping.

Tip:

You may also use regular yogurt if you are not vegan.

Green Plantain Chips

Make plantain chips without any hassle using this recipe.
Prep Time and Cooking Time: 20 minutes | Serves: 2

Ingredients to Use:

- Avocado oil spray
- 1 green plantain, cut into strips
- Salt to taste

Step-by-Step Directions

1. Spray the air fryer basket and the plantain strips with avocado oil.
2. Arrange in the basket without overlapping.
3. Cook on air fryer setting at 350°F for 10 to 15 minutes, flipping with tongs halfway through.

Serving Suggestion:

Sprinkle with sugar.

Tip:

Use a vegetable peeler to make thin chips.

Chapter 10: Cakes, Cookies & Muffins

Banana Bundt Cake with Cream Cheese Icing

Wow your family and friends with this excellent air fryer banana cake.
Prep Time and Cooking Time: 40 minutes | Serves: 8

Ingredients to Use:

- 1 cup all-purpose flour
- 1 teaspoon baking powder
- 2 teaspoons vanilla extract
- 1/3 cup vegetable oil
- 1 egg
- 1/2 teaspoon cinnamon
- 1/2 teaspoon baking soda
- 2 bananas, peeled
- 2 oz. cream cheese, softened
- 2 tablespoons heavy cream
- 2 tablespoons butter, softened
- 3/4 cup sugar
- 1 cup powdered sugar
- 1/2 teaspoon salt

Step-by-Step Directions

1. In a bowl, mash the bananas then mix in the egg.
2. Next add the oil, sugar, and 1 teaspoon vanilla extract. Mix well.
3. Gently sift the flour, baking soda, and cinnamon into the bowl with the banana.
4. Pour the mixture into a Bundt pan.
5. Choose the bake function in your air fryer oven.
6. Bake for 14 minutes at 32o°F.
7. Rotate the pan and continue baking for 16 minutes.
8. Let rest for 10 minutes.
9. Put butter and cream cheese in a microwavable bowl.
10. Microwave for 8 seconds until butter is melted.
11. Stir and cook for another 8 seconds.
12. Add powdered sugar and the remaining 1 teaspoon vanilla extract.
13. Add cream and whisk until you get your preferred consistency. More cream creates a thicker consistency.

Serving Suggestion:

Drizzle some cream cheese icing before serving.

Tip:

If the top of the cake seems to be cooking faster or is turning brown quickly, place a sheet of foil on top.

Luscious Triple Berry Cobbler

A wonderful recipe to make if you have a variety of fresh berries at hand.
Prep Time and Cooking Time: 22 minutes | Serves: 6

Ingredients to Use:

- 3 tablespoons melted butter
- 1/4 cup flour
- 1/2 cup quick oats
- 1/2 cup raspberries or blackberries
- 1/2 cup strawberries
- 1 cup blueberries
- 2-1/8 cups of white sugar, divided
- 1 teaspoon lemon juice
- 1/4 cup brown sugar
- 1 teaspoon vanilla

Step-by-Step Directions

1. Combine berries, 1/8 cup white sugar, and lemon juice in a large mixing bowl.
2. In a separate bowl, mix flour, vanilla, oats, melted butter, brown sugar, and the other 1/8 cup of white sugar.
3. Mix well.
4. Coat pan with non-stick cooking spray.
5. Put the oats mixture in first.
6. Then add the berries.
7. Choose the bake function in your air fryer oven.
8. Bake for 12 minutes at 390°F.

Serving Suggestion:

Let the cake cool for 10 minutes before serving. Can be served with vanilla ice cream or whipped cream.

Tip:

Garnish with fresh berries and mint leaves.

Chocolate Raspberry Lava Cake

Delicious mini lava cakes with a soft gooey center.
Prep Time and Cooking Time: 15 minutes | Serves: 3

Ingredients to Use:

- 1 large egg
- 3 tablespoons all-purpose flour
- 3 tablespoons white sugar
- 6 tablespoons unsalted butter
- 1 large egg yolk
- A pinch of salt
- 1/2 teaspoon vanilla extract
- 4 oz. semi-sweet chocolate bar, broker into smaller pieces
- Fresh raspberries

Step-by-Step Directions

1. Combine butter and chocolate in a microwavable bowl.

2. Microwave for 1 minute, stirring every few seconds until melted. Set aside.
3. Grease 3 ramekins that are 6 oz. each. Set aside.
4. In a large bowl, combine the chocolate, flour, and salt. Mix well.
5. Fill each ramekin halfway.
6. Choose the air fry function.
7. Air fry for 8-10 minutes at 370°F.

Serving Suggestion:

Allow to cool for 1 minute before serving and sprinkle top with powdered sugar and add fresh raspberries.

Tip:

You may also use whipped cream and vanilla ice cream as toppings.

Crumbly Air Fryer Carrot Cake

Easy carrot cake that pairs perfectly with your afternoon coffee or tea.
Prep Time and Cooking Time: 50 minutes | Serves: 6

Ingredients to Use:

- 2/3 cup all-purpose flour
- 2 tablespoons dark brown sugar
- 1/2 cup buttermilk
- 1 teaspoon baking powder
- 1/4 teaspoon baking soda
- 3 tablespoons canola oil
- 2 teaspoons pumpkin pie spice
- 1/3 cup white whole wheat flour
- 1/3 cup walnuts, chopped and toasted
- 1/4 cup dried cranberries
- 1 large egg, lightly beaten
- 1 cup shredded carrots
- 1 teaspoon vanilla extract
- 1/3 cup white sugar plus another 2 more tablespoons
- 1/4 teaspoon salt
- 1 teaspoon orange zest, grated

1. Preheat air fryer to 350°F.
2. Grease a 6-inch round baking pan and lightly dust with flour. Set aside.
3. Whisk together orange zest, buttermilk, vanilla, brown sugar, white sugar, oil, and egg in a large bowl.
4. In a separate bowl, combine flours, baking soda, salt, 1 teaspoon pumpkin spice, and baking powder.
5. Slowly add the egg mixture to the dry ingredients.
6. Add dried cranberries and carrots.
7. Pour batter into baking pan.
8. Combine the remaining 2 tablespoons white sugar, 1 teaspoon pumpkin spice, and walnuts in a small bowl.
9. Sprinkle this mixture over the batter evenly.
10. Choose the air fry function in your air fryer oven.
11. Air fry for 35 minutes or until the toothpick comes out clean when checked.

Serving Suggestion:

Let the cake rest for 10 minutes and serve while still warm.

Tip:

If the top appears to cook quicker than the rest of the cake, cover the top with foil.

Keto-Friendly Chocolate Cake

A 3-step chocolate cake recipe to keep you within your keto goals.
Prep Time and Cooking Time: 15 minutes | Serves: 6

Ingredients to Use:
- 2 large eggs
- 1/3 cup unsweetened cocoa powder
- 1 teaspoon baking powder
- 1-1/2 cups almond flour
- 1/3 cup unsweetened almond milk
- 1 teaspoon vanilla extract
- 1/2 cup powdered swerve
- 1/4 teaspoon salt

Step-by-Step Directions

1. Mix all the ingredients in a large bowl.
2. Grease baking tin and pour in the batter.
3. Air fry for 10 minutes at 350°F.

Serving Suggestion:

Sprinkle powdered swerve before serving.

Tip:

You can also chill the cake before serving.

Air Fryer Pandan Cake

A fun and easy to make fluffy cake that the kids will love.
Prep Time and Cooking Time: 35 minutes | Serves: 2

Ingredients to Use:
- 4-1/2 tablespoons plain flour
- 2 egg whites
- 2 egg yolks
- 1/4 tablespoon baking powder
- 2-1/3 tablespoon sugar
- 1 tablespoon coconut milk
- 1 teaspoon pandan essence or extract
- 1-1/3 teaspoon olive oil

Step-by-Step Directions

1. Sift the flour and baking powder in a bowl and set aside.
2. Preheat air fryer to 302°F.
3. Using a hand mixer, mix the egg white with half the sugar to make the meringue.
4. Add olive oil and mix.
5. Next add coconut milk, pandan essence, and flour.

6. Add 1/3 of the meringue to the flour mixture. Fold with a spatula.
7. Add the rest of the meringue and stir gently.
8. Pour mixture to a baking pan or tray.
9. Cover with foil and poke small holes on it with a toothpick.
10. Choose the air fry function in your air fryer oven.
11. Bake for 25 minutes.
12. Remove foil and bake for 5 more minutes.

Serving Suggestion:

Serve with whip cream or syrup.

Tip:

Goes well with coffee or tea.

3-Ingredient Chocolate Mug Cake

The perfect recipe when you need that chocolate fix.
Prep Time and Cooking Time: 16 minutes | Serves: 1

Ingredients to Use:

- 1 tablespoon water
- 2 tablespoons unsweetened applesauce
- 6 tablespoons chocolate cake mix

Step-by-Step Directions

1. Whisk all ingredients until smooth.
2. Pour batter into an 8-oz. mug that can withstand high heat.
3. Choose the air fry function in your air fryer oven.
4. Air fry for 13 minutes or until cooked.

Serving Suggestion:

Let the mug cool first before serving. Top with chocolate syrup or frosting.

Tip:

Be careful when taking out the mug.

Zesty Orange Drizzle Cake

This spongy cake brings refreshingly tangy flavors that will remind you of summer days.
Prep Time and Cooking Time: 1 hour 2 minutes | Serves: 6

Ingredients to Use:

- 1 cup all-purpose flour
- 4 egg yolks
- 1/4 cup vegetable oil
- 1-1/2 teaspoon baking powder
- 1/4 cup water
- 1/3 cup plus sugar for the batter
- 1/3 cup sugar for egg white mixture
- 1/2 teaspoon kosher salt
- 4 egg whites
- 1 can chilled condensed milk
- 1 teaspoon vinegar
- 3 tablespoons orange juice plus more for frosting
- Orange zest

Step-by-Step Directions

1. Mix egg yolks and sugar until fluffy.
2. Add orange juice, water, and oil.
3. Sift baking soda, flour, and salt on top of the egg mixture.
4. Add zest and mix well.
5. Whisk the egg whites, sugar, and vinegar in a separate bowl until stiff.
6. Slowly fold the egg white mixture into the batter until well combined.
7. Line pan with parchment paper.
8. Choose the bake function in your air fryer oven.
9. Bake for 42 minutes at 310°F.
10. To make the frosting, combine condensed milk, orange juice, and orange zest in a bowl.
11. Mix using a hand mixer for 4 minutes.

Serving Suggestion:

Once cool, turn the pan upside down and remove parchment paper. Add frosting on top and serve.

Tip:

Be careful not to over bake the cake. Check cake for doneness from time to time using a toothpick and take it out immediately once cooked.

Banana Fluffy Cake

They may not look picture-perfect, but the taste will surely change your mind.
Prep Time and Cooking Time: 20 minutes | Serves: 3

Ingredients to Use:

- 1-1/2 tablespoons castor sugar
- 2 tablespoons rice flour
- 1 banana mashed
- 1 banana sliced
- 1 large egg, white and yolk separated

Step-by-Step Directions

1. Preheat air fryer to 356°F.
2. Whisk the egg white until foamy.
3. Add sugar until soft peaks.
4. Add egg yolk, flour, then the mashed banana.
5. Put batter into paper cups or lined muffin trays and top with a sliced banana.
6. Choose the air fry function.
7. Air fry for 8 minutes.

Serving Suggestion:

Can be served with syrup.

Tip:

You can skip the sugar if you are using very ripe bananas. Make this recipe if you have bananas that have gone overripe to avoid tossing them in the trash.

Durian Burnt Cheesecake

A bittersweet cheesecake that melts in your mouth.
Prep Time and Cooking Time: 23 minutes | Serves: X

Ingredients to Use:

- 9 oz. chilled cream cheese
- 8 fl. cream
- 2 large eggs
- 5 tablespoons caster sugar
- 3-1/2 tablespoons cake flour
- 1 cup durian flesh

Step-by-Step Directions

1. Preheat air fryer to 392°F.
2. Line a 6-inch round baking tin.
3. Combine all ingredients in a food processor until smooth.
4. Gently pour into a lined baking tin.
5. Choose bake function.
6. Bake for 23 minutes.

Serving Suggestion:

Let the cake cool for at least 20 minutes before serving. Garnish as desired.

Tip:

Let some parchment paper protrude from the tin to make it easier to take out the cake.

Air Fryer Lemon Berry Cakes

A delightful recipe to try during the summer season.
Prep Time and Cooking Time: 30 minutes | Serves: 4

Ingredients to Use:

- 2 eggs
- 1 cup fresh blueberries
- 2 tablespoons lemon juice

- 3/4 cup sugar
- 1 tablespoon olive oil
- 6 oz. strawberry or raspberry yogurt
- 1-1/2 teaspoon sea salt
- 1-1/2 cup all-purpose flour
- 2 teaspoons baking powder
- 1/2 cup milk

1. Combine all wet ingredients in a large bowl.
2. Slowly incorporate the dry ingredients until runny.
3. Fold in the berries.
4. Grease Bundt pans.
5. Pour batter into pans.
6. Choose the bake function.
7. Bake for 25 minutes at 400°F.

Serving Suggestion:

Allow cake to cool to be able to take it out easily. Sprinkle with powdered sugar and garnish with fresh berries.

Tip:

You can add 1 tablespoon of milk at a time if the batter becomes too thick.

Air Fryer Blueberry Swirl Cake

A delectable blueberry cake that pairs well with your morning coffee or as a dessert.
Prep Time and Cooking Time: 40 minutes | Serves: 8

Ingredients to Use:

- 1/3 cup vegetable oil
- 1 box yellow cake mix
- Non-stick cooking spray
- 2 eggs
- 1/2 cup butter, room temperature
- 21 oz. blueberry pie filling

Step-by-Step Directions

1. Combine the cake mix, butter, and vegetable oil in a large bowl.

2. Pour batter into greased baking pan.
3. Add the blueberry pie filling on top and create swirls.
4. Choose the bake function.
5. Bake for 15 minutes at 320°F.

Serving Suggestion:

Top with whipped cream and fresh berries.

Tip:

Goes well with a hot cup of coffee or cold milk.

Air Fryer Apple Cake

A lovely air fryer cake only has 4 ingredients and takes less than half an hour to make.
Prep Time and Cooking Time: 20 minutes | Serves: 8

Ingredients to Use:

- 1 cup all-purpose flours
- 3 eggs
- 1 cup brown sugar
- 1 cup apples, peeled and diced

Step-by-Step Directions

1. Combine eggs and sugar in a bowl until smooth.
2. Add flour and mix.
3. Add the apples making sure that all they are evenly coated with the batter.
4. Pour batter into a greased pan.
5. Choose the air fry function.
6. Air fry for 12-15 minutes at 320°F.

Serving Suggestion:

Sprinkle with powdered sugar and serve.

Tip:

Cooking time will vary depending on how thick the baking pan is and the type of air fryer you are using. Use the toothpick method to check if the cake is cooked.

Toothsome Nutella Cake

A light and fluffy cake for Nutella lovers.
Prep Time and Cooking Time: 18 minutes |
Serves: 2

Ingredients to Use:

- 1-1/2 cup Nutella
- 1/2 cup Nutella for frosting
- 4 eggs
- 1/2 cup all-purpose flour

Step-by-Step Directions

1. Mix Nutella, eggs, and flour in a large bowl until smooth.
2. Grease pan with oil or spray with non-stick oil.
3. Pour batter into pan.
4. Choose the air fry function.
5. Set temperature to°F.
6. Air fry for 13 minutes or until the center is fully cooked.

Serving Suggestion:

Let the cake cool for 10 minutes then apply the frosting.

Tip:

Letting the cake cool will make it easier to remove from the pan.

Air Fryer Pumpkin Cake

The ultimate fall air fryer recipe that the entire family will love.
Prep Time and Cooking Time: 20 minutes |
Serves: 10

Ingredients to Use:

- 1 tablespoon pumpkin pie spice
- 12 oz. evaporated milk
- 3 large room temperature eggs
- 1 cup walnuts, diced
- 1 package yellow cake mix
- 1 cup granulated sugar
- 15 oz. pumpkin puree
- 3/4 cup melted unsalted butter
- 8 tablespoons room temperature butter for frosting
- 1 teaspoon ground cinnamon
- 8 oz. room temperature cream cheese
- 1 cup powdered sugar
- 2 tablespoons vanilla extract

Step-by-Step Directions

1. Combine pumpkin puree, eggs, sugar, milk, ground cinnamon, and pumpkin spice in a large bowl.
2. Next add the cake mix, diced walnuts, and melted unsalted butter. Mix well.
3. Pour batter on greased pan or skillet.
4. Choose the bake function.
5. Bake for 15 minutes at 320°F.
6. In a separate bowl create frosting by combining cream cheese, butter, sugar, vanilla extract, and walnuts.

Serving Suggestion:

Let the cake cool down then apply the frosting. Garnish with more walnuts and a sprinkle of pumpkin spice on top.

Tip:

Once the 15 minutes is up, stick a toothpick to check if the cake is done cooking. If not, add a few more minutes.

Mini Berry Cheese Cakes

A super simple cake recipe that's perfect for beginners.
Prep Time and Cooking Time: 3 hours 20 minutes | Serves: 8

Ingredients to Use:

- 1/2 cup plus 2 teaspoons granulated sugar
- 1-1/2 cups graham cracker crumbs
- 8 oz. cream cheese, room temperature
- 1/4 cup melted butter

- 1/2 cup sour cream
- 8 oz. fresh blackberries
- 1 egg
- 1/2 teaspoon vanilla extract
- 1 teaspoon lemon juice

1. Mix butter, sugar, and graham crumbs.
2. Scoop and push graham mixture to the bottom of each muffin liner.
3. In a separate bowl, combine cream cheese, sour cream, sugar, vanilla, egg, and lemon juice until smooth.
4. Add the cream cheese mixture on top of graham crumbs until the muffin liner is almost filled.
5. Choose the air fry function.
6. Air fry for 15 minutes at 320°F or until the center is set.
7. Let cakes cool and refrigerate for 3-4 hours.

Serving Suggestion:

Sprinkle with powdered sugar and garnish with fresh blackberries.

Tip:

You can put one blackberry at the center of the cheesecake for a pleasant surprise.

Copycat Recipe Starbucks Coffee Cake

Now you can enjoy this Starbucks classic right at the comfort of your home.
Prep Time and Cooking Time: 32 minutes | Serves: 6

Ingredients to Use:

- 1 teaspoon ground cinnamon plus 1 teaspoon for topping
- 1/3 cup half and half or light cream
- 1 cup room temperature butter plus ½ cup for topping
- 1 teaspoon salt
- 3/4 cup brown sugar plus 1 cup for topping
- 1/2 cup white sugar
- 1 teaspoon baking powder
- 2 eggs
- 2 cups flour plus 1 cup for topping
- 1 teaspoon vanilla
- 1/2 cup pecan, diced

Step-by-Step Directions

1. Combine 1 cup butter, ¾ cup brown sugar, and white sugar in a bowl until creamy.
2. Add baking powder, eggs, flour, vanilla, salt, and half & half. Mix well.
3. Coat pan with olive oil and pour the batter in.
4. In a separate bowl, combine 1 cup brown sugar, 1 cup flour, ½ cup butter, and 1 teaspoon cinnamon.
5. Fold in the pecans.
6. Spread the pecan mixture over the batter.
7. Choose the air fry function.
8. Set temperature for 320°F.
9. Air fry for 12 minutes or until the toothpick comes out clean.

Serving Suggestion:

Let the cake cool for a few minutes before serving.

Tip:

You can leave out the salt if you are using salted butter.

Heavenly Chocolate-Cherry Dump Cake

This super easy double chocolate cake is perfect for the holiday season or whenever you need a pick-me-up.
Prep Time and Cooking Time: 17 minutes |

Serves: 6

- 1 package Devil's Food Cake mix
- 1 container chocolate frosting
- 2 large eggs
- 1/2 cup chocolate chips
- 1 teaspoon vanilla
- 21 oz. canned cherry

Step-by-Step Directions

1. Combine cherries, cake mix, eggs, chocolate chips, and vanilla in a large mixing bowl.
2. Pour batter on a greased pan.
3. Choose the air fry function.
4. Set temperature to 320°F.
5. Air fry for 12 minutes or until the toothpick comes out clean when the center is poked.

Serving Suggestion:

Let the cake cool for a few minutes then spread the chocolate frosting.

Tip:

Garnish with cherries.

Air Fryer Strawberry Shortcake

This is a showstopper cake that's fun to make and decorate.
Prep Time and Cooking Time: 40 minutes | Serves: 6

Ingredients to Use:

- 1 tablespoon vanilla extract
- 1 white cake mix
- 2 cups heavy cream
- 32 oz. fresh strawberries, diced
- 1/4 cup sugar

Step-by-Step Directions

1. Follow the instructions on the cake mix.
2. Pour batter into a greased pan.

3. Choose the bake function.
4. Bake for 20 minutes at 320°F.
5. In a mixing bowl, combine vanilla and heavy cream.
6. Add sugar and mix until frothy.
7. Cut the cake crosswise.
8. Put a layer of strawberries on top of the bottom half of the cake.
9. Then a layer of cream filling.
10. Place the other half of the cake on top of the filling.
11. Add another layer of filling.
12. Finally, decorate the top with strawberries.

Serving Suggestion:

Garnish with mint leaves on top.

Tip:

Use a non-stick cooking spray to coat your baking pan.

Upside Down Pineapple Cake

This sweet dessert will surely give everyone a festive mood.
Prep Time and Cooking Time: 40 minutes | Serves: 6

Ingredients to Use:

- 1/4 cup brown sugar
- 1 package yellow cake mix
- 2 tablespoons melted butter
- 2-3 maraschino cherries
- 20 oz. can pineapple slices
- Ingredients needed to make cake mix

Step-by-Step Directions

1. Spray the bottom of the baking pan with non-stick spray.
2. Melt butter in the microwave and pour it on the baking pan bottom.
3. Next, sprinkle brown sugar on top of melted butter.
4. Put the pineapples on top of the sugar.

5. Add cherries in the pineapple holes.
6. Follow the instructions on the cake mix box to make the batter.
7. Pour batter in the pan on top of pineapples.
8. Choose the bake function.
9. Bake for 25 minutes at 320°F.

Serving Suggestion:

Let the cake cool down before flipping the pan.

Tip:

Check the middle with a toothpick to see if the cake is done cooking. The ingredients will vary depending on the cake mix package you will use.

Easiest Air Fryer Brownies

Make air fryer brownies that are crisp on the outside and soft and moist on the inside.
Prep Time and Cooking Time: 20 minutes | Serves: 4

Ingredients to Use:

- 2 large eggs
- 1/4 teaspoon baking powder
- 1/2 cup all-purpose flour
- 1/4 cup unsalted butter, melted
- 6 tablespoons unsweetened cocoa powder
- 1/2 teaspoon vanilla extract
- 3/4 cup sugar
- 1 tablespoon vegetable oil
- 1/4 teaspoon salt

Step-by-Step Directions

1. Grease a 7-inch baking pan. Set aside.
2. Preheat air fryer to 330°F.
3. Combine all the ingredients in a large bowl and mix well.
4. Gently pour into pan.
5. Choose the bake function.

6. Bake for 15 minutes in the air fryer.

Serving Suggestion:

Let the brownie cool down before slicing and serving.

Tip:

Garnish with powdered sugar.

Oatmeal & Chocolate Chip Cookies

This big batch of chewy cookies is perfect for a big family or for sharing with friends.
Prep Time and Cooking Time: 40 minutes | Serves: 20

Ingredients to Use:

- 1 cup nuts, chopped
- 1 cup softened butter
- 2 cups semi-sweet chocolate chips
- 3/4 cup sugar
- 1 teaspoon salt
- 3/4 cup packed brown sugar
- 1 teaspoon baking soda
- 2 large room temperature eggs
- 1 teaspoon vanilla extract
- 1 package instant vanilla pudding mix
- 3 cups quick-cooking oats
- 1-1/2 cups all-purpose flour

Step-by-Step Directions

1. Preheat air fryer to 325°F.
2. Combine sugars and butter and whisk until fluffy.
3. Add eggs and vanilla extract.
4. In a separate bowl, combine pudding mix, oats, flour, salt, and baking soda.
5. Gradually add dry ingredients to the first bowl of fluffy cream mixture.
6. Fold in nuts and chocolate chips.
7. Using a spoon, scoop and drop dough into a greased baking tray.
8. Slightly flatten the top to create a cookie

shape.

9. Arrange cookies at least 1 inch apart.
10. Choose the air fry function.
11. Air fry for 8-10 minutes or until the edges turn brown.

Serving Suggestion:

Remove from tray and let cookies cool on a wire rack before serving.

Tip:

Make sure that all ingredients are cold so the biscuit shape can hold up. These biscuits can be made ahead and stored in the freezer.

Banana, Peanut Butter, & Oatmeal Air Fryer Cookies

Chewy and chunky cookies with cranberry bits in every bite.
Prep Time and Cooking Time: 15 minutes | Serves: 6

Ingredients to Use:

- 1/2 cup whole wheat flour
- 1/2 cup chunky peanut butter
- 2 teaspoons ground cinnamon
- 1/4 teaspoon baking soda
- 1/4 cup non-fat milk powder
- 1 cup ripe banana, mashed
- 1 cup dried raisins or cranberries
- 1/2 teaspoon vanilla extract
- 1/2 cup honey
- 1 cup old-fashioned oats
- 1/2 teaspoon salt

Step-by-Step Directions

1. Preheat air fryer to 300°F.
2. Combine honey, peanut butter, banana, and vanilla extract in a bowl.
3. in a separate bowl, mix milk, flour, oats, baking soda, salt, and cinnamon.
4. Slowly add and mix flour mixture to the bowl with banana.

5. Add dried cranberries.
6. Grease baking tray.
7. Scoop 1/4 cup of batter and arrange in the tray with 2 inches of space apart.
8. Slightly flatten to achieve cookie shape.
9. Choose the air fry function.
10. Air fry for 7 minutes.

Serving Suggestion:

Let cookies cool down for 1 minute before serving.

Tip:

You can freeze the cookies and reheat them in the air fryer at 300°F.

Classic Chocolate Chip Cookies

This is a crowd favorite that will only take under 15 minutes to make in an air fryer.
Prep Time and Cooking Time: 13 minutes | Serves: 18

Ingredients to Use:

- 2 cups semi-sweet chocolate chips
- 1 teaspoon vanilla extract
- 1 teaspoon baking soda
- 1/2 cup unsalted butter
- 1 egg
- 1/2 cup brown sugar
- 1/4 cup white sugar
- 1/2 teaspoon almond extract
- 1-1/2 cups all-purpose flour
- 1/2 teaspoon salt

Step-by-Step Directions

1. Soften butter in a microwave oven. It should be partially melted but not completely.
2. Mix in the sugars.
3. Add vanilla extract and egg. Mix.
4. Add the dry ingredients followed by the chocolate chips. Stir gently.
5. Form into 2-inch balls.
6. Line air fryer basket with parchment

paper.
7. Choose bake function.
8. Arrange cookies and bake for 8 minutes at 300°F.

Serving Suggestion:

Let cookies cool down for 4 minutes before removing from the air fryer.

Tip:

Use an egg that is within room temperature to get the best results. You can refrigerate the dough for an hour to make it easier to form into cookie shapes.

Chocolate Applesauce Ramekin Cookies

This cake recipe makes a lovely dessert for two in under 30 minutes.
Prep Time and Cooking Time: 25 minutes | Serves: 2

Ingredients to Use:

- 1/4 teaspoon baking powder
- 1/8 teaspoon salt
- 2 tablespoons sugar
- 1/8 teaspoon baking soda
- 2 tablespoons mini chocolate chips
- 2 tablespoons milk
- 1/4 cup flour
- 1/4 teaspoon vanilla
- 2 tablespoon applesauce
- 1 tablespoon melted butter

Step-by-Step Directions

1. In a large bowl, combine flour, baking soda, baking powder, sugar, and salt.
2. Make a crater in the middle and add butter, applesauce, and vanilla.
3. Mix and add the chocolate chips.
4. Grease ramekins.
5. Choose the bake function.
6. Pour batter in ramekins and bake for 15

minutes at 375°F.

Serving Suggestion:

Let ramekins cool and serve with a scoop of vanilla ice cream.

Tip:

Garnish with mint leaves.

Soft &Chewy Air Fryer Molasses Cookies

These deliciously sweet cookies have a hint of spicy ginger and a soft and chewy center.
Prep Time and Cooking Time: 15 minutes | Serves: 15

Ingredients to Use:

- 2 teaspoon ground cinnamon
- 1-1/2 teaspoon Celtic sea salt
- 1-1/2 cups softened butter
- 1 cup brown sugar
- 1/4 cup granulated sugar
- 4 teaspoons baking soda
- 1/2 cup molasses
- 4 cups all-purpose flour
- 1 teaspoon ground cloves
- 2 eggs
- 1 teaspoon ground ginger

Step-by-Step Directions

1. Ina bowl, mix salt, ginger, flour, cloves, cinnamon, and baking soda.
2. In a separate bowl, combine sugar and butter until fluffy using a mixer at a medium setting.
3. Add molasses and eggs with a low setting.
4. Add the dry ingredients. Mix well.
5. Make 1-inch balls from the dough.
6. Roll the balls into the granulated sugar and coat each piece completely.
7. Arrange dough in a baking tray with 1 inch of space in between.

8. Choose the air fry function.
9. Air fry for 8-10 minutes at 375°F.

Cool for 2 minutes before removing from tray.

Tip:

The center is meant to be gooey. If the edges are firm, the cookies are ready. Cookies may be stored in an airtight cookie jar and will last for a week.

Air Fried Oreo Cookies

A 3-ingredient cookie recipe that will surely delight Oreo lovers.
Prep Time and Cooking Time: 14 minutes | Serves: 6

Ingredients to Use:
- 1 tablespoon melted butter
- 12 pieces Oreo cookies
- 1 sheet puff pastry

Step-by-Step Directions
1. Roll out puff pastry on a flat surface.
2. Put a cookie on top of the dough and cut a circle big enough to wrap the cookie.
3. Wrap all cookies with dough and brush melted butter on the surface.
4. Choose the air fry function.
5. Air fry for 12 minutes at 350°F.
6. Turn cookies halfway to brown evenly.

Serving Suggestion:

Plate and sprinkle powdered sugar on top.

Tip:

You can store the cookies in the fridge and reheat them in the air fryer for a few minutes.

Air Fryer Red Velvet Cookies

A cookie version of the red velvet cake that we love.
Prep Time and Cooking Time: 20 minutes |

Serves: 10
Ingredients to Use:
- 2 eggs
- 8 oz. softened butter
- 1/4 cup milk
- 8 oz. softened cream cheese
- 1 package cake mix red velvet
- 1/2 cup powdered sugar

Step-by-Step Directions
1. Preheat air fryer to 350°F.
2. Combine butter and cream cheese using a mixer.
3. Add the eggs and mix.
4. Add the cake mix and milk until creamy and soft.
5. Create balls and roll them in powdered sugar.
6. Arrange cookies in a lined baking tray.
7. Choose the air fry function.
8. Air fry for 10-15 minutes.

Serving Suggestion:

Serve while still warm with a glass of milk.

Tip:

Monitor the baking closely as time may vary depending on the type of air fryer used. Cookies are done if the center has set.

Oatmeal Caramel Cookie Bar

A giant crumbly cookie best shared with friends and family.
Prep Time and Cooking Time: 20 minutes | Serves: 10

Ingredients to Use:
- 1 cup old fashioned oats
- 1/2 cup sea salt caramel chips
- 1 cup whole wheat flour
- 1 large egg
- 1/2 teaspoon baking soda
- 1/4 cup milk

- 1/4 teaspoon salt
- 2 tablespoons melted butter
- 1/3 cup brown sugar
- 1 teaspoon vanilla extract

1. Combine flour, salt, oats, and baking soda in a bowl. Set aside.
2. Mix egg, brown sugar, butter, milk, and vanilla in a separate bowl.
3. Preheat air fryer to 330°F.
4. Slowly add the dry ingredients to the wet ingredients until fully combined.
5. Add caramel chips.
6. Line tray with parchment paper.
7. Put the dough in the tray and smoothen the top with a spatula.
8. Choose the bake function.
9. Bake for 15 minutes or until the surface turns brown.

Serving Suggestion:

Let the cookie cool for a few minutes before serving. Slice or break into smaller pieces.

Tip:

You may use a toothpick to check if the cookie is done. These cookies may be stored in an airtight container for 5 days or refrigerated for up to 3 months.

Easy Peanut Butter Cookies

This 10-minute recipe is perfect for a quick treat for the kids and those who are still kids at heart.
Prep Time and Cooking Time: 10 minutes | Serves: 8

Ingredients to Use:

- 1 cup sugar
- 1 cup peanut butter
- 1 egg

Step-by-Step Directions

1. Mix all ingredients in a bowl until well combined.
2. Line tray with parchment paper.
3. Using an ice cream scoop or spoon, arrange the dough in the tray.
4. Use a fork to flatten the top.
5. Choose the air fry function.
6. Air fry for 5 minutes at 350°F.

Serving Suggestion:

Serve with coffee, tea, or milk.

Tip:

Make a big batch and store it in airtight containers.

Air Fried Nutella Cookies

This is a simple cookie recipe that uses ingredients you already have in your pantry.
Prep Time and Cooking Time: 14 minutes | Serves: 10

Ingredients to Use:

- 1 cup flour
- 1-1/4 cup Nutella
- 2 large eggs

Step-by-Step Directions

1. In a large mixing bowl, mix all ingredients until well blended.
2. Line baking tray with parchment paper.
3. Use an ice cream scoop or large spoon and arrange cookies in the tray.
4. Choose the air fry function.
5. Air fry for 4 minutes at 340°F.

Serving Suggestion:

Sprinkle some powdered sugar on top and serve.

Tip:

These cookies can be stored in airtight containers and will last for a few days.

French Vanilla Cookies

This 3-ingredient cookie recipe only takes 10 minutes to make.
Prep Time and Cooking Time: 10 minutes | Serves: 12

- 2 large eggs
- 1/4 cup vegetable oil
- 1 package cake mix French Vanilla flavor

Step-by-Step Directions

1. Whisk all the ingredients in a bowl.
2. Spray or coat tray with oil.
3. Arrange cookies leaving at least 2 inches of space in between.
4. Using a fork, slightly flatten the surface.
5. Choose the air fry function.
6. Air fry for 5 minutes at 350°F.

Serving Suggestion:

Sprinkle some sugar on top and serve.

Tip:

You may use any flavor of cake mix for this recipe. You may substitute canola with vegetable oil.

Air Fryer Blueberry Cookies

Lovely cookies to eat as a dessert or paired with your morning coffee or tea.
Prep Time and Cooking Time: 9 minutes | Serves: 4

Ingredients to Use:

- 1 tablespoon melted butter
- 1 teaspoon vanilla extract
- 1 package Jiffy blueberry muffin mix
- 1 large egg

Step-by-Step Directions

1. Combine muffin mix, vanilla extract, egg, and butter.
2. Scoop dough and arrange in greased baking trays.
3. Choose the air fry function.

4. Air fry for 4 minutes at 320°F.

Serving Suggestion:

Cookies are ready once the edges turn brown. Plate and serve with your beverage of choice.

Tip:

You can make a big batch to store in airtight containers or the fridge.

Milo Krispies Cookies

This recipe yields exquisite-looking cookies that are hard to resist.
Prep Time and Cooking Time: 20 minutes | Serves: 5

Ingredients to Use:

- 1/3 cup butter
- 1 tablespoon corn flour
- 2 oz. milk or dark chocolate pieces
- 13-in-1 Milo packet
- 1/3 cup sugar
- 1 cup flour
- 3 cups rice krispies or puffs

Step-by-Step Directions

1. Preheat air fryer to 338°F.
2. Mix sugar and butter until fluffy.
3. Add flour and Milo.
4. Form into balls and flatten into cookie shapes.
5. Coat with rice puffs.
6. Line tray or basket with foil.
7. Arrange cookies in the tray.
8. Choose the bake function.
9. Bake for 12 minutes.

Serving Suggestion:

Drizzle melted chocolate on top and serve.

Tip:

Make sure that you leave some space in between the cookies before baking.

Fluffy Bran Muffins

This muffin recipe is not only tasty but is also great for digestion.

Prep Time and Cooking Time: 35 minutes | Serves: 8

Ingredients to Use:

- 1 cup all-purpose flour
- 1/3 cup unsweetened applesauce
- 1 teaspoon salt
- 1 teaspoon baking powder
- 1-1/2 cups Fiber One cereal
- 1 egg
- 1 teaspoon vanilla
- 2/3 cup brown sugar
- 1 teaspoon baking soda
- 1 cup buttermilk

Step-by-Step Directions

1. Combine buttermilk and cereal in a mixing bowl. Set aside for 20 minutes.
2. Combine all the wet ingredients in a separate bowl.
3. In another bowl, combine the dry ingredients.
4. Combine all three mixtures in a large bowl and mix well.
5. Coat muffin tins with non-stick cooking spray.
6. Fill muffin tins up to 2/3 full with batter.
7. Choose the air fry function.
8. Air fry for 12-15 minutes at 320°F.

Serving Suggestion:

Plate and serve with butter.

Tip:

Make this recipe for family members that have trouble with indigestion.

Easy Blueberry Streusel muffins

These wonderfully filling muffins are great for breakfast with your favorite beverage.

Prep Time and Cooking Time: 24 minutes |

Serves: 12

Ingredients to Use:

- 1/2 cup fresh blueberries
- 2 eggs
- 1 cup flour plus 4 tablespoons for topping
- 1 teaspoon baking powder
- 1/3 cup milk
- 1 tablespoon vanilla
- 2 tablespoons sugar plus 4 tablespoons for topping
- 3 tablespoons melted butter
- 4 tablespoons butter for topping
- 4 tablespoons brown sugar

Step-by-Step Directions

1. Combine flour, baking powder, and sugar in a mixing bowl.
2. Add the milk, melted butter, eggs, and vanilla extract.
3. Add fresh blueberries.
4. To create topping, mix brown sugar, 4 tablespoons sugar, 4 tablespoons butter, and 4 tablespoons flour.
5. Pour batter into greased or lined muffin tins about 2/3 full.
6. Add the topping over the batter.
7. Choose the bake function.
8. Bake for 12-14 minutes at 320°F.

Serving Suggestion:

Garnish with fresh berries.

Tip:

These will last for 2-3 days in airtight containers at room temperature.

Pumpkin Muffins with Cream Cheese Frosting

This is a neat recipe to try if you love pumpkin. Pair these delicious muffins with pumpkin spice latte too.

Prep Time and Cooking Time: 35 minutes |

Serves: 8

- 1 cup canned pumpkin
- 1-1/2 cups all-purpose flour
- 1 teaspoon pumpkin pie spice
- 2 eggs
- 1 teaspoon baking powder
- 1-/4 cup sugar
- 1 teaspoon baking soda
- 1/3 cup vegetable oil
- 1 teaspoon ground cinnamon
- 1 teaspoon salt plus ½ teaspoon for frosting
- 1/2 cup unsalted butter, room temperature
- 4 cups powdered sugar
- 8 oz. cream cheese, room temperature
- 1 teaspoon vanilla extract

Step-by-Step Directions

1. Combine eggs, 1-1/4 cup sugar, and vegetable oil in a bowl.
2. In a separate bowl, mix baking powder, soda, flour, cinnamon, pumpkin spice, and 1 teaspoon salt.
3. Combine both mixtures and mix well.
4. Pour batter into lined or greased muffin tins about 2/3 full.
5. Choose the bake function.
6. Bake for 10-12 minutes at 320°F.
7. To make the frosting, combine unsalted butter, cream cheese, vanilla, 1/2 teaspoon salt, and powdered sugar in a mixing bowl.

Serving Suggestion:

Muffins need to cool completely before adding the frosting.

Tip:

Sprinkle with pumpkin spice powder or sprinkles.

Orange & Cranberry Muffins

This is a great recipe to make if you have plenty of fresh cranberries available.
Prep Time and Cooking Time: 32 minutes | Serves: 8

Ingredients to Use:

- 1 teaspoon lemon zest, grated
- 2 tablespoons orange zest
- 1 teaspoon grated orange zest
- 1 cup diced cranberries
- 1/3 cup vegetable oil
- 8 tablespoons sugar
- 3/4 cup milk
- 1-3/4 cup flour
- 1 large egg
- 1/2 teaspoon salt
- 3 teaspoons baking powder

Step-by-Step Directions

1. Put cranberries in a bowl.
2. Add 2 tablespoons sugar and orange zest. Mix well.
3. In a separate bowl, mix the remaining sugar, flour, salt, and baking powder.
4. Add egg, oil, and milk. Mix until everything is well combined.
5. Add cranberries, lemon zest, and orange zest.
6. Fill greased muffin tin with batter.
7. Choose the bake function.
8. Bake in the air fryer at 325°F for 15 minutes.

Serving Suggestion:

Let muffins cool for a few minutes before serving.

Tip:

Use a toothpick to tell if muffins are ready.

Double Choco Chip Muffins

These chocolate loaded muffins are not only

toothsome, but incredibly moist as well.
Prep Time and Cooking Time: 35 minutes | Serves: 12

Ingredients to Use:

- 2 teaspoons vanilla extract
- 1/2 cup unsweetened cocoa powder
- 1-1/4 cup all-purpose flour
- 1 cup bittersweet chocolate chips
- 1 tablespoon vegetable oil
- 3/4 cup milk
- 1 teaspoon baking powder
- 1 teaspoon baking soda
- 1/2 cup brown sugar
- 2 eggs
- 1 teaspoon salt
- 4 tablespoons melted unsalted butter

Step-by-Step Directions

1. Combine cocoa, chocolate chips, flour, baking soda, salt, and baking powder in a bowl and mix well.
2. Add eggs, melted butter, milk, brown sugar, vanilla extract, and vegetable oil. Mix until well combined.
3. Coat muffin tins with non-stick cooking spray.
4. Fill with batter about 2/3 full.
5. Sprinkle sugar on top.
6. Choose the air fry function.
7. Air fry for 12-15 minutes at 320°F.

Serving Suggestion:

Sprinkle with powdered sugar and serve.

Tip:

You may also use silicone muffin cups for this recipe.

Air Fryer Apple Muffins

This air fryer recipe is a perfect way to use fresh apples while they are in season.
Prep Time and Cooking Time: 24 minutes | Serves: 2

Ingredients to Use:

- 1/2 cup apples, diced
- 1/2 teaspoon salt
- 1/2 cup all-purpose flour plus 4 tablespoons for topping
- 2 tablespoons melted butter
- 3 tablespoons butter for topping
- 1 teaspoon ground cinnamon plus 1 teaspoon for topping
- 3 tablespoons heavy cream
- 1 egg yolk
- 1 teaspoon baking powder
- 3 tablespoons brown sugar plus 4 tablespoons for topping
- 1 teaspoon vanilla extract

Step-by-Step Directions

1. Combine 1 teaspoon cinnamon, 3 tablespoons sugar, ½ cup flour, salt, and baking powder in a bowl.
2. Next add the cream, egg, melted butter, and vanilla. Mix well.
3. Fold in apples.
4. To make the topping, combine 4 tablespoons flour, 1 teaspoon cinnamon, and 4 tablespoons brown sugar.
5. Pour batter into greased ramekins.
6. Sprinkle topping on batter.
7. Choose the air fry function.
8. Air fry for 320°F for 12-14 minutes.

Serving Suggestion:

Let muffins cool for a few minutes before serving.

Tip:

You can tweak this recipe to include ingredients you love. Try adding some frosting or nuts.

Easy Cornmeal Muffins

This super easy to make muffin is perfect as a side dish for your savory dishes.

Prep Time and Cooking Time: 17 minutes | Serves: 12

Ingredients to Use:

- 1/3 cup vegetable oil
- 1 cup flour
- 1/4 cup sugar
- 1 cup yellow cornmeal
- 2 large eggs
- 1 teaspoon salt
- 1 teaspoon baking soda
- 1-1/4 cups buttermilk
- 1 tablespoon baking powder

Step-by-Step Directions

1. Combine cornmeal, salt, baking soda, baking powder, sugar, and flour.
2. Add the oil, eggs, and buttermilk. Mix well.
3. Pour batter into greased or lined muffin trays.
4. Fill muffin cups about 2/3 full.
5. Choose the bake function.
6. Bake for 12 minutes at 330°F.

Serving Suggestion:

Serve while still warm and with a slice of butter on top.

Tip:

Leftover muffins can be refrigerated and quickly reheated in the air fryer.

Banana Walnut Muffins

This muffin recipe is a great way to save very ripe bananas from ending up in the bin.
Prep Time and Cooking Time: 22 minutes | Serves: 6

Ingredients to Use:

- 1 cup walnuts, chopped
- 3 ripe bananas
- 1-1/2 cups flour
- 1/3 cup melted butter
- 1/2 teaspoon salt

- 3/4 cup sugar
- 1/4 teaspoon ground cinnamon
- 1 teaspoon baking soda
- 1 teaspoon vanilla extract
- 1 teaspoon baking powder
- 1 egg

Step-by-Step Directions

1. In a large bowl, mix flour, cinnamon, bananas, sugar, butter, egg, baking soda, vanilla, and baking powder until smooth.
2. Add walnuts.
3. Pour batter into greased muffin trays.
4. Choose the bake function.
5. Bake in the air fryer at 320°F for 12 minutes.

Serving Suggestion:

Top with frosting or a sprinkle of powdered sugar.

Tip:

Use non-stick cooking spray to grease muffin trays. Once the 12 minutes are up, check if muffins are ready. Add a minute or two until muffins are done.

Bacon & Cheese Savory Muffins

These savory muffins are excellent snacks or even meal-replacements while on the go.
Prep Time and Cooking Time: 22 minutes | Serves: 6

Ingredients to Use:

- 2 tablespoons olive oil
- 1 cup cheddar cheese, shredded
- 1 cup milk
- 2-1/2 cups all-purpose flour
- 2 teaspoons baking powder
- 1 egg
- 1 teaspoon dried basil
- 1/4 cup cooked bacon, crumbled
- 1/2 teaspoon salt

1. In a mixing bowl, combine cheese, basil, salt, flour, and baking powder.
2. Add egg, olive oil, milk, and bacon. Mix well.
3. Fill a greased muffin tray with batter up to 2/3's full.
4. Choose the bake function.
5. Bake for 15 minutes at 350°F.

Serving Suggestion:

Let the tray cool before taking out the muffins. Plate and serve.

Tip:

Exercise caution when taking out the muffin tray. After 15 minutes of baking, check for doneness using a toothpick. If the toothpick comes out clean, the muffins are ready.

Lemon & Blueberry Muffins

This recipe highlights the zesty and sweet flavors of lemon and blueberries.
Prep Time and Cooking Time: 24 minutes | Serves: 5

Ingredients to Use:

- 2 tablespoons lemon juice
- 1 cup flour
- 1/4 cup butter
- 1/2 cup sugar
- 1/2 teaspoon salt
- 1/4 cup milk
- 1/2 cup blueberries
- 1 teaspoon baking powder
- 1 teaspoon vanilla
- 1 tablespoon lemon zest
- 1 egg

Step-by-Step Directions

1. Spray a muffin tray with non-stick cooking spray.

2. In a large mixing bowl, mix all the ingredients until fully combined.
3. Pour batter into muffin cups up to ¾ full.
4. Choose the bake function.
5. Bake for 14 minutes at 320°F.

Serving Suggestion:

Let the muffins slightly cool before serving. Garnish with fresh blueberries and mint leaves.

Tip:

Make a big batch and store in Ziploc bags in the fridge. Reheat anytime in the air fryer for a few minutes.

Easy Homemade Honey Muffins

This delightfully tasty recipe is great with almost any pairing, especially with a homemade jam.
Prep Time and Cooking Time: 22 minutes | Serves: 12

Ingredients to Use:

- 1/4 cup honey
- 5 cups flour
- 1/4 cup melted butter
- 1 tablespoon baking powder
- 1 cup milk
- 1 large egg
- 1/2 cup sugar
- 1/2 teaspoon salt

Step-by-Step Directions

1. Combine baking powder, flour, sugar, and salt in a mixing bowl.
2. Add melted butter, milk, egg, and honey.
3. Pour into lined muffin tins up to 2/3 full.
4. Choose the bake function.
5. Bake for 12 minutes at 320°F.

Serving Suggestion:

Let muffins cool and serve with butter. You

can also sprinkle some sugar on top.

Tip:

When the 12 minutes are up, check muffins for doneness. Bake further if needed.

Easy Chocolate & Espresso Muffins

These soft and moist muffins that combine two ingredients that we love are just divine.
Prep Time and Cooking Time: 25 minutes | Serves: 8

Ingredients to Use:

- 1/3 cup vegetable oil
- 1 cup all-purpose flour
- 1 teaspoon apple cider vinegar
- 3/4 cup light brown sugar
- 1 teaspoon vanilla extract
- 1/2 cocoa powder
- 3/4 cup milk
- 1/2 teaspoon baking powder
- 1 large egg
- 1/2 teaspoon salt
- 1/2 teaspoon baking soda
- 1/2 teaspoon espresso powder

Step-by-Step Directions

1. Preheat air fryer to 300°F.
2. Whisk together cocoa, flour, baking powder, espresso powder, baking soda, salt, and sugar in a mixing bowl.
3. In another bowl combine apple cider vinegar, oil, vanilla, egg, and milk.
4. Pour wet ingredients into the bowl with dry ingredients.
5. Mix well until smooth.
6. Pour batter into lined muffin cups up to about 3/4 full.
7. Choose the bake function.
8. Bake for 13-15 minutes.

Serving Suggestion:

Let the muffins cool for 5 minutes before serving.

Tip:

You can substitute ¾ teaspoon finely ground instant coffee for the espresso powder.

Sugar Cinnamon Donut Muffins

Definitely on the sweeter side, this light and airy muffin recipe are perfect as a dessert or a snack.
Prep Time and Cooking Time: 30 minutes | Serves: 16

Ingredients to Use:

- 1 cup buttermilk
- 1 cup sugar plus ¾ cup sugar for coating
- 1/2 teaspoon nutmeg, ground
- 8 tablespoons melted unsalted butter plus another 8 tablespoons melted for coating
- 2-3/4 cups all-purpose flour
- 2 large eggs
- 1/4 corn starch
- 1 teaspoon salt
- 1 large egg yolk
- 1 tablespoon baking powder
- 1 teaspoon ground cinnamon

Step-by-Step Directions

1. Preheat air fryer to 350°F.
2. Combine corn starch, flour, salt, baking powder, sugar, and nutmeg in a bowl.
3. Add wet ingredients and mix until combined. Be careful not to over mix.
4. Pour batter into lined muffin cups about 1/2 full.
5. Choose the bake function.
6. Bake for 12-14 minutes at 340°F.
7. In a bowl, combine 3/4 cup sugar and 1 teaspoon cinnamon.
8. Dip and roll donuts into melted butter then coat with the sugar-cinnamon

granules.

After coating, return donuts to the rack and allow to cool for 5 minutes before serving.

Tip:

Use an ice cream scoop to help you transfer the batter into the muffin cups.

Spaghetti & Meatball Muffins

This savory muffin recipe is the perfect lunchbox treat for pasta lovers.
Prep Time and Cooking Time: 21 minutes | Serves: 24

Ingredients to Use:

- 1 egg slightly beaten
- 8.8 oz. cooked pasta
- 2 cups mozzarella cheese, shredded
- 2 cups pasta sauce
- 24 cooked meatballs
- 1/2 cup parmesan cheese, shredded

Step-by-Step Directions

1. Put the cooked pasta in a bowl and add 1 1/2 cup of pasta sauce.
2. Add egg and stir.
3. Add 1 cup of the mozzarella cheese and 1/2 cup parmesan cheese. Mix well.
4. Fill each muffin cup with the pasta.
5. Choose the air fry function.
6. Air fry for 4-5 minutes at 390°F.
7. Put a meatball on top and push it into the center.
8. Add some more pasta sauce and mozzarella on top.
9. Air fry for 2 minutes more with the same air fryer settings until cheese melts.

Serving Suggestion:

Let muffins cool down before serving.

Tip:

Be careful when taking out the muffin cups to add the meatballs. Use silicone-tipped tongs. These muffins can be stored in the fridge and reheated in the air fryer.

Cheesy Tuna Melt

Try this savory muffin recipe when you get hungry and have little time to spare for preparation.
Prep Time and Cooking Time: 22 minutes | Serves: 4

Ingredients to Use:

- 1 tablespoon Dijon mustard
- 3/4 cup packaged coleslaw mix
- 2 cans white tuna chunks, drained
- 1/2 cup shredded cheese
- 1/2 teaspoon dried dill
- 3 tablespoon mayonnaise
- 3 green onions sliced
- 4 English muffins, halved

Step-by-Step Directions

1. Preheat air fryer to 370°F.
2. In a bowl, combine coleslaw mix, green onion, and tuna.
3. In a separate bowl, mix mustard, mayonnaise, and dill.
4. Add mixture to the bowl with tuna and mix well.
5. Put 2 tablespoons of the tuna mixture on top of the halved muffin.
6. Choose the air fry function.
7. Air fry for 3-4 minutes.
8. Add the cheese on top and air fry for another 1-2 minutes.

Serving Suggestion:

Let the muffins cool down for a few minutes before serving as melted cheese can burn.

Tip:

Garnish with basil or dill.

Chapter 11: Appetizer Recipes

Mozzarella Stuffed Mushrooms

The perfect appetizer for anyone who's on a low-carb diet.

Prep Time and Cooking Time: 20 minutes | Serves: 12

Ingredients to Use:

- 1 cup tomato sauce
- 2 teaspoons fresh basil, chopped
- 12 large mushroom caps
- 1 cup mozzarella cheese, shredded

Step-by-Step Directions

1. Mix the tomato sauce and basil leaves in a bowl.
2. Stuff the mushrooms with the mixture.
3. Sprinkle cheese on top.
4. Arrange mushroom caps inside the air fryer oven.
5. Select roast function.
6. Cook at 380 degrees F for 7 minutes.

Serving Suggestion:

Garnish with sliced basil leaves.

Tip:

Do not rinse mushrooms. Instead, clean with a damp paper towel.

Tortilla Chips with Salsa

Parties start great with appetizers like this one.

Prep Time and Cooking Time: 20 minutes | Serves: 6

Ingredients to Use:

- 10 tortillas
- Cooking spray
- Salt to taste
- 3 cups salsa

Step-by-Step Directions

1. Spray both sides of tortillas with oil.
2. Sprinkle with salt.
3. Slice into wedges.
4. Place the wedges in the air crisper tray.
5. Choose air fry option.
6. Cook at 350 degrees F for 4 minutes.
7. Flip and cook for another 3 minutes.
8. Serve with salsa.

Serving Suggestion:

Sprinkle with a little salt before serving.

Tip:

Drain on a plate lined with paper towels.

Vegan Flautas

These tortilla rolls can be sliced into smaller pieces and serve as appetizers during parties.

Prep Time and Cooking Time: 30 minutes | Serves: 8

Ingredients to Use:

- 1 white onion, sliced
- 2 cups black beans, rinsed and drained
- 1 cup Poblano peppers, sliced
- 1 teaspoon garlic powder
- 1 teaspoon chili powder
- 1/2 teaspoon oregano
- 1/2 teaspoon ground cumin
- Pinch cayenne pepper
- Salt to taste
- 4 corn tortillas
- 1/2 cup Pepper Jack cheese, grated
- Cooking spray

Step-by-Step Directions

1. Add onions, black beans and peppers to a pan over medium heat.
2. Season with garlic powder, chili powder, oregano, cumin cayenne and salt.
3. Cook while stirring for 5 minutes.
4. Top the tortillas with the mixture.
5. Sprinkle cheese on top.
6. Roll up the tortillas and seal.
7. Spray tortillas with oil.
8. Place these in the air crisper tray.
9. Set the air fryer oven to air fry.
10. Cook at 330 degrees F for 5 minutes.
11. Let cool.
12. Slice carefully the rolls into bite size pieces.

Serving Suggestion:

Serve with guacamole, chopped tomatoes and sour cream.

Tip:

You can also use flour tortillas for this recipe.

Baked Ricotta with Herbs

Serve this baked ricotta with crackers, veggie dips or chips.
Prep Time and Cooking Time: 20 minutes | Serves: 8 to 10

Ingredients to Use:

- 30 oz. ricotta
- 4 teaspoons rosemary, chopped
- 4 eggs, beaten
- 1 tablespoon lemon zest
- 6 tablespoons Parmesan cheese
- Salt and pepper to taste

Step-by-Step Directions

1. Combine all the ingredients in a bowl.
2. Spread mixture into a small baking pan.
3. Set the air fryer oven to air fry.
4. Cook at 380 degrees F for 10 minutes.

Serving Suggestion:

Sprinkle with a little pepper before serving.

Tip:

Stop cooking when the edges turn brown.

Mini Taco Cups

These taco cups will be the life of any gathering.
Prep Time and Cooking Time: 30 minutes | Serves: 8

Ingredients to Use:

- 1 lb. lean ground beef
- 2 tablespoons taco seasoning
- 1/4 cup green chili, chopped
- 1/4 cup tomatoes, chopped
- 12 wonton wrappers
- 1 cup cheddar cheese, shredded

Step-by-Step Directions

1. Add ground beef to a pan over medium heat.
2. Break up and crumble the beef.
3. Cook for 5 minutes, stirring.
4. Drain and transfer to a bowl.
5. Add to the bowl the tomatoes and green chilli.
6. Season with taco seasoning.
7. Mix well.
8. Add the wonton wrappers to a muffin pan.
9. Top with the beef mixture and cheddar cheese.
10. Place in the air fryer oven.
11. Set it to bake.
12. Bake for 3 to 5 minutes.

Serving Suggestion:

Top with salsa, guacamole and shredded cheese. Drizzle with hot pepper sauce.

Tip:

Use 90 percent lean ground beef.

Dumplings

Quick and easy to make, dumplings are perfect appetizers for Asian-themed parties.
Prep Time and Cooking Time: 20 minutes | Serves: 4

Ingredients to Use:

- 1 pack frozen dumplings
- Cooking spray

Step-by-Step Directions

1. Spread frozen dumplings in a single layer in the air crisper tray.
2. Spray with oil.
3. Set the air fryer oven to air fry.
4. Cook at 380 degrees F for 6 minutes.
5. Flip and cook for another 6 minutes.

Serving Suggestion:

Serve with soy sauce mixed with lemon juice, and chili garlic paste for dipping.

Tip:

Do not thaw the dumplings.

Roasted Goat Cheese & Tomato Tarts

This is one irresistible idea for appetizer that's actually a cinch to prepare.
Prep Time and Cooking Time: 20 minutes | Serves: 8

Ingredients to Use:

- 1 tablespoon honey
- 1 teaspoon dried Italian seasoning
- 1/2 cup goat cheese, crumbled
- 1 pack crescent rounds, sliced into 8 rounds
- 2 tomatoes, sliced
- 2 tablespoons olive oil

Step-by-Step Directions

1. In a bowl, mix honey, Italian seasoning

and goat cheese.
2. Press the dough to form a flat circle.
3. Top the dough rounds with the honey mixture.
4. Put tomato slices on top.
5. Drizzle with olive oil.
6. Place these inside the air fryer oven.
7. Set the air fryer oven to roast.
8. Cook at 350 degrees F for 5 minutes.

Serving Suggestion:

Sprinkle with pepper.

Tip:

You can also use cream cheese for this recipe.

Chicken Nachos

When you're pressed for time and friends are coming over, this recipe will save the day.
Prep Time and Cooking Time: 20 minutes | Serves: 4

Ingredients to Use:

- 2 cups tortilla chips
- 1/2 cup chicken, cooked and shredded
- 1/2 cup black beans, rinsed and drained
- 1 jalapeno, sliced
- 1/2 cup fresh cheese, grated
- 1/2 cup cheddar cheese, shredded

Step-by-Step Directions

1. Spread the tortillas chips in a baking pan.
2. Sprinkle the chicken, beans, jalapeno and cheeses on top.
3. Set the pan inside the air fryer oven.
4. Choose bake setting.
5. Cook at 350 degrees F for 3 to 5 minutes or until cheese has melted.

Serving Suggestion:

Serve with guacamole, lime wedges, sour cream and salsa.

You can also top nachos with chopped tomatoes.

Frico Cups

These are sure to be a big hit in your next party. And they're easy to make too.
Prep Time and Cooking Time: 15 minutes | Serves: 12

Ingredients to Use:

- 3 cups Parmesan cheese, grated
- 12 cherry tomatoes
- 1 cup guacamole
- 1/4 cup cheddar, grated

Step-by-Step Directions

1. Line your muffin pan with 2 tablespoons Parmesan cheese per cup.
2. Place the pan inside the air fryer oven.
3. Set it to air fry.
4. Cook at 350 degrees F for 5 minutes.
5. Let cool.
6. Once hardened, top with guacamole, cherry tomatoes and cheddar cheese.

Serving Suggestion:

Sprinkle with Italian herbs.

Tip:

You can also air fry the frico cups to melt the cheddar cheese.

Mini Pizza Cups

Turn pizza into an interesting appetizer with the help of this recipe.
Prep Time and Cooking Time: 15 minutes | Serves: 8

Ingredients to Use:

- 8 flour tortillas
- 2 cups pizza sauce
- 1 cup mozzarella cheese

Step-by-Step Directions

1. Make smaller round shapes with your flour tortillas using a biscuit cutter.
2. Add these to the muffin cups of a muffin pan.
3. Top with the tomato sauce and cheese.
4. Place inside the air fryer oven.
5. Choose bake function.
6. Bake at 350 degrees F for 8 to 10 minutes.

Serving Suggestion:

Sprinkle with dried herbs.

Tip:

You can also use other pizza toppings that you like such as crumbed Italian sausage, white onion, bell pepper and so on.

Dry Rubbed Chicken Wings

There's nothing like this dry rubbed chicken wings to make your guests go wow.
Prep Time and Cooking Time: 45 minutes | Serves: 6

Ingredients to Use:

- 2 lb. chicken wings
- 2 tablespoons olive oil

Dry rub

- 1 tablespoon brown sugar
- 1 teaspoon garlic powder
- 1 teaspoon smoked paprika
- 1 teaspoon chili powder
- 1 teaspoon onion powder
- 1 teaspoon dried mustard powder
- 1 teaspoon cumin
- 1 teaspoon paprika
- 1/2 teaspoon oregano
- 1/2 teaspoon ground thyme
- Pinch cayenne pepper
- Salt and pepper to taste

1. Combine the dry rub ingredients in a bowl.
2. In another bowl, toss wings in oil.
3. Sprinkle all sides with the dry rub.
4. Place inside the air fryer oven.
5. Choose bake function.
6. Bake at 370 degrees F for 8 to 10 minutes per side.

Serving Suggestion:

Garnish with lettuce leaves and cucumber slices.

Tip:

Thaw first if you are using frozen chicken wings.

Chili Cheese Fries

Top your fries with chili and cheese, and serve as appetizer to your guests.
Prep Time and Cooking Time: 20 minutes |
Serves: 6

Ingredients to Use:

- 1 pack French fries
- Salt and pepper to taste
- 15 oz. chili
- 1/2 cup cheddar cheese, shredded

Step-by-Step Directions

1. Spread the fries in the air crisper tray.
2. Choose air fry setting in your air fryer oven.
3. Cook at 400 degrees F for 7 to 8 minutes, stirring once or twice.
4. In a pan over medium heat, warm up the chili.
5. Top the fries with the chili.
6. Sprinkle with cheese.
7. Place in the air fryer oven.
8. Choose bake setting.
9. Bake at 350 degrees F for 3 minutes or

until cheese has melted.

Serving Suggestion:

Top with a dollop of sour cream.

Tip:

You can also use homemade potato fries for this recipe.

Baked Potato Rounds

These baked potato rounds will definitely be the highlight of the party.
Prep Time and Cooking Time: 30 minutes |
Serves: 8

Ingredients to Use:

- 2 potatoes, sliced into ½ inch thick rounds
- Cooking spray
- Salt and pepper to taste
- 1 cup sour cream
- 1 cup cheddar cheese, shredded

Step-by-Step Directions

1. Spray potato rounds with oil.
2. Sprinkle with salt and pepper.
3. Add the potato rounds to the air crisper tray.
4. Select air fry setting.
5. Cook at 370 degrees F for 15 minutes, flipping once.
6. Let cool.
7. Top with sour cream and cheddar cheese.
8. Put these back to the air fryer oven.
9. Choose bake setting.
10. Bake at 350 degrees F for 3 minutes or until cheese has melted.

Serving Suggestion:

Sprinkle with dried herbs.

Tip:

Use Russet potatoes for this recipe.

Mediterranean Nachos

This kind of appetizer will certainly make you look like a kitchen pro.
Prep Time and Cooking Time: 20 minutes | Serves: 8

Ingredients to Use:

- 10 corn tortillas
- 4 tablespoons olive oil
- Salt to taste

Toppings
- 2 cups cooked pulled pork
- 1 cup cucumbers, chopped
- 1 cup tomatoes, chopped
- 1/2 cup black olives, pitted and sliced
- 1/2 cup feta cheese
- 1/2 cup tzatziki sauce
- Fresh dill

Step-by-Step Directions

1. Slice tortillas into wedges.
2. Coat with olive oil and sprinkle with salt.
3. Arrange in a single layer in the air crisper tray.
4. Set it to air fry.
5. Cook at 320 degrees F for 1 to 2 minutes per side.
6. Let cool and transfer to a serving platter.
7. Sprinkle all the toppings on top of the chips.

Serving Suggestion:

Drizzle with hot pepper sauce.

Tip:

You can also use tortilla chips for this recipe.

Teriyaki Beef Skewers

If you want something heavy for your appetizers, here's a recipe you should consider.
Prep Time and Cooking Time: 6 hours and 30 minutes | Serves: 8

Ingredients to Use:

- 3 cups brown sugar
- 2 cups soy sauce
- 1 cup pineapple juice
- 1 cup water
- 2 teaspoons garlic powder
- 1/2 cup vegetable oil
- 2 lb. steak, sliced

Step-by-Step Directions

1. Toss all the ingredients in a bowl.
2. Coat the steak slices evenly with the marinade.
3. Cover and marinate for 6 hours in the refrigerator.
4. Thread beef onto skewers.
5. Place inside the air fryer oven.
6. Set it to grill.
7. Cook at 400 degrees F for 5 to 7 minutes per side.

Serving Suggestion:

Serve with garlic sauce.

Tip:

Use lean beef.

Bacon Wrapped Asparagus

This is a no-fail recipe that gives you beautiful appetizers each time.
Prep Time and Cooking Time: 15 minutes | Serves: 8

Ingredients to Use:

- 1 lb. asparagus, trimmed
- 6 slices bacon

Step-by-Step Directions

1. Wrap a couple of asparagus with bacon slices.
2. Arrange in a single layer in the air crisper tray.
3. Set your air fryer oven to air fry.
4. Cook at 380 degrees F for 10 minutes.

You can also drizzle with maple syrup before air frying.

Italian Olives

Your friends who love olives will definitely enjoy this appetizer.
Prep Time and Cooking Time: 15 minutes | Serves: 8

Ingredients to Use:

- 2 cups green olives, pitted
- 2 cups black olives, pitted
- 2 tablespoons olive oil
- 2 cloves garlic, minced
- ½ teaspoon dried fennel seeds
- ½ teaspoon dried oregano
- Pinch red pepper flakes
- Salt and pepper to taste

Step-by-Step Directions

1. Toss all the ingredients in a bowl.
2. Mix well.
3. Spread the olives in the air crisper tray.
4. Choose air fry setting.
5. Set temperature to 300 degrees F.
6. Cook for 5 minutes.

Serving Suggestion:

Serve immediately.

Tip:

You can also use garlic powder instead of minced garlic.

Mini Lemon Crab Cakes

These are miniature crab cakes that you can serve as appetizer in your next gathering.
Prep Time and Cooking Time: 45 minutes | Serves: 12

Ingredients to Use:

- 24 oz. crab meat
- 3 green onions, chopped
- 3 tablespoons lemon juice
- 3 teaspoons lemon zest
- 6 tablespoons breadcrumbs
- 6 tablespoons mayonnaise

Step-by-Step Directions

1. Combine all the ingredients in a bowl.
2. Shape into 24 small patties.
3. Refrigerate for 30 minutes.
4. Add the mini crab cakes to the air crisper tray.
5. Set your air fryer oven to air fry.
6. Cook at 370 degrees F for 5 minutes per side or until golden and crispy.

Serving Suggestion:

Garnish with half lemon slices.

Tip:

You can also add fish flakes to the mixture.

Bacon Wrapped Dates

Bacon surely makes everything taste better including dates!
Prep Time and Cooking Time: 15 | Serves: 12

Ingredients to Use:

- 12 slices bacon
- 24 dates, pitted

Step-by-Step Directions

1. Slice the bacon in half.
2. Wrap each date with a bacon slice.
3. Arrange in a single layer in the air crisper tray.
4. Choose air fry setting.
5. Cook at 400 degrees F for 7 to 8 minutes.

Serving Suggestion:

Insert toothpick before serving.

Tip:

You can also dip in balsamic vinegar before air frying.

Pizza Chips

Pizza chips are even smaller versions of pizza than pizza cups but they taste just as great.
Prep Time and Cooking Time: 15 minutes | Serves: 12

Ingredients to Use:

- 12 cheddar cheese slices, sliced into 4 smaller pieces
- 12 pepperoni slices, chopped
- 2 tablespoons dried oregano

Step-by-Step Directions

1. Top the cheese slices with pepperoni and oregano.
2. Place these in the air crisper tray.
3. Choose air fry setting in your air fryer oven.
4. Cook at 350 degrees F for 5 minutes.

Serving Suggestion:

Let cool to harden before serving.

Tip:

You can also use a cracker and top it with the cheese.

Mini Clam Patties

This is a unique take to the famous crab cakes that uses clam meat instead of crabmeat.
Prep Time and Cooking Time: 15 minutes | Serves: 8

Ingredients to Use:

- 2 lb. clam meat, chopped
- 1 onion, minced
- 1 teaspoon garlic powder
- 2 stalks green onion, chopped
- 1/4 cup breadcrumbs
- 1 egg, beaten
- Cooking spray

Step-by-Step Directions

Combine all the ingredients in a bowl.
Shape into 16 small patties.
Spray with oil.
Transfer patties to the air crisper tray.
Set your air fryer oven to air fry.
Cook at 350 degrees F for 5 minutes per side or until golden and crispy.

Serving Suggestion:

Serve with sweet chili sauce.

Tip:

You can also add fish flakes to the mixture.

Cheese Chips

You and your friends will be delighted at these tasty appetizers.
Prep Time and Cooking Time: 15 minutes | Serves: 12

Ingredients to Use:

- 12 cheddar slices, sliced into 4 pieces
- Cooking spray

Step-by-Step Directions

1. Spray cheese slices with oil.
2. Arrange in a single layer in the air crisper tray.
3. Choose air fry setting.
4. Cook at 350 degrees F for 5 minutes, turning once.

Serving Suggestion:

Sprinkle with dried Italian herbs.

Tip:

Store in an airtight container for up to 3 days.

Mushrooms with Bacon & Cheese

Mushrooms, bacon and cheese go perfectly together as what you'll find out from this recipe.

Prep Time and Cooking Time: 15 minutes |
Serves: 12

- 3 tablespoons butter, melted
- 8 oz. cream cheese
- 8 strips bacon, cooked and chopped
- Salt and pepper to taste
- 24 mushrooms

Step-by-Step Directions

1. Combine butter, cream cheese, bacon, salt and pepper in a bowl.
2. Top mushrooms with the mixture.
3. Place the mushrooms inside the air fryer oven.
4. Set the air fryer oven to roast.
5. Cook at 350 degrees F for 5 minutes.

Serving Suggestion:

Garnish with chopped chives.

Tip:

Use baby bell mushrooms or button mushrooms for this recipe.

Blueberry Empanada with Goat Cheese

This is not like any other appetizer you've tasted.
Prep Time and Cooking Time: 20 minutes |
Serves: 8

Ingredients to Use:

- 2 cups blueberries, chopped
- 1/2 cup goat cheese, crumbled
- 1 tablespoon flour
- 1/4 cup sugar
- 1 refrigerated pie dough
- 1 egg, beaten

Step-by-Step Directions

1. Combine blueberries, goat cheese, flour and sugar in a bowl.

2. Cut 8 circles from the refrigerated dough.
3. Top each dough slice with the mixture.
4. Fold and seal the edges by pinching with a fork.
5. Brush the outside with egg.
6. Place inside the air fryer oven.
7. Choose bake function.
8. Bake at 320 degrees F for 5 minutes per side

Serving Suggestion:

Garnish with fresh blueberries.

Tip:

You can use frozen or fresh blueberries for this recipe.

Lime Tortilla Chips & Guacamole

Dip your crunchy tortilla chips in creamy guacamole.
Prep Time and Cooking Time: 10 minutes |
Serves: 12

Ingredients to Use:

- 10 corn tortillas
- 6 tablespoons olive oil
- 1/4 cup lime juice
- Salt to taste
- 1 cup guacamole

Step-by-Step Directions

1. Use a pizza or biscuit cutter to slice the tortillas into wedges.
2. Coat the wedges with oil, lime juice and salt.
3. Place these in the air crisper tray.
4. Set the air fryer oven to air fry.
5. Cook at 320 degrees F for 2 minutes per side.
6. Serve with guacamole.

Serving Suggestion:

Let cool to harden before serving.

Use freshly squeezed lime juice.

Cranberry Brie Bites

These sweet and crispy appetizers are so delicious, they're gone in a blink of an eye.
Prep Time and Cooking Time: 15 minutes | Serves: 12

Ingredients to Use:

- 24 wonton wrappers
- 8 oz. brie cheese
- 2 cups cranberry sauce

Step-by-Step Directions

1. Line your muffin pan with wonton wrappers.
2. Place the muffin pan inside the air fryer oven.
3. Choose air fry setting.
4. Cook at 300 degrees F for 3 minutes.
5. Top the wonton cups with cheese.
6. Place it back to the oven.
7. Select bake function.
8. Bake for 3 minutes or until cheese has melted.
9. Top with cranberry sauce and serve.

Serving Suggestion:

Garnish with cranberry slices.

Tip:

You can also use other melty cheese.

Bacon Wrapped Cracker

Wrap your crackers with bacon and toast in the air fryer oven to create simple but appetizing starters.
Prep Time and Cooking Time: 10 minutes | Serves: 12

Ingredients to Use:

- 12 crackers
- 12 slices bacon
- 1/4 cup Parmesan cheese, grated

Step-by-Step Directions

1. Wrap crackers with bacon slices.
2. Sprinkle with Parmesan cheese.
3. Place in the air crisper tray.
4. Choose air fry setting.
5. Cook at 350 degrees F for 5 minutes per side or until bacon is crispy.

Serving Suggestion:

Serve with sweet chili sauce.

Tip:

Do not overcrowd the air crisper tray.

Bruschetta

This is a simple and easy to prepare appetizer that you'd enjoy serving to your friends.
Prep Time and Cooking Time: 20 minutes | Serves: 12

Ingredients to Use:

- 4 tomatoes, chopped
- 1/4 cup fresh basil leaves, diced
- 1/4 cup Parmesan cheese, shredded
- 1 clove garlic, minced
- 1 tablespoon balsamic vinegar
- 1 teaspoon olive oil
- Salt and pepper to taste
- 1 loaf French bread, sliced
- Cooking spray

Step-by-Step Directions

1. In a bowl, combine all the ingredients except French bread.
2. Top the bread slices with the mixture.
3. Spray the bread with oil.
4. Arrange in a single layer in the air crisper tray.
5. Choose toast or air fry setting.
6. Cook at 250 degrees F for 2 to 3 minutes.

Sprinkle with pepper.

You can also use Italian bread for this recipe.

Pita Chips

These pita chips are versatile and can be paired with most dips.
Prep Time and Cooking Time: 10 minutes | Serves: 8

Ingredients to Use:

- 6 pita breads
- 4 tablespoons olive oil
- 2 teaspoons dried oregano
- Pinch salt

Step-by-Step Directions

1. Slice pita bread into wedges.
2. Brush each side with olive oil.
3. Sprinkle with oregano and salt.
4. Arrange in a single layer in the air crisper tray.
5. Set your air fryer oven to air fry.
6. Cook at 350 degrees F for 1 to 2 minutes per side.

Serving Suggestion:

Serve with ranch dip or French onion dip.

Tip:

You can also season pita chips with Italian herbs.

Bacon-Wrapped with Scallops

Wrap your scallops with bacon and you have appetizers that will surely impress everyone.
Prep Time and Cooking Time: 30 minutes | Serves: 4

Ingredients to Use:

- 16 scallops
- 8 slices bacon

- Salt and pepper to taste
- Cooking spray

Step-by-Step Directions

1. Pat scallops dry with paper towel.
2. Slice bacon in half.
3. Wrap scallops with bacon.
4. Secure with toothpick.
5. Spray with oil.
6. Transfer to the air crisper tray.
7. Set the air fryer oven to air fry.
8. Cook at 370 degrees F for 5 minutes per side.

Serving Suggestion:

Drizzle with honey.

Tip:

You can also use turkey bacon to reduce fat and calorie content.

Toasted Caprese Salad

Here's a different take on the famous Italian appetizer.
Prep Time and Cooking Time: 10 | Serves: 6

Ingredients to Use:

- 2 ripe tomatoes, sliced into rounds
- 16 oz. fresh mozzarella cheese, sliced into rounds
- Basil leaves
- 2 tablespoons olive oil
- 3 teaspoons balsamic vinegar
- Pinch Italian seasoning
- Salt and pepper to taste

Step-by-Step Directions

1. Alternate the tomato, mozzarella and basil leaves in a baking pan.
2. Mix oil and vinegar.
3. Drizzle mixture on top of the appetizer.
4. Season with Italian herbs, salt and pepper.
5. Place inside the air fryer oven.

6. Select toast setting.
7. Cook at 320 degrees F for 2 minutes.

Serving Suggestion:

Garnish with herbs.

Tip:

Serve immediately.

Spanakopita

This is a well-known Greek appetizer that you'd surely love.
Prep Time and Cooking Time: 20 minutes|
Serves: 4

Ingredients to Use:

- 2 eggs, beaten
- 10 oz. spinach, chopped
- 4 oz. feta cheese
- Salt and pepper to taste
- 8 mini phyllo shells

Step-by-Step Directions

1. Combine all the ingredients except phyllo shells in a bowl.
2. Top the shells with the mixture.
3. Place the shells inside the air fryer oven.
4. Set it to air fry.
5. Cook at 220 degrees F for 3 minutes.

Serving Suggestion:

Sprinkle with pepper and serve.

Tip:

You can also use frozen spinach for this recipe but thaw first.

Mac & Cheese Balls

Here's a good way to make use of leftover mac and cheese from last night's dinner.
Prep Time and Cooking Time: 30 minutes |
Serves: 12

Ingredients to Use:

- 4 cups mac and cheese
- 1 egg, beaten
- 1-1/2 cups breadcrumbs
- 1 tablespoon milk
- Cooking spray

Step-by-Step Directions

1. Combine mac and cheese, egg, breadcrumbs and milk in a bowl.
2. Shape into 24 balls.
3. Spray with oil.
4. Place the balls in the air crisper tray.
5. Set the air fryer oven to air fry.
6. Cook at 350 degrees F for 5 to 7 minutes per side or until golden and crispy.

Serving Suggestion:

Serve with honey mustard sauce.

Tip:

Refrigerate for 1 hour before serving.

Pizza Egg Rolls

These pizza egg rolls explode with so much flavor with each bite.
Prep Time and Cooking Time: 20 minutes |
Serves: 12

Ingredients to Use:

- 1 cup pizza sauce
- 24 egg wrappers
- 24 cubes mozzarella cheese
- Italian herbs

Step-by-Step Directions

1. Spread pizza sauce on top of the egg wrappers.
2. Top with the mozzarella cheese.
3. Sprinkle with herbs.
4. Roll or fold the wrapper and seal.
5. Place in the air crisper tray.
6. Choose air fry setting.
7. Cook at 380 degrees F for 10 minutes, flipping once.

Let cool for 15 minutes before serving.

You can also add pepperoni or crumbled sausage to the filling.

Spinach Dip

Use this recipe to prepare this simple but flavorful spinach dip.
Prep Time and Cooking Time: 1 hour | Serves: 12

Ingredients to Use:

- 8 oz. cream cheese, softened
- 1/2 cup onion, minced
- 1/4 teaspoon garlic powder
- 1 cup spinach
- 1 cup mayonnaise
- 1 cup Parmesan cheese, grated
- 1/4 cup water chestnuts , drained and chopped
- Pepper to taste

Step-by-Step Directions

1. Combine all the ingredients in a baking pan.
2. Mix well.
3. Place the baking pan inside the air fryer oven.
4. Set the air fryer oven to bake.
5. Bake at 300 degrees F for 30 minutes.
6. Stir and cook for another 20 minutes or until edges turn golden.

Serving Suggestion:

Serve with crackers or chips.

Tip:

If using frozen spinach, thaw first before mixing.

Lasagna Egg Rolls

Transform your favorite lasagna into egg rolls with this recipe.
Prep Time and Cooking Time: 45 | Serves: 8

Ingredients to Use:

- 3 cups lasagna noodles, cooked, cooled and diced
- 1/2 cup Italian pasta sauce
- 1/4 cup lean ground beef, cooked
- 1 cup mozzarella cheese, shredded
- 16 egg roll wrappers
- Cooking spray

Step-by-Step Directions

1. In a bowl, mix lasagna noodles, pasta sauce, ground beef and cheese.
2. Top the wrappers with the mixture.
3. Roll up and seal.
4. Spray with oil.
5. Arrange the rolls in the air crisper tray.
6. Set the air fryer oven to air fry.
7. Cook at 380 degrees F for 6 to 8 minutes.

Serving Suggestion:

Serve with marinara dipping sauce.

Tip:

You can also use leftover lasagne for this recipe.

Scotch Eggs

Scotch eggs are delicious and filling appetizer that would surely be a hit in your next get together.
Prep Time and Cooking Time: 30 minutes | Serves: 6

Ingredients to Use:

- 1 lb. bulk sausage, crumbled
- 1 onion, chopped
- 1 teaspoon garlic powder
- 6 hard boiled eggs, peeled

- 1 egg, beaten
- 1 cup coconut flour
- Cooking spray

1. Combine sausage, onion and garlic powder in a bowl.
2. Mix well.
3. Form patties from the mixture.
4. Wrap the eggs with this mixture.
5. Dip the Scotch eggs in egg and coat with coconut flour.
6. Spray with oil.
7. Add to the air crisper tray.
8. Set the air fryer oven to air fry.
9. Cook at 400 degrees F for 8 to 10 minutes per side or until golden.

Serving Suggestion:

Serve with hot sauce or mustard.

Tip:

You can also use almond flour.

Green Chili Biscuits

Expect everyone to be impressed with this incredibly simple but delicious appetizer recipe.
Prep Time and Cooking Time: 20 minutes | Serves: 10

Ingredients to Use:

- 2 cups all purpose flour
- 1 teaspoon sugar
- 1 tablespoon baking powder
- 1 teaspoon baking soda
- 1/2 cup butter, melted
- 1/2 cup green chili, chopped
- 1-1/4 cup sour cream
- 1/4 cup cheddar, shredded
- Salt to taste
- Cooking spray

Step-by-Step Directions

1. Combine all the ingredients in a bowl.
2. Mix well.
3. Shape into 20 balls or more.
4. Spray the balls with oil.
5. Place the balls in the air crisper tray.
6. Select bake function.
7. Bake at 340 degrees F for 10 minutes, turning once.

Serving Suggestion:

Serve with garlic butter dip.

Tip:

Use low-fat sour cream.

Sausage & Pineapple Bites

These are some of the simplest yet enticing appetizers recipes you'll ever try.
Prep Time and Cooking Time: 30 minutes | Serves: 10

Ingredients to Use:

- 14 oz. kielbasa sausage, sliced
- 20 oz. pineapple chunks

Step-by-Step Directions

1. Place a pineapple slice on top of the sausage.
2. Insert a toothpick to attach together.
3. Place in the air fryer oven.
4. Set it to grill.
5. Cook at 350 degrees F for 5 minutes.

Serving Suggestion:

Serve with barbecue sauce.

Tip:

You can use either fresh or canned pineapple.

Shrimp & Chorizo Appetizer

Everyone will look forward to your parties when you serve appetizers like this.

Prep Time and Cooking Time: 20 | Serves: 12

Ingredients to Use:

- 24 medium shrimp, peeled and deveined
- 6 links chorizo, sliced into 4 rounds each

Step-by-Step Directions

1. Thread a toothpick through shrimp and chorizo.
2. Add these to the air crisper tray.
3. Select air fry setting.
4. Cook at 370 degrees F for 5 minutes per side.

Serving Suggestion:

Serve in shot glasses with marinara sauce. Garnish with chopped parsley.

Tip:

Cook in batches.

Crunchy Deviled Eggs

Here's a unique twist to the popular deviled eggs appetizer.
Prep Time and Cooking Time: 30 | Serves: 6

Ingredients to Use:

- 6 hard boiled eggs, peeled and sliced in half
- 1 tablespoon yellow mustard
- 1 teaspoon chili powder
- 2 tablespoons mayonnaise
- Salt and pepper to taste
- 3/4 cup all-purpose flour
- 1 egg, beaten
- 1 teaspoon hot pepper sauce
- 1-1/2 cups breadcrumbs
- Cooking spray

Step-by-Step Directions

1. Scoop out the yolks.
2. Add yolks to a bowl.
3. Stir in mustard, chili powder, mayo, salt and pepper.
4. Mash the mixture using a fork. Set aside.

5. Coat the egg white shells with flour.
6. Dip in egg mixed with hot sauce.
7. Dredge with breadcrumbs.
8. Spray with oil.
9. Place these in the air fryer oven.
10. Select air fry function.
11. Cook at 400 degrees F for 3 to 5 minutes per side or until golden.
12. Top with a dollop of egg yolk mixture and serve.

Serving Suggestion:

Sprinkle chopped parsley or green onion on top.

Tip:

You can also skip the chili powder and hot sauce if you don't like your appetizer spicy.

Crostini Tuna Melt Appetizer

These are delicious but easy to prepare appetizer that you won't regret serving to your special guests.
Prep Time and Cooking Time: 10 minutes | Serves: 8

Ingredients to Use:

- 1 French bread loaf, sliced
- 7 oz. canned tuna flakes in oil
- 3/4 cup Parmesan cheese, shaved

Step-by-Step Directions

1. Top the bread slices with tuna flakes and Parmesan cheese.
2. Arrange the bread slices inside the air fryer oven.
3. Select toast setting.
4. Cook at 350 degrees F for 5 minutes.

Serving Suggestion:

Garnish with paprika and fresh dill.

Tip:

You can also use mozzarella cheese for this recipe.

Open Faced Cajun Chicken Sandwich

These are not only an eye candy but are also delightful for your taste buds.
Prep Time and Cooking Time: 20 minutes | Serves: 6-8

Ingredients to Use:

- 1 chicken breast fillet, sliced into cubes
- 2 teaspoons Cajun seasoning
- 1 Italian bread loaf, sliced
- 1/2 cup mozzarella cheese, grated

Step-by-Step Directions

1. Coat the chicken breast cubes with Cajun seasoning.
2. Transfer to the air fryer oven.
3. Select roast function.
4. Cook at 350 degrees F for 10 minutes, flipping once.
5. Top the bread slices with the chicken and cheese.
6. Add to the air crisper tray.
7. Air fry at 400 degrees F for 2 minutes.

Serving Suggestion:

Serve with roasted sausage pepper soup.

Tip:

You can also use French loaf slices for this recipe.

Potato Pancake Appetizer

These appetizers are surprisingly easier than they look.
Prep Time and Cooking Time: 20 minutes | Serves: 6

Ingredients to Use:

- 3 potatoes, grated
- 1 onion, minced
- 1 egg, beaten
- 1 tablespoon flour

- Salt and pepper to taste
- 1 cup sour cream
- 8 oz. smoked salmon

Step-by-Step Directions

1. Mix potatoes, onion, egg, flour, salt and pepper in a bowl.
2. Spread a tablespoon of the mixture in a baking pan.
3. Repeat until batter is used, leaving 2 inches space between.
4. Place inside the air fryer oven.
5. Choose bake function.
6. Bake at 370 degrees F for 5 minutes per side or until golden.
7. Top with sour cream and smoked salmon.

Serving Suggestion:

Sprinkle with chopped chives or fresh dill.

Tip:

You can also use pickled herring for this recipe.

Bacon, Garlic & Cheese Crostini

Expect these appetizers to be gone within a few seconds of serving. They're that good.
Prep Time and Cooking Time: 10 minutes | Serves: 8

Ingredients to Use:

- 3 tablespoons mayonnaise
- 4 oz. cream cheese, softened
- 1/4 teaspoon garlic powder
- 1 French baguette, sliced
- 8 slices bacon, cooked crisp and chopped
- 1 cup cheddar cheese, shredded

Step-by-Step Directions

1. Mix mayo, cream cheese and garlic powder in a bowl.
2. Top the baguette slices with mayo

mixture.

3. Sprinkle bacon and cheese on top.
4. Place inside the air fryer oven.
5. Select toast or grill setting.
6. Cook at 350 degrees F for 3 minutes.

Serving Suggestion:

Garnish with herbs.

Tip:

You can also use other types of loaf bread for this recipe.

Crab & Cranberry Bites

Crab meat and cranberry jam may seem like an unlikely pair but they actually go well together.
Prep Time and Cooking Time: 15 minutes | Serves: 8

Ingredients to Use:

- 1/4 cup cream cheese
- 1/4 cup crab meat
- 2 tablespoons green onion, chopped
- 16 mini phyllo shells
- 1/2 cup cranberry sauce

Step-by-Step Directions

1. Mix cream cheese, crab meat and green onion in a bowl.
2. Add phyllo shells to a muffin pan.
3. Top with crab mixture.
4. Place in the air fryer oven.
5. Choose air fry setting.
6. Cook at 370 degrees F for 5 minutes.
7. Top with the cranberry sauce.

Serving Suggestion:

Let cool for 5 minutes before serving.

Tip:

You can also use wonton wrappers for this recipe.

Apple & Goat Cheese Crostini Appetizer

Crunchy, creamy and full of flavor—it's hard to find fault in this wonderful appetizer.
Prep Time and Cooking Time: 10 minutes | Serves: 8

Ingredients to Use:

- 4 oz. goat cheese, crumbled
- 1 tablespoon lemon juice
- 1 teaspoon lemon zest
- 1 French bread, sliced
- 1 apple, sliced thinly

Step-by-Step Directions

1. Mix goat cheese, lemon juice and lemon zest in a bowl.
2. Spread this mixture on top of bread slices.
3. Top with apples.
4. Set inside the air fryer oven.
5. Choose toast function.
6. Cook at 350 degrees F for 5 minutes.

Serving Suggestion:

Garnish with fresh thyme.

Tip:

Use Granny Smith apple if available.

Roasted Sweet Potato Appetizer

This is the kind of appetizer that will impress even the most discerning guests.
Prep Time and Cooking Time: 20 | Serves: 6

Ingredients to Use:

- 3 sweet potatoes, sliced thickly
- 2 tablespoons olive oil
- 1 teaspoon Italian herbs
- 4 oz. feta cheese, crumbled
- 3 tablespoons Greek yogurt

Step-by-Step Directions

1. Toss the sweet potatoes in olive oil.
2. Transfer to the air fryer oven.
3. Select roast setting.
4. Cook at 390 degrees F for 5 minutes per side.
5. Arrange roasted sweet potatoes on a serving platter.
6. Mix cheese and yogurt.
7. Top sweet potatoes with yogurt mixture and serve.

Serving Suggestion:

Sprinkle with Italian herbs before serving.

Tip:

Use low-fat plain yogurt.

Chili Lime Shrimp Appetizer

This appetizer is not only full of color but also with enticing flavors.
Prep Time and Cooking Time: 15 minutes | Serves: 12

Ingredients to Use:

- 1/2 cup guacamole
- Round tortilla chips
- 1 cup shrimp, cooked
- 1/2 red onion, minced
- 1/2 cup corn kernels
- 1 cup tomatoes, chopped

Dressing
- 2 tablespoons avocado oil
- 3 tablespoons lime juice
- 1 teaspoon garlic powder
- 1 teaspoon onion powder
- 3 teaspoons chili powder
- Salt to taste

Step-by-Step Directions

1. Spread guacamole on top of tortilla chips.
2. Top with shrimp, onion, corn and tomatoes.
3. Mix the dressing ingredients in a bowl.
4. Pour dressing on top of the shrimp mixture.
5. Place inside the air fryer oven.
6. Choose toast setting.
7. Cook at 350 degrees F for 3 minutes.

Serving Suggestion:

Garnish with cilantro.

Tip:

Thaw first if using frozen cooked shrimp or corn kernels.

Sweet & Spicy Sausage Bites

These are incredible appetizers that only take a few minutes of your time.
Prep Time and Cooking Time: 15 minutes | Serves: 8

Ingredients to Use:

- 8 Italian sausage links, sliced into rounds
- 1 cup barbecue sauce
- 2 tablespoons hot pepper sauce
- 1 tablespoon honey

Step-by-Step Directions

1. Mix barbecue sauce, hot pepper sauce and honey in a bowl.
2. Toss sausage slices in the sauce.
3. Insert toothpicks.
4. Place inside the air fryer oven.
5. Choose bake setting.
6. Bake at 370 degrees F for 7 to 10 minutes.

Serving Suggestion:

Serve with mustard.

Tip:

You can also use kielbasa for this recipe.

Conclusion

As a generation who grew up with toaster ovens, seeing it evolve into a remarkable multifunctional cooker that can cook almost anything is a delight.

Having to own and use one will surely be even more exciting. And there's no better way to start your venture with your air fryer toast oven than with a nifty recipe book to let you get the best out of your shiny new appliance.

Air fryer toast ovens have so much to offer when it comes to functionality. They may be small, but they pack solid hardware that can execute even the trickiest recipes.

From cooking frozen foods to roasting an entire chicken and serving an entire full course meal, air fryer toast ovens prove that they may soon be replacing most of your old kitchen appliances.

Printed in the USA
CPSIA information can be obtained
at www.ICGtesting.com
LVHW080718161023
761142LV00057B/24